The Scout and Ranger

JAMES PIKE

The Scout and Ranger
With the Texas Rangers Against the Indians of the South West and With the 4th Ohio Cavalry During the American Civil War

James Pike

The Scout and Ranger
With the Texas Rangers Against the Indians of the South West and
With the 4th Ohio Cavalry During the American Civil War
by James Pike

First published under the title
*The Scout and Ranger: Being the Personal Adventures of Corporal Pike
of the Fourth Ohio Cavalry*

Leonaur is an imprint of Oakpast Ltd

Copyright in this form © 2013 Oakpast Ltd

ISBN: 978-1-78282-104-5 (hardcover)
ISBN: 978-1-78282-105-2 (softcover)

http://www.leonaur.com

Publisher's Notes

The views expressed in this book are not necessarily
those of the publisher.

Contents

Preface	9
My First Effort at Seeing Life	11
My First Indian Campaign	22
More Adventure	41
With the Rangers Again	46
Another Lonely Ride	62
More Adventures	66
Kickapoo Campaign	72
Indian Warfare	77
Scouting	85
Col. Johnston's Comanche Campaign	90
Knights of the Golden Circle	104
Tyranny and Perfidy of the Secessionists	110
Out in the Wilderness	115
Farewell to Dixie	119
In the Union Service	134
After John Morgan	146
Reconnoitring Middle Tennessee	152
Trip to Decatur	161

Carrying an Important Dispatch to General Buell	176
Reconnoitring Bridgeport	181
Arrival of Wounded from Fredericksburg	198
At Home—French Leave	200
Scout to Woodbury	206
Gen. Stanley's Great Raid	210
After John Morgan in Ohio	215
Off to the Hiawasse in Search of Steamboats	217
After Steamboats Again	227
Battles of Dug Gap and Chickamauga	238
Personal Adventures During the Battle	247
Wheeler Badly Whipped	254
Raid in North Carolina	263
Bridge Burning Expedition to Augusta	271
Bloodhound Chase	278
The Whipping Post	291
"Adieu" to Charleston	299
The North Carolina Campaign	308
Personal—Conclusion	317

DEDICATION
TO
MY LATE COMRADES IN ARMS,
THIS BOOK
IS RESPECTFULLY DEDICATED
BY THE AUTHOR

Preface

Whatever aids in illustrating the spirit of the late great struggle, through which the nation has so successfully passed, must be of interest to the American reader. The occurrences of the late rebellion will ever form a study for the free citizens of the Republic, of far deeper interest than those of any other event in the world's history; and few will be content with the perusal of mere outlines, or of battle descriptions, however vivid, but which are only repetitions, though of a magnified type, of what the world has witnessed at almost every decade, since the dawn of civilization; and hence they will search out details, and incidents, which will lead them into the spirit of a conflict, to which they are indebted for their national greatness, material prosperity, and civil and religious freedom; and those incidents may be as readily learned in connection with the career of the private soldier, as with that of the major general.

The simple but touching narratives of one who has survived the horrors of a rebel prison; or the little hillock which covers the remains of one of the murdered victims of rebel cruelty, are far more perfect illustrations of the civilization of the ruling classes in the South, and the malignity of their character, than the whole career of the ablest of our commanders.

Thousands of incidents in the life of every soldier, were they recorded, would be invaluable in illustrating the history of the late war; but the mass of these will soon be forgotten, and the actors themselves fill unknown graves. Men who, in any other era, would be singled out, and known as heroes to a whole nation for their gallant deeds, will pass through life as but one of millions, and must rest content with a general tribute to the great mass.

We are now to have a national literature, as well as a national existence. American writers of romance and the drama, will no longer seek the antiquated regions of Europe for scenes and heroes; America has supplied all that is necessary to the most vivid of pictures; and no pen, even though the plot be fiction, need ever exaggerate in incidents or descriptions. He who tells the simple truth, narrates more of the strange and the heroic, than could be conceived by the fertility of a Dickens, or a Dumas.

The writer of this narrative, throughout, has adhered strictly to facts, without any attempt at embellishment. The wild chases after the Comanches; the stern duties of war; and the hardships of prison life, have left him little time to cultivate elegant diction, and as he has an abiding conviction that unvarnished truth is ever more acceptable than high wrought fiction, he is content with the simple narrative, which is spread before the reader in the pages which follow.

The Author.

Hillsboro, Ohio, June 21, 1865.

Chapter 1

My First Effort at Seeing Life

I have not the vanity to suppose the details of my career in life, other than as it has been connected with the public service, would be of the slightest interest to the reader; and, therefore, I shall not dwell upon them. But I cannot but believe that my adventures in that most dangerous and romantic of all branches of the service—while acting the part of a scout—during the late long and bloody war against the most gigantic rebellion known to history, will be read with interest, not only by the patriotic people of the loyal states, for whom my life was risked, but by thousands in the South—violent rebels—who will, in these pages first recognize me, in my true character, as a soldier of the Union; though oft I have partaken of their hospitalities, and been their familiar companion; and many a rebel officer will, in the following narrative, for the first time learn that they have communicated much valuable information to one who was in the service of the nation against which they had arrayed the whole power, and chivalry of half a score of powerful and flourishing states, extending from the Gulf of Mexico to the thirty-seventh parallel of north latitude.

My career as a scout was commenced under Gen. O. M. Mitchell, who, in 1862, commanded the Third Division of the Cumberland Army; General Mitchell, who united in himself the qualities of a noble man, a thorough scholar, and a dashing officer, and whose death, before the nation could well spare his services, caused a deep despondency to pervade every loyal breast. When he was removed from command in Tennessee, I was turned over to General Rosecrans; who, in turn, on leaving, recommended me to General Thomas. I have also served with Gens. D. S. Stanley, George Crook, Lytle, Sheridan, Grant, and Sherman; so that the reader will not be at a loss to imagine that my term of service has been an eventful one; and that vanity does not inspire me to write an account of those wild and almost incredible adventures, which are naturally incident to the branch of the service to which I was devoted.

But why engage in the dangerous vocation, and risk life, amid enemies who, had they known my character, would gladly have suspended me to the nearest limb? Say, like Shylock, it was my nature, and the reader has it all. I had been well trained in such service, having left my home in Ohio, long since, and migrated to Texas, where I was schooled as a "Ranger" and hunter—the latter character being a necessary accompaniment of the former, as the ranger draws little or no subsistence from the government, but obeys the injunction of Scripture, and takes neither brass nor postal currency in his purse, nor hard tack in his haversack, relying almost entirely on his trusty rifle, for subsistence, from the first to the last of his term of enlistment.

But why should an Ohioan, and a printer, be induced to migrate to Texas, where civilization has but begun, and where men still fancy that there is something diabolical in the process of producing books and newspapers? In Texas—a land of contrarieties, where all is abundance, by the mere act of nature, or sterility beyond the power of art to fertilize; where one only looks up stream for water; where rivers are narrow at their mouths, and wide at their fountains; where the ground is never dusty, though parched with drouth; where grass grows green in winter; where neither the horse nor the cow can be tempted to eat corn; where the widest extremes of heat and cold are often felt in a day; and where the unfortunate immigrant, if he murmurs, or shows surprise, at all he sees and feels, is at once pronounced "green from the states," and looked upon as an object of commiseration? Well, perhaps it is strange that I should find myself there—but it is not more strange than true.

I had been working at my trade in Jefferson City, Missouri, during the winter of 1858-9, and in the spring resolved to go to Kansas, which was yet disturbed by factions, and consequently the very place for one fond of adventure; and, as my nature prompted me to ramble, I saw no other section half so inviting; and accordingly, having armed myself, "as the law directs," I started for the territory on foot.

I had travelled but half a day, however, when I stopped for dinner at a wayside inn, kept by a plethoric old man, the possessor of a young wife and half a dozen worthless darkies. While at dinner, someone rode up to the gate and inquired of the landlord if there was a young man there, who was travelling on foot.

"That's my name," I said, and went to the door, to ascertain: what was wanted.

"Say, young man," said the party, "don't you want to go to Texas?"

"Don't care if I do," said I.

"Well," he replied, "my name is Colonel Johnston; I live twelve miles south of Dallas; I am taking down a drove of horses, and want help; I will furnish you with a horse, saddle, and bridle, and pay your way."

In an instant, all desire to visit Kansas, and participate in the partisan turmoils, which were continually agitating the territory, "vanished into thin air," and in their stead arose visions of wild horse chases, buffalo hunts, Indian fights, and a thousand other "manly sports," which I knew to be the chief sources of amusement and excitement, in that wild, celebrated region.

"But where were you going?" queried the colonel.

"To Kansas," I replied.

"What were you going there for?" he continued.

"For fun," was my sententious, but truthful answer.

"Well," he responded, "if you want fun, just go to Texas; that is the place to find it; plenty of all sorts of game, fine horses, and clever people. It's just the spot for a young man. If ever you go there, you will like the country so well, that you will never leave it."

"Hold on, then, till I get my dinner, and I'll go," was the only reply I stopped to make, till I had satisfied my appetite.

Dinner over, I mounted the animal designated, and we proceeded to gather up the horses, which had scattered about to graze, while the colonel was waiting on me. There were in the drove an unusually fine lot of northern mares, which Johnston stated would be very valuable in Texas, besides a number of magnificent geldings.

As soon as we were fairly on our way, my employer took care to remind me that his name was *Colonel* Johnston, and inquired mine. He then went on to enlighten me, by saying, that, in Texas, every man of any note had some title; was either dubbed general, colonel, major, captain, judge, or esquire; that his friends had given him the title of colonel, though he had never held any military position, the term being merely complimentary. He further informed me, that at one time in his life, he had been a mate on board of a river steamer, and then began to relate various feats of personal prowess, which at once inspired me with a high regard for both his physical and intellectual endowments. He was really a fine looking, robust man, about thirty-five years of age, of a very generous, and manly disposition; and but for a superfluity of vanity and self-importance, was an exceedingly agreeable companion. He had been in Illinois, settling up his wife's estate, and had taken her share of the property in horses; and, by the way, one of the first things he told me was, that he had married a widow.

We travelled fast; I thought *very fast*; and as day after day came and went, and we were in the saddle early and late, I began to imagine something must be wrong about the man and his horses; but I said nothing. On the second day after we had joined fortunes, he began to deprecate the fact that he would have to force a sale of a horse in order to raise money; whereupon I loaned him a sufficient sum (I think about forty dollars in gold), to take him through. The reader will say that this was indiscreet on such a short acquaintance, and that I ought not to have been so free with my money with a stranger. But it was always a fault of mine to confide in strangers, and in this case I did not lose anything, though at one time I believed the chances good to lose all; for Johnston sought a quarrel with me in the Indian Nation, while near Boggy River, and I detected him in the act of drawing his six-shooter on me, at a time when he thought I did not observe him.

My rifle was near at hand, and I quickly had him at my mercy, with my piece levelled on his breast, and my finger on the trigger. We had differed the evening before as to which side of the mountain the road went, and I was found to be in the right. But this was such a trifling excuse for a quarrel, that I naturally concluded he entertained the notion of putting me out of the way, and thus get, not only all I had loaned him, but all I had on my person. My advice to young men is, not to be too free in showing money to strangers; nor ought they to do as I have often done, make loans when there was no way of getting the money back when it is wanted. In this instance I might have lost every dollar I possessed, and my life, too, by my freedom in letting a stranger know my resources. I was green then, but am wiser now.

Our route lay through South Missouri, along a high barren ridge, for eighty miles. If I remember rightly, we passed no town till we came to Linn creek, where we crossed the Osage river, which, I believe, is the head of navigation. It is a small town but is a very businesslike little place. As we crossed the river a little boat steamed away from the landing, loaded, as I afterward learned, with nineteen tons of deer hides, besides other peltries and furs. The town is hemmed in by the Osage range, which although very high and abrupt, should rather be called hills than mountains. The rock of this range is a sort of lava concrete on the surface, while the tops of the ridges and level benches in the mountains were covered with bowlders, evidently of volcanic origin, as they have the appearance of having been melted in a little round-bottomed pot, from which, after cooling, they had been dumped. This portion of the country abounds in minerals, especially lead and iron; and it is, perhaps, the best watered region in the United States; thousands of large, clear springs burst out from beneath the mountain ranges; but very few issue from their sides, however, which is somewhat remarkable.

We passed through Springfield, which at that time was a beautiful and flourishing little city. A school dismissed while we were riding through the streets, and from the walls of the large seminary issued such a swarm of pretty girls, as would make any young man's head swim with delight as he viewed them. I have always had a curiosity to go back there.

From Springfield our route was through a good country for some distance, until we reached Barry county, in which the land is too poor and rocky to talk about. While travelling through it, we managed to tear off nearly every shoe from the horses' feet, and this caused some delay, in getting them reset.

Getting on our way again, we passed through Cassville. The country was still so rocky that the geese couldn't walk about to graze; at least so I concluded, from the fact that I saw one sitting on a hill-side, some distance from a house, and a woman carrying it food. The goose made no effort to help itself, and the woman had to rough it over the rocks the entire distance.

Crossing the Arkansas line, we reached Bentonville, a very thriving village in the Ozark mountains; thence we went to Fayetteville, a town of considerable importance, to the north, but in sight of the Boston mountain, a spur of the Ozark range. As we passed through, we met the overland mail stage, coming at full speed, or at least as fast as mule flesh could move it.

When stages were first put on this line, considerable excitement was created in Western Arkansas; it was a new thing—an eighth wonder of the world; and to the great disgust of the "natives," some of the managers and their wives, feeling the importance of their "posish," put on considerable "style;" and the popular disgust would manifest itself on every possible occasion, much to the annoyance, both of employees and passengers. The children readily imbibed the spirit of their seniors and would continually reiterate the slang of their parents. On this particular occasion, as the coach came down a steep hill into the town, a crowd of little urchins was standing by the roadside, waiting to see the "sights;" when one of them, a bright looking boy, but as ragged as only Arkansas children are, elbows and knees out, with a huge rent in that part of his pants covering the spot "where mothers smite their young," from which protruded a piece of muslin very much the colour of the surrounding soil,—shouted at the top of his voice: "The g-r-e-a-t O-v-e-r-l-a-n-d M-a-i-l C-o-m-p-a-n-y—" and was, evidently, going to add something more, when a huge, muscular, six-footer of a passenger thrust his head out of the window and yelled: "Dry up, you little reprobate, or I'll jump out and raise a crowd and clean you out in a minute."

The little urchin and his party, not exactly expecting such a reception, took to their heels, each with his flag of truce flying behind him almost horizontally. The sight was immensely enjoyed by the wearied passengers, who greeted the retreating boys with roars of laughter. The lumbering of the coach and the shouts of the passengers so frightened our horses that we had a stampede for the next five miles, but fortunately, no harm resulted.

Boston mountain was the next difficulty we had to surmount. The road over it is fifteen miles long, and the ascent was exceedingly steep; but there are several *steppes*, or benches, on the sides, and these afford good resting places for travellers. Every acre on these *steppes* is good tillable land, and would be admirably adapted to vine growing; while upon the very summit is one of the finest farms in Arkansas. We stopped here for the night and were generously entertained, as indeed we always were; for the people of this State, before the war, were ever noted for their hospitality.

On the following morning we started down the mountain. The sky wore a threatening appearance; great banks of clouds seemed to rise from the horizon, and, as it were, to be sucked or drawn from every direction toward the mountain by some powerful current or attraction, until, finally, as we reached the first bench from the top, they met with such violence that the concussion seemed to jar the mountain itself, as if it had been shaken by an earthquake. Peal upon peal of thunder rolled through the clouds, accompanied by terrific flashes of glittering lightning, that seemed to leap from heaven to earth, and from earth again through boundless space. To add to the terrific noise of the thunder, it bellowed through the mountain gorges, reverberating from cliff to cliff, like volleys of musketry, and was accompanied by the sound of creaking boughs, falling trees, and of rocks loosed by the winds, tumbling from the summit of the mountain to the abysses below. The falling rain soon accumulated into torrents, and these added to the din, as they fell over precipices, until one could scarcely do other than conclude that harmony had been broken up in the heavens and that the elements were engaging in one long, desperate, and terrific strife.

We did not stop—we could not; the storm came sweeping down the mountain with a fury that was irresistible; and nearly carried our animals over the cliffs. The clouds themselves seemed to be falling, for in addition to the torrents of rain which drenched us, we were closely enveloped in a thick mist which shut out from our view all surrounding objects. The horses entirely bewildered, became frantic, and dashed off in all directions, but chiefly up the sides of the gorge, down which our route lay. Some were speedily lost to view, while others almost precipitated themselves down the mountain side, regardless of danger. As for ourselves, we were powerless, and could only await the dispersion of the clouds that we might see what to do; and fortunately we were not compelled to wait long, as the storm was brief; it however made up in fury what it lacked in duration.

One by one we discovered our horses on the mountain side, trembling at the giddy height to which, in their terror, and while enveloped in fog, they had clambered. To get them down was a work of no little difficulty and danger, but it was accomplished, however, without accident, and we sped away for Lee's creek, a mountain stream which was known to rise with great rapidity, and when up was not fordable. The prospect of being water bound in the mountains for two or three days without provisions, the reader will admit, was not very inviting; and so we concluded, and we put on our best speed and gained the ford just in time; for five minutes later and it was a roaring torrent.

Not far from the foot of Boston mountain we passed through a little village of sixty or eighty houses, the inhabitants of which appeared to be settling some question of vital importance to the community, as they were engaged in a free fight after the most approved style—everybody being in; and oaths, rocks, clubs, and pistol-shots were the order of the day. Not receiving any invitation to participate, and being firm adherents of the theory that every community should be allowed to settle its domestic affairs in its own way, subject only to the Constitution of the United States—even though that way was a little rough—we passed along on our route, through a shower of ill-aimed missiles; and for once denied ourselves the luxury of engaging in a free fight.

We crossed the Arkansas River at Van Buren, and stopped with very good will at a plantation owned by a handsome widow, whose husband had been an officer in the regular service. Our entertainment was superb, and at nine o'clock we retired, and, being wearied, were soon enjoying a profound sleep. Toward midnight we were aroused by a loud barking in the yard from half a score or so of dogs. On going to the door I looked out and discovered a man in the act of turning our horses out of the lot. Seizing my rifle, I aroused Johnston, and started for the scene of operations. Luckily the animals were tired, and moved slowly, so that I was on the thief in a minute; and he, seeing that I was armed, loosed his hold, fired a shot, and fled. I returned his fire in haste and at random; so the ball did not take effect. The thief ran down the lane, at the end of which an accomplice was standing, and in a moment they both mounted their horses, and were soon out of sight.

At Fort Smith we entered the Indian Nation—the first we met being Choctaws. They had long been on friendly terms with the whites, and travelling through their country was as safe as, and perhaps safer than, in Arkansas. But few of the Indians build their houses on public roads, the exceptions generally being half-breeds. The full Indian always seeks some secluded spot on which to build. There were some handsomely improved farms through the country, but they were mostly owned by white men who had married Indian wives.

We camped out through the Nation, and procured our food, ready cooked, from the people. The squaws make excellent bread, and they supplied us bountifully with stewed venison. One may go to the Indian's house when he will, and he will find the kettle on and boiling, filled with the choicest meat. I invariably found the natives kind and obliging, and very reasonable in their charges. I often left Johnston to wait in the woods for his rations, while I sat down with the Indians, and enjoyed a warm meal. They had milk, eggs, and butter in abundance. All eat soup, succotash, and other "spoon victuals," out of the same dish, and with the same spoon; not from a scarcity of either, but from their laws of etiquette. He is regarded as exceedingly rude who refuses to eat soup from the same bowl with them, though each is supplied with separate plates, knives, and forks for the eating of meat, eggs, fruit, etc.

Although I did not discover any malicious disposition among the natives, I was informed that human life was held very cheap by them;

although they seldom molest white men travelling through their country, they frequently engage in deadly strife among themselves. I do not think much of their progress in civilization as a general thing. Here and there a farm and residence evinced industry and taste; but on the next, perhaps, one will see a crowd of grown young men and women, stark naked, playing marbles.

Their police regulations were well adapted to preserve order. In every township of six miles square there was a mounted force of ten men, one relief of whom was almost constantly in the saddle, travelling the country in all directions; and their mode of transmitting intelligence from one beat to another was only excelled by the telegraph.

The country is beautifully diversified with mountains, bold, rugged, and often isolated, rising from the surface of a level valley. They are covered with pine and cedar and other evergreens. The valleys are well adapted to grazing, and hence the principal wealth of the country is in horses, cattle, and hogs. We were often stopped at the bridges to pay toll. As the streams throughout the entire region usually have quicksand bottoms, it is a great convenience to travellers to have these bridges, although it is rather disagreeable to encounter a squaw every few miles vigorously demanding toll.

On Boggy River we were out in the rain for some time, and, being wet without, we were naturally dry within; and as the water in the Indian Nation does not possess sufficient consistency to quench thirst on such occasions, we resolved to procure some whisky. But how? That was the question. The law was very strict in prohibiting its importation or manufacture, and it was not easy to evade it. However, we must procure some; and, seeing a house at a short distance from the road, we stopped the horses to graze while I set out on the questionable mission of purchasing whisky, without knowing what to call it in Choctaw.

At the house I found no one at home except a squaw so old that her teeth were worn off even with her gums, and a young girl—very pretty, but very shy. I made known the object of my visit by telling her, in the very best English I could command, that I desired to purchase some whisky; but she failed to comprehend my meaning. I thought for a moment, and then concluded that as they had to smuggle it, perhaps they would be more familiar with bottled liquors, and I said "brandy," but was still not understood. "Morning-glory," "eye-opener," "whisky-cocktail," "gin-sling," "stone-wall," and the names of a host of other drinks arose in my mind, but were discarded, one after another, as altogether unknown in that barbarous locality; and I began to indulge in unavailing regrets that I had not learned to speak Choctaw before visiting the country. But at this moment a happy idea presented itself, and I forthwith proceeded to put it into execution. Up to this time the Indian girl had stood resolutely in the middle of the floor, as if prepared to dispute my further advance. I now passed by her, and walked to a table where there was a gourd.

Seeing the movement, she sprang to it, and filled it with water from a bucket nearby, and presented it to me to drink with every expression of kindness. Reader, I must own it was a most eloquent temperance lecture; and, perhaps, had I been alone, I should have made no further attempt to make myself understood; but Johnston was out on the prairie, thoroughly *drenched*, while I—well, for my part, I was *dry*. Pouring the water back into the bucket, I raised the gourd to my mouth, pretended to take a long drink, then made a wry face, smacked my lips, touched my breast with my forefinger, and then staggered a little. In an instant I was understood. Her black eye sparkled with delight, and she indulged in a merry laugh. Running out into the yard, she spent some time looking up and down as if in fear; then hastily entering the house, she lifted a board in the floor under the table, and drew forth a quart flask nearly full of the desired article, and handed it to me. I produced some money to pay for it, but she put back my hand in an agitated manner, pointed to the path by which I came, and patted her hands together several times hastily, which I interpreted into "go quick;" so without waiting to return thanks which she could not understand, to her evident satisfaction, I left.

That night we encamped on Boggy River, which, I believe, divides the lands of the Choctaws and Chickasaws. It is a very considerable stream, with broad, rich valleys, finely timbered. The land has been but little improved by labour. It was here that Johnston took it into his head to be "unlawful;" but that was the only difficulty I ever had with him.

At Boggy Depot we saw a great many Choctaws and Chickasaws assembled to hold a grand council, and, like all political gatherings, it was a mixed crowd. Some were gay, some were quiet, some were noisy, and, despite of stringent prohibition, some were *drunk*, and consequently boisterous. This depot is a great resort for all classes of traders.

From Boggy we travelled through a well-timbered country, occupied by the Chickasaws. It is not so mountainous as the Choctaw country, and I do not consider the people nearly so far advanced in civilization as the Choctaws, but far more docile and kind in their manners.

We crossed the Red River at Colbert's ferry, when the Colonel gave a shout of delight as he once more landed in Texas. My first impressions of the country were not pleasing. For twelve miles our way lay through a country heavily timbered and thickly interlaced with vines. A sandy soil, with, once in a while, a badly-managed farm and shabby log house, did not agree with my preconceived notions of the State; but after having travelled twelve miles, the landscape began to change. We reached high prairies, covered with luxuriant grass, and dotted with highly-cultivated plantations and beautiful groves. Immense herds of cattle were seen in every direction, and although this is not the chief grazing part of the State, there were many herds of horses, and flocks of sheep interspersed among the cattle. The soil is black and waxy, and no matter how much the roads are travelled they are never dusty, but become beaten down, like a cake of beeswax; and this species of soil extends as far south as Austin.

We passed through Sherman, a place of great commercial importance in Northern Texas, which at that time bid fair to be a large city; and the next place we reached was Dallas, celebrated for its mills which produce the best flour in Texas. The staple of the surrounding country is wheat, the soil being peculiarly adapted to its culture. Northern Texas is settled almost exclusively by people from Kentucky, Tennessee, and the West; and there is consequently more energy displayed in that section than in other portions of the State.

We reached Mr. Johnston's house, twelve miles south of Dallas, and were welcomed by his wife and daughter. They went out on the prairie to examine the stock; and as part of the horses had been represented as belonging to the estate of his wife's first husband, I naturally expected that the lady would recognize some of them, and call them by name, or otherwise particularly designate them; but to my astonishment she seemed never to have seen any of them before. I now remembered our haste, and the colonel's unaccountable excitement at times; and I could not escape the conviction that I had helped to run off a drove of stolen horses.

As my contract was now up, the colonel pressed me to continue with him; and his solicitations were cordially seconded by his wife and daughter; but as soon as I had secured a settlement with him, and received my money, I pushed on to Austin, where I expected to find employment as a printer.

Chapter 2

My First Indian Campaign

My expectations of finding employment as a printer, at Austin, were not realized, and I went back to Bell County, and turned my attention for a while to horse taming; but it was not long before there was found more congenial employment for me. The Kiowa, Comanche, and Kickapoo Indians suddenly began to wage a most relentless and cruel warfare upon the frontier settlements. Their first act of barbarity was committed far down in the country, within a few miles of where I was employed. About the 1st of May, 1859, a small detachment of Comanches appeared on the west side of Bell County, stole some horses, and drove a lance through the body of a little boy about twelve years of age; the act being done in the presence of an agonized mother, and of sisters frantic with grief and fear. The Indians, after mocking their terrified actions, galloped away, laughing and sneering at their agony.

The neighbourhood was at once aroused, and a few men went in pursuit; I, myself, constituting one of the party. The savages fled toward the mountains, at the head waters of the Colorado River; and high up on the San Gabriel, we came in sight of them; and at once the chase became so hot that the Indians "scattered,"—always their last strategic resort. We only succeeded in finding one, a gigantic fellow, who had long been known on the frontier, and was recognized by some of the pursuing party, as a famous Comanche warrior, called Big Foot. True to his own manhood, he sustained his reputation as a warrior to the very last, and ceased to resist only as he fell into the rolling waters of the San Gabriel, pierced with more than a dozen bullets from trusty Texan rifles. His body was swept away by the swift running stream; but his rifle, lance, and bow and arrows were captured, and divided out among the party as trophies. Big Foot was a giant in size and strength, being about seven feet high, and in all respects well proportioned; and his loss must have been severely felt by his tribe.

Their next outrage worthy of note, was the capture of two beautiful young ladies, named Whitson, whose persons they brutally violated. The ladies were walking home from a neighbour's house, where they had been on a visit, when they were suddenly surrounded by twenty-five savages, who committed the fearful deed already indicated, and then carried them away into a captivity a thousand times worse than death.

They lived near Weatherford, on the Brazos River, and after capturing them, the Indians carried them far out on the Staked Plains, stripped them, and left them on the open prairie, without a morsel of food, or a drop of water, and far away from any civilized habitation. When found they were lying beneath a little *mesquit* bush, locked in each other's arms, and quietly awaiting the approach of death. It was evident that they had been crazed by hunger, thirst, and cruel treatment, as their hands and arms were lacerated, as if they had struggled to tear the flesh from their own limbs. Luckily, we had a skilful surgeon and physician among our party, who immediately set about restoring them. We gave them liberally of our clothing and sewed blankets into skirts, so that they were soon as comfortable as could be expected. It was about two hours before sundown when we discovered them on a high plain, between the waters of the Colorado and the Double Mountain Fork of the Brazos; and I do not think they could have survived more than thirty-six hours longer if left to themselves.

We started that night and went a short distance, and in the morning began our journey to the settlements in earnest. On the Clear Fork of the Brazos the party separated; those of us who belonged down the country taking the route to Gatesville, while the friends and neighbours of the girls made haste to restore them to their sorrow-stricken parents and family. It was some time before they were sufficiently recovered to tell us their heart-rending story. Although they expressed their gratitude in the most fervent manner, and their eyes beamed with delight at the prospect of being restored to their home, their features wore a sad expression; and although we did all in our power to revive their spirits while they were with us, they were never seen to smile.

This outrage threw the whole frontier into a frenzy of excitement, and wherever the story of their wrongs was repeated, it enkindled a blaze of indignation which only the blood of the Comanche could quench.

From this time every species of depredation became common. Horses were stolen; cattle shot; men, women, and children murdered, and their residences committed to the flames; the mangled bodies being thrown within and consumed by the devouring element; and to make matters worse, the people were unfortunately divided in sentiment, relative to which was the guilty tribe. One faction, led by the redoubtable John R. Baylor, ascribed the murders to the Reserve Indians of Texas; notwithstanding the fact that these tribes were under the care and supervision of Major Neighbors, a careful, energetic, and strictly honest agent, who had the roll called frequently; and no warriors were allowed to be absent from either of the two reservations without a written permission.

Capt. Ross was the recognized leader of the other party, and contended stoutly for the innocence of the Reserve Indians, and alleged that the depredations were committed by the Comanches. But the fact that Baylor had once been the agent of the upper, or Clear Fork Reserves, caused his statements to be believed, and secured him numerous followers. Major Neighbors, the agent of the Reserve Indians, denounced him as a liar; and this was the cause, and the only cause, of Baylor's warlike demonstration. Raising about four hundred men, he marched to the Lower Reserve, vowing vengeance at every step. He was met about a mile from the agency by a small body of Caddoes, Tonchues,[1] and Wacos, and a skirmish ensued, and Baylor was handsomely whipped, and compelled to retreat toward the Clear Fork of the Brazos. His men then soon began to break up in squads, and scatter off—some to go home, others to hunt, while a few of the most daring ones pushed out after the wild Comanches.

While these stirring events were transpiring, Governor Runnells was not idle. He hastily fitted out a squadron of rangers, under command of Capt. John Henry Brown, an energetic and courageous man, who had had a wide experience in previous contests with the Indians, and was perfectly familiar with the frontier. This command was mustered at Belton, in Bell county, and left for the Indian country about the middle of June. I enlisted for six months, unless sooner discharged, and I presume the others entered for the same term.

Perhaps a description of our appearance will interest the reader. Imagine two hundred men dressed in every variety of costume, except the ordinary uniform, armed with double-barrelled shot-guns, squir-

---

1. Pronounced Tone-oo-a.

rel rifles, and Colt's six shooters, mounted on small, wiry, half wild horses, with Spanish saddles and Mexican spurs; unshaven, unwashed, undisciplined, but brave and generous men, riding pell-mell along roads, over the prairies, and through the woods, and you will be able to form a correct conception of a squad of Texan Rangers on the march. In such a band it is impossible to distinguish officers from privates, as the former have no distinct dress; and all act alike.

Usually, we encamped in a hollow square, placing our tents at regular intervals around the outside. The horses were tied to stakes by a forty foot rope, and allowed to graze outside the camp until "retreat," when they were led inside, and the rope shortened. Guards were posted outside the tents, and at some distance off; while the horse guards were inside the square. From Belton, we started in the direction of Gatesville, going up Cow House Creek, and crossing the Owl Creek mountains. Encamping on Owl Creek, we disposed ourselves for the night, and felt felicitated at the prospect of several hours' rest after a hard day's travel; but our hopes were fallacious.

At about two o'clock in the morning, when all were wrapped in deep slumber—the previous quiet having been perfect—we were suddenly aroused by a terrific scream; the horses surged, and pranced around their stakes, their eyes glittering, and their nostrils distended, while they made the air reverberate with sharp piercing snorts of rage and fear. It became evident that an enemy of no mean pretensions was upon us; and the men, springing to their guns, at once prepared for a defence. For perhaps five minutes the camp was hushed and still; then again that fearful shriek rang out, and a large panther sprang from a tree almost over the captain's tent, seized a piece of raw beef, which lay convenient, and was off with his booty so suddenly, that not a shot was fired. The animal was so large and powerful, that although the beef weighed at least thirty pounds, yet its flight was not in the least impeded. After indulging in a hearty laugh, and numerous speculations as to how the animal passed the guards unobserved, quiet was restored in the camp; and while most of the men again resigned themselves to slumber, the old hunters gathered in groups around the camp-fires, "spinning yarns," and relating remarkable adventures with "panter," "bar," and catamount, till daylight.

On the following day we passed through Gatesville, and encamped on the north side of town. The inhabitants insisted on presenting us with cakes, and pies, in lavish profusion, simply because, as one old man expressed it, while dealing out a basket full: "youre gwine whar you won't git no more soon." From Gatesville, our route lay through the "Cross Timbers," to the Red Fork of the Brazos. We hunted deer, wild turkeys, and musk hogs; fished in the little streams on the route; had bullfights at almost every camp; had horse-races, foot-races, and all sorts of sports; had plenty to eat and drink; and, in short, a good time generally.

About the 8th of July, we reached the Caddoe village, and encamped at a famous chalybeate spring, the waters of which are slightly tinctured with salt. It was some time before we could reconcile ourselves to the drinking of salt water, but as it was all that was to be had, we were compelled to come to it. After we had pitched our tents, I was detailed with a squad of fifteen, to accompany Captain Brown to the agency, where he had orders to report.

After scrambling over a very high mountain, and getting a horse killed, and a man accidently shot in the leg, we came in sight of the agency, where everything appeared to be in a high state of excitement. Captain Ross, the sub-agent, and Captain Plummer, commanding the United States regulars, at the post, had mistaken us for Baylor's men, and had accordingly prepared for a vigorous defence. The Indians were mustered in the rear of the regulars, who were drawn up in line, so as to command the approaches to the palisade fort; while two pieces of artillery, loaded with grape, were placed so as to sweep the road, by which we were approaching, and a small body of cavalry stood prepared to distinguish itself, whenever opportunity offered.

We held on the even tenor of our way, until arriving within short pistol range, when the troops were dismissed, and all gathered around us, to know who we were, where we came from, what we were going to do, and *how* we were going to do it? They were glad to see us, and treated us with every kindness. When Captain Brown explained his business to the Indians, and told them he had orders to whip Baylor off and away from their country, they were so delighted, that they could scarcely find words or means to express their joy. The chiefs of the different tribes crowded around the Captain, followed by their principal warriors, and in their eloquent sign language, and in broken English, expressed their friendship, as manifestly, as the most polished phrases could have portrayed it.

This was the Lower Reserve—the upper manifesting a different temper. Their head chief, Katampsie, possessed a warlike disposition. Exceedingly suspicious in all his dealings with the whites, and crafty as a fox, he was not so easily satisfied of our good intentions. He was at a loss to understand how one portion of the people of Texas should want to wage war on him, while another party, claiming to be the troops of the governor, should come professing friendship to the Indians, and hostilities to the white men, who had recently paid him a visit. He knew, and recognized no authority but the United States, and his own free will. When, therefore, he was informed that we were ordered to shoot any of his warriors found off the reservation, he regarded us as open enemies, and he himself was the first to set our authority at defiance.

After the first interview, we went back to our camp at the Caddoe village. A few days afterward, Lieut. Tob. Carmack, with twelve men was sent up the Clear Fork of the Brazos, with orders to scour the river bottom, in every direction, to see that none of the wild Comanches were lurking in the thick timber along the river—a very dangerous service; and we had orders not to fire a shot in any emergency, unless at an Indian.

After scouting the country a considerable time, we discovered signs of Indians, of a nature to lead us to believe that we were in the vicinity of a considerable force of Comanche, or Kiowa warriors. We struck the trail just before night, and consequently had but little daylight by which to follow it; and we consequently left it, and went down near the river bank to encamp. We tied our horses in a well concealed place, and established ourselves in a strongly defensive position, by the side of a bluff, on the second bank of the river, and kindled but a single small fire, to favour the guard, who had to watch both camps, and horses; after which we laid down to sleep. I came on guard, as the first relief, and Old Sharp as the second; and I was also to stand the last relief, in place of a young man who was sick; so that the guard duty for that night fell exclusively on Old Sharp and myself. Sharp was an experienced hunter and woodsman, and had had many an encounter with the Indians. He was social and lively, and about forty years of age; well built, with dark, keen eyes, black hair, and of swarthy complexion, with wiry frame; he was active and brave, and he received the name of "Old Sharp," not on account of age, but because of his expression and quaint manner. Never was the camp safer from surprise, than when he stood sentinel.

Time wore on slowly that night, as it is a lonely task to stand guard, in the depths of the trackless forests of the southwest, with no sound reaching the ear, except the twitter of the night bird, the hoot of the owl, the occasional sighing of a tired horse, or the breathing of one's wearied companions. Perhaps the sentinel, at such a time, may find that his thoughts have left him, and are wandering away amid more pleasant scenes—by chance revelling with delighted friends, or lingering around loved ones at home, who anxiously await his tardy coming. It is a cruel thing, when one is lost in sweet reverie, to be recalled to a sense of his isolated and dangerous situation, by the melancholy howl of a wolf, the agonized screaming of the panther, or, as is often the case, by the muffled sound of *moccasined* feet, stealing around him. Not unfrequently is the sentinel first made aware of the danger which surrounds him, by the sharp twang of the bowstring, and the plunging of an arrow deep into his flesh.

I had become wearied with watching on this night, and my mind was lost in a dreamy reverie; I had done my best to pierce the gloom of the forest with my eye, in order to detect the slightest movement; I had listened to every sound, with an eagerness, which those who have stood sentinel, and have had the lives of hundreds of their companions entrusted to their care, can readily comprehend; I saw around me the sleeping forms of my companions, and felt, and knew, that upon my watchfulness, and fidelity, depended their safety, and their lives. My time had passed away slowly enough. Not an unwonted sound had broken in upon the solemn stillness of the night; and at length, when my time had expired, I went to arouse Old Sharp; but had scarcely touched him, when a loud rattling of rocks at the water edge, brought him to his feet instantaneously. "What's that?" said he, in a whisper. "Horse loose, I reckon," was my reply, in an undertone, and leaving Sharp on guard, I slipped down to the river bank, which was here about eight feet high, and perpendicular.

I was advancing rapidly, with my left hand raised before me, to protect my face from overhanging boughs, and my right on the stock of my "Navy Six," when the sound of rattling rocks was repeated, but I failed to detect the hard ring of horses' hoofs, and I therefore at once concluded an Indian was secreted in the vicinity. I was going rapidly toward the sound, which, in turn, seemed to approach me, when I suddenly stepped over the bank down on the hard rocks, and found myself confronted by a full grown black bear; indeed, I had almost fallen on his head.

I sprang to my feet without delay, and drew my pistol as quickly as possible, but it was too late. Just as I regained my feet, the bear reared upon his hind legs, bellowed piteously with fright, almost turned a back summersault, and then fled precipitately across the shoal, and into the thickets on the opposite bank of the river.

Returning to Sharp, he wanted to know what the "row" was, and I informed him that it was a bear that had made the noise. "Yes, yes," he replied, "but I allowed you had knifed the 'cuss,' from the way he 'bellered.'" This was the first time I thought of my knife, though I then carried a splendid Bowie knife in my belt. The bear had awaked some of the men by his bellowing, but as soon as they discovered that no harm had been done, and that the "varmint" had made his escape, they lazily rolled themselves up in their blankets and slept again.

Sharp was fully aroused by this little incident, but was not at all pleased that I had suffered the "bar" to escape. "You had oughter have knifed him," he insisted; but I was satisfied to let the bear off with Uncle Toby's address to the fly: "go, poor devil, the world is big enough for me and thee."

Old Sharp now seated himself on the ranger's chair, that is, an inverted saddle, and I took a seat beside him, to see what would turn up next, or if our nocturnal friend would pay us another visit. The little affair at once roused in Old Sharp's mind the recollection of many a scene, and hair-breadth escape, and he went on to relate several adventures of his own, with "bar;" our conversation, of course, being carried on in a whisper; and he concluded his narratives with: "but la, boy, the bars a'in't savage in this country like they are furder north; they git plenty to eat in the southern country, but furder north, 'specially in the winter season, when pressed with hunger, they git terribly severe."

By the time he had concluded his stories, I was too sleepy to continue the confab, so I picked out a good place by the side of an old log, where there were plenty of dry leaves, for a bed, and laid down to sleep, although I was some distance from the remainder of the party. I had been asleep some time, when I felt a sense of closeness or warmness, and woke up; and judge my surprise on finding myself entirely covered up with the leaves, and I felt Sharp's hand upon me, at the same moment.

"Come, my boy," said he, "there is danger here."

In an instant I was on my feet, rifle in hand, ready for any emergency. "Injuns?" I asked.

"Look thar," said he, pointing to a dark object, slowly retreating into the shadows of the timber.

Instantly I brought my rifle to bear upon it, when Sharp laid his hand on my shoulder, saying, in a whisper,

"Stop, boy, thar's Injuns about, and ye musn't shoot."

At this moment, the animal turned around, and came back a few paces toward us, stopped with one fore foot partially raised, and glared upon us in an apparently mingled rage and astonishment. Sharp only tightened his grip on my shoulder, and whispered:

"Look him right straight in the eyes, boy."

Instinctively I did as I was ordered; never moving a muscle, but gazing straight into those two great, fiery eyeballs. We stood thus for perhaps twenty seconds, when the animal, putting its foot softly to the ground, stepped half a dozen paces toward us, and stooped upon its hinder legs for a moment, while its tail moved gracefully to and fro. It eyed us thus for perhaps five seconds, then turned itself and again retreated into the depths of the forest, looking back as it went, until it got a considerable distance from us, when it uttered a scream so loud and shrill, that it echoed through the woods like the shriek of a terrified woman, except that it was louder than the human voice. It was a panther of the largest size; and as it disappeared, Old Sharp relaxed his grasp upon my shoulder, saying slowly:

"I thought that varmint war about to give us some trouble. Pick up your blanket, boy, and come up where we kin see the horses, thar's danger here; thar's Injuns in these woods. I've bin oneasy for some time; wake up t'other chap if you're sleepy, we must have two men out at onct."

I declined, however, to awaken the sick man, who, though an agreeable companion and a good soldier, was in too feeble health to endure the fatigues of so rugged a service. I then informed Sharp that I was willing to stand with him till morning; and from that time till daylight nothing occurred to further disturb the camp.

Early next morning we dispatched our breakfast, mounted our horses and again struck out on the trail, keeping a good lookout for Indians. It was scarcely half an hour after sunrise when we descried a faint smoke curling up through the timber on the river bottoms, but apparently not in the direction in which we were travelling. Leaving the trail, we moved directly toward the smoke at a charge; and as we entered the timber, we could see ten or a dozen Indians spring up from the ground, rifles in hand, the whole party scampering off toward a thicket some distance away. There was no chance to cut them off from the thicket before they could enter it; but we kept up the charge until we had come within two hundred yards of it, when we received a pretty well-directed volley from behind the bushes. We then hastened to surround the thicket as quickly as possible; but while we were doing this, the savages mounted their horses, and charged out upon and over us, I might almost say, for we had deployed too far to be able to rally in time to prevent it.

Lieut. Carmack rallied his men and made preparations for a pursuit. We had discharged a portion of our *yagers* and pistols in the *mêlée*, which had to be reloaded; and one of our men had received a wound in the arm from an arrow, and two horses had been hurt in the charge. It was a short job to extract the arrows from the horses, though they fought and kicked frantically; but not so with the man. Carmack tried to pull the arrow out, but it was no go. Next Sharp proposed to try it; he had had some experience in such matters, having been wounded more than once with arrows in his time. Opening his hands, he took the arrow between his palms and began rolling and lifting it, at the same time. The wounded man whose name was Williams, sat still on a log and endured the torture heroically. It lasted a full minute—this rolling and twisting—before the dull arrow had cut its way out of the flesh. His success so elated Sharp, that he held it up triumphantly, saying:

"Thar, now, I told you so; ef you'd a pulled agin on that arrer, you'd a did the business for that arm. Do you see that?" he continued, pointing to where the arrow was bent against the bone; "now the wonder is, that the spike hadn't a come out the fust pull you made."

Hastily bandaging Williams' arm, we mounted and commenced the pursuit. The Indians had headed directly for the Upper Reserve, now about twelve miles distant. We pursued till we were satisfied they belonged to Katampsie's band of Reserve Comanches, when turning, we struck out on our return to the Caddoe village. While passing through the settlements we were informed of a great many petty outrages committed by both Reserves, since their fight with Baylor's party. At one place they had robbed a man's dwelling; at another, thrown down the fences, and rode through and trampled down whole fields of corn; one man had been robbed of a fine mare; several watermelon patches had been plundered; and in one of the last-named offenses, we chanced to catch a party; but they mounted their horses and were quickly off. Not content with what they could eat, each man had some sort of a sack, and some of them, two or three, all filled with melons. As they fled we closed in on them at a charge, but our horses were tired, and no match for their fresh ponies. When the pursuit was at its height, they hastily cut their sacks loose from their saddles and dropped them on the trail.

Not desiring to provoke hostilities with the Lower Reserve, to which these Indians belonged, we did not fire upon them; nor did they attempt to fire upon us. They perfectly understood our orders whenever found off their reserves; but they evidently did not fear us much, for when they were high up on the mountain, one of them turned in his saddle and shouted back:

"White man's hoss no good; Injun's hoss heap good; white man no catch um. You go home; hoss heap sick; me see um." Then, with a loud laugh, he pressed on with his companions. Carmack did not fancy following them into the mountain, for there were at least thirty of them; and they would have been more than a match for us, if they assumed a hostile attitude. We dismounted here and helped ourselves to the captured melons and encamped nearby for the night. We procured milk from the settlers in the vicinity; and the women brought us warm bread, fresh butter, etc., which proved a great treat, as we had been living for some days on meat alone.

On the following day we rode back to the Caddoe village and once more found everything in excitement; the cause being a report to the effect that the wild Comanches had come down on the Lower Reserve and stolen seventy-five head of horses, and then made good their escape. Captain Brown, with as many of his men as could be spared, and a large force of regulars and friendly Indians, were soon on the trail, while a party of us that were left, had nothing to do but to rest ourselves and horses until they returned.

About the first of August, Captain Brown sent Captain Knowlin to the fork, with similar orders given to Lieut. Carmack, *viz*: to fire on any of Katampsie's band who might be found off their reservation. We had the usual amount of sport all the way up the Brazos, killing deer, turkeys and antelope in abundance, together with a venerable bear, so old she was nearly toothless. We saw no Indian signs until we got within about three miles of the reserve line on the east, when we were suddenly attacked while at dinner, by about ninety Comanches. Our horses were concealed in a thicket nearby, and were not discovered by the Indians at all, or it would have been impossible for us to have saved them. We were seated round in a ring, with our smoking mess pans filled with stewed venison, in the centre, when we were suddenly startled by the long, fierce war-hoop, and looking up, we saw a large party of Comanches in full war paint and costume, each with every feather that his vanity, or the custom of his tribe would prompt or allow him to wear, streaming in the wind, while their horses were literally bedizened with paint and silver plate. The warriors' shields and clothing were likewise spangled all over with silver; but we had no time to enjoy this splendid array of barbaric pomp, although it was one possessed of fearful interest to us.

When we first discovered them they were under full headway, coming around a point of timber; and the next instant they came down upon us at a charge. We had barely time to seize our rifles, which were lying beside us, and spring to the side of a house nearby, when they sent a shower of arrows among us. We delivered a hasty but well directed volley as we ran, and emptied seven of their saddles. Staggered and annoyed at resistance from so small a party, they circled away to a safe distance, reformed and charged down upon us again; this time sweeping around us in a complete circle and getting between us and our horses. But their arrows flew among us harmlessly, while five more of the assailants fell from our well directed fire. But they were not yet defeated, and returned upon us a third time. We were then ordered to aim at their horses, and I think the bullet of every man must have taken effect, and some must have got two shots, for we killed fifteen horses, and there were but thirteen of us in our party.

The Indians now circled away out of sight, around the point of timber where we had first observed them, and did not return. Presently we saw a runner start for the village at full speed, and in about half an hour we could see squaws and boys carrying guns and shot pouches to the Indians in the timber. Seeing this the Lieutenant inquired:

"What do you say, boys, shall we fight with them?"

"Fight them," was the answer on all sides.

We had a hope of being relieved by the regulars from Camp Cooper, and this, with our recent success, made us confident of victory. By this time we could see the Indians filing around the point of timber and approaching us on foot, in the fullest confidence. They moved on toward us until nearly within rifle range, when they went down into a deep ravine, which ran nearly in a half circle around the house, and about one hundred and eighty yards distant from it. It was evident from their deliberate movements, that they intended to make sure work of it this time, even if it was slow. For my part, I could almost feel the scalp slip on my head. The savages followed down the ravine and were soon within short range, and began to peep over the bank at us.

We kept a close watch but did not fire a gun, for we were expect-

"When we first discovered them, they were under full headway, coming around a point of timber; and the next instant they came down upon us at a charge."

ing a charge. We kept ourselves well sheltered by the corners of the house, while the Indians hugged the bank. Presently the report of a rifle was heard in the ravine, which was followed by a volley, almost as well delivered as if fired by disciplined soldiers. Then was heard the war-whoop, and the fire became general, but irregular—each man loading and shooting as fast as possible. We only discharged our rifles when we saw a sure mark, always taking care that not more than two or three pieces were fired at a time, holding our loaded guns and pistols ready to receive a charge; but it did not come, and the Indians, after keeping up a desultory firing for an hour and a half, struck out for their village, carrying with them their dead and wounded.

It was apparent that they had been expecting us, their horses being ornamented and feathered with great care. Their own faces were also elaborately painted, and they were decked out in their most fanciful war dress. After they dismounted they fought us with Mississippi rifles; and, as evidence of the skill with which they were handled, it is only necessary to state that over fourteen hundred bullets struck the house, and perhaps as many more whistled disagreeably near to it. As there were no loop holes in the house, we were compelled to fight around the corners, which prevented us from doing as much execution as we otherwise would have done; but with all this, the savages were severely punished, as we counted eighteen litters taking off dead and wounded, and found, beside, three corpses which they had been unable to carry away.

As soon as they commenced leaving we began to fear they would be reinforced and return, and we immediately dispatched a voting man named Gus Sublett, for the Caddoe village for more men. He was a manly fellow, and would do as he promised—*go through or die!* We immediately began to put the house in a good state of defence, cutting loop holes on every side, and covering the roof with raw hides, to prevent it from being fired by burning arrows. We had two men badly wounded who claimed considerable attention, as they suffered severely; one of them, Patrick O'Brien, having received a ball in his hip, and the other, whose name was Terry, had been shot in the calf of the leg.

After twenty-eight hours our reinforcements arrived, when we felt a perfect ability to hold our own; but we were not attacked; the Indians remaining on the reserve without any further admonitions. I do not know that the savages would have left off where they did, had it not been for the intervention of Major Lieper, their agent, who appeared on the ground just after the fight was over; and, on our promise to cease firing, rode over and had a *powwow* with Katampsie, in which the latter expressed a willingness to "quit and call it even," provided we would do the same; but Captain Knowlin insisted that Katampsie should give us six sacks of flour and two hundred pounds of bacon, as "blood money;" and to this he agreed, but refused to let more than three of our men go into his village after it.

The Indians then gathered up their fallen braves and returned in sullen silence to their village; but that silence was not long maintained, for their women speedily began to "howl" the dead. This is a regular ceremony among them, at which, in addition to outbursts of grief and exclamations of sorrow from relatives and friends of the deceased, all the old crones of the tribe join in howling over the remains. An Indian "wake" is a noisy concern—especially if the deceased is a man of note. A wife crops her hair off, even around her neck, and scarifies her breasts, arms, and thighs, as a token of mourning for her husband; and a daughter undergoes similar manipulations on the death of her father. The scarifying knife is fixed in the end of a stick, so as to gauge the cut to a certain depth, generally well through the skin, in order to form a tolerably broad scar. Although the process is a severe one, they not only readily endure it, but use the knife on themselves.

On the day following the fight Sterling White, Sublett, and myself went into the village after our "blood money." When Katampsie saw us coming he sprang to his feet, vowing vengeance. The old fellow had several squaws about his tent, who, I suppose were his wives, as they all seized hold of him and held him tightly as soon as they saw us prepare to defend ourselves. The chief raved and tore, jumped up and down, and cursed us in Spanish, finally worrying the women down till they were obliged to turn him loose; when, instead of carrying out his threats, he quietly sat down on a dilapidated cracker box, folded his arms across his breast, and appeared for some time lost in meditation.

Again we pressed our demand, when he arose, and in company with some of his leading warriors, went with us to Major Lieper, and requested him to fill our requisition from the government stores, which was promptly done, and we left the inhospitable village for camp, well satisfied that Katampsie's warriors were not inclined to back their chief in his hostile intentions toward the whites.

A small force was left to patrol the country up and down, to see that the Indians obeyed orders, while the remainder of our party returned to the camp at the Caddoe village. The men at the upper agency were left under charge of Captain Knowlin, while Captain Brown, with the main force, went down the country to guard the more exposed settlements.

While we were near the Caddoe village, a reliable citizen came into our camp and reported having seen a considerable force of Indians on Rock Creek, a little over twenty miles distant. Judging from the intelligence received as to the number of warriors, Captain Brown thought it prudent to prepare for a defence of his camp rather than to start in pursuit. We were out of ammunition; and to procure a supply, it was necessary for someone to go to Belknap, twenty-two miles distant, and it fell to my lot to be the messenger. It was by no means a pleasant task, partly because the weather was exceedingly hot, but especially because all the Indians in that region had come to look upon the Rangers as enemies. I passed through the agency, and as long as I was near the regulars I felt perfectly safe; but was a little doubtful as to personal safety outside of their jurisdiction. About half way between the agency and Belknap, in going around a short turn in the road, I met sixteen warriors riding along at a walk. Instantly the foremost of them strung their bows and unslung their quivers; but I rode deliberately and boldly up, till within the length of a lance of them, when one of them made signs for me to stop, which I did. Four of them tried to ride behind me, but having seen them string their bows, I refused to let them pass; at the same time throwing my horse around so that a gigantic forest tree covered my back.

They affected not to understand me, when I drew my pistol from my belt, and said to them in Mexican, "*parreti, amigos!*"[2] and immediately they stopped, with a cunning laugh, and turned to their chief, as if awaiting orders. The chief, whose name I learned was Placido, and who was afterward my firm friend, seemed to regard me with suspicion. Eyeing me from head to foot, he asked me some questions in his own tongue; but I told him I did not understand him; but he went on, delivering a lengthy discourse, still speaking in Indian; and seemed to regard me with an air that said, "I know very well what I am saying, and you must understand it."

I now said in Mexican—"*no entiende*"—I don't understand. He then looked at me, for some time, and inquired my name, speaking in Mexican, and I told him my patronymic. He then accused me of being a Texan and an enemy. I understood him now perfectly; his eyes fairly blazed with malicious anger, as I deliberately eyed him from head to

---
2. "Stop, friends."

foot. I began to think it was a mixed case as to whether or not I passed further inspection. The savages stood around me, in a half circle, seemingly determined to know, for certain, all about me; and at the same time, the lack of a medium to convey ideas, rendered our situation peculiarly embarrassing, particularly as they had already begun to show unmistakable signs of hostility. They held a short consultation in their own tongue, after which the Chief again asked me my name, speaking in Mexican. I again favoured him with it, but it was evidently not the information he sought; and he hesitated a moment as if to recall some forgotten word, when he said:

"*Donde vienne usted?*" (where do you come from?)

Without hesitation, I answered, "From Fort Arbuckle."

"*Por donde vamos?*" (where are you going?) he continued.

"To Fort Belknap," was my answer.

"*Que quiere alla?*" he persisted in inquiring.

I told him I had a "big letter" for Captain Thompson, from Captain Plummer, and that I was a United States soldier, and not a Texan; and that I was friendly to them so long as they were friendly to the United States soldiers; and this being delivered in a very earnest manner, and tolerable lingo, made some impression; for, pointing to my drawn pistol, he indicated a desire to have it returned to its scabbard. I pointed to their bows, and intimated that I wanted them returned to their quivers. They looked at one another, and laughed, and then unstrung their bows, while I, at the same time, put my pistol in my belt.

After expressing great love for the United States soldiers, and undying hatred to all Texans, they bid me "*Adios,*" and galloped away; not, however, until they had bantered me for a horse race and a horse "swap." I watched them till they had disappeared, and then resumed my journey. I got through all right, and with my ammunition and carts, returned to Caddoe Village.

On my way back, I heard most piercing cries of pain, near an Indian camp; and as it was quite dark, I approached as nearly as possible, in order to discover whence it proceeded. Riding cautiously, and keeping on soft ground, I approached within one hundred and fifty yards of a large fire, from which the shrieks appeared to emanate, when I discovered about forty warriors in a circle around a tree to which a prisoner was tied. From his appearance, I took him to be a Comanche; and his captors were trying his manhood by threshing him with a raw-hide rope. His sufferings were excruciating; and the crackling fire was built so as to throw out a strong heat on his lacerated back.

"His sufferings were excruciating, and the crackling fire was built so as to throw out a strong heat on his lacerated back."

He was greatly exhausted when I saw him, and he was not bearing himself with that stoicism which the Indian is supposed to possess. He was probably put to death that night. His captors were exceedingly grave, and quiet, during the short time I watched them; not one moving from his place except the one who applied the lash.

The victim had probably ventured too far, while following the avocation of a Comanche warrior, *viz.*: horse stealing, and had fallen into the hands of the Philistines, who, although they themselves might not set a better example, were determined to convince the unlucky one that it was a great crime to be caught. Fearing that, if discovered, I might become more than a disinterested spectator of the scene, and not relishing the idea of assisting the prisoner in playing his particular role, I rode away as quietly as I approached, and put out for our camp, in a hurry. Residents of a civilized country will find it difficult to believe that I witnessed this scene within three miles of the agency, and that the actors were Delawares, who have been for years under the supervision of the United States authorities; yet the statement is as true as it is lamentable.

CHAPTER 3

More Adventure

The people on the frontier became daily more and more incensed against the Indians; and although they knew the government intended to remove them at the earliest practicable moment, to the head waters of the False Washita River, it required the utmost vigilance to keep citizens off the Reserves and the Indians on them. At length the preparations for the removal were complete, and on the 15th of August, 1859, the march to the Washita Agency began. The affair was superintended exclusively by United States troops, under command of Major Geo. H. Thomas, now Major General Thomas, who managed matters in an able manner, and gave complete satisfaction to the people of the frontier. Every warrior was compelled to be present and answer to his name, at roll call, in the same manner as the regular soldiers; and in this way, very few had an opportunity to drop out and lay back, to wreak private vengeance on the settlers; nevertheless, fearing that some might escape the vigilance of the regulars, we had orders to follow up, and arrest or kill any Indian found straggling more than three miles to the rear of the column. We had but little to do except exercise vigilance.

One adventure, however, shows the partiality of the Indian for horse-flesh. We discovered a party of horsemen, one day, at a distance from us, and near the west bank of the Trinity river. We were on rising ground, and they had not discovered us, and we therefore hastily withdrew and took down the river under cover of the timber, directly toward them; they were on one side of the river and we on the other. There were ten or a dozen of them, and were apparently leading more horses than they were riding. We rode on till within about a mile of the party, when we could plainly discern that they were Indians, and immediately we gave chase. Our horses were put to their best speed, and we rapidly gained on the savages. One by one their led horses were turned loose, while the "quirt"[1] was mercilessly used to those they were riding. Soon their baggage was cut loose and left on the trail to facilitate their escape; and after this the Indians made much better time, and it became, for a while, about an even race, we neither gaining nor losing anything; when at length the Indians began to scatter, with a view to keeping out of our way till night, when they hoped to escape. Two of their horses were evidently badly wearied, and were rapidly "giving out;" and, therefore, Jack Anderson and myself singled them out and followed them, till they abandoned the animals, which they did in the mouth of the rocky gorge which led up into a mountain.

The savages were about a quarter of a mile ahead of us, and consequently when we reached the spot, they were already far up the side of the mountain, which was almost inaccessible; and seeing that it would be impossible to overtake them, we caught the abandoned horses and started for our rendezvous on the Little Washita River. We were much wearied, having run our horses, as we afterward discovered, about thirty-two miles. We had a rough time finding our way through a strange country to an unknown place during the night; but it was accomplished. We found about one-half of the command assembled on our arrival.

A small detachment was sent out to scout through the country in the rear of the Indians as far as Red River crossing, while the remainder lay encamped on the Little Washita, up which stream we reconnoitred till we reached its head. We then proceeded across to the headwaters of the Brazos, near the junction of the Double Mountain Fork, where we encamped in an old, deserted cabin on the waters of the Red Fork, picketing our horses on short rope, and putting out a strong guard, for we had been following a trail all day which seemed to be about two days old. During the night we were once more visited by a panther, which got in among our horses, and made them perfectly frantic with fear. I was on guard at the time, and as it passed very near me I was in nearly the same condition as the animals. As it was between myself and the camp, I dare not shoot without danger of hurting either the men or horses, so that I was obliged to let it pass.

It walked along very slowly and deliberately, apparently inspecting each horse separately; when presently, as if satisfied in its own mind on some important point, it turned and trotted out over my beat, eyeing

---

1. A short, heavy riding whip, with a bone or iron handle.

me suspiciously all the time. It made for the timber, and when it got about thirty yards from where I stood, I blazed away with my shotgun, which was charged with heavy buckshot. The panther bounded into the air, and as it again reached the ground, it whirled its head around, and bit its side, at the same time uttering most doleful screams. Knowing that I had done a rash thing in wounding it in the night, I was considering the propriety of "falling back on the reserve," when it suddenly seemed to comprehend my intentions, and started for me.

I now saw that there was no chance for retreat. He cleared nearly half the distance which separated us at the first bound. Quick as thought I brought down my gun to fire the other barrel; but before I had time to pull, half a dozen guns cracked near me, and the panther once more bounded in the air, and fell again to the earth in the agonies of death. This was the first time I thought of the camp. The men in it, having heard my shot, rushed out ready for any emergency. I was considerably relieved when I saw the panther fall, but fearing lest he might rise again, I fired my remaining load into his side. Some of the men brought a chunk of fire, and we examined the body, and found it literally riddled with shot. The animal was both large and old.

This was during the last relief, and as daylight was near at hand, the men did not again go to bed, and I was accordingly relieved from watch, and I determined to pay my respects to some turkeys which I had heard for some time "gobbling" in the distance. Following the direction of the sound I came to a tree on the bank of a creek, and about three quarters of a mile from camp. Its branches were literally covered by turkeys—the number being not less than forty or fifty. I fired and brought down two, and was tying their feet together, when in the distance I heard a yell as if from a single Indian. Now, thought I, here's for glory; I'm in for a single-handed fight, and off I started in the direction of the sound, taking good care to scrutinize every place that could conceal a foe.

I advanced rapidly, but cautiously, for nearly a mile when again the shrill whoop rang out, but apparently as far off as ever, and in the same direction. But this time the yell was answered, and by at least thirty voices. This was decidedly more than I had bargained for; it was a perfect extinguisher upon my desire to distinguish myself, and my ambition for a single-handed fight gave way to apprehensions for personal safety. I felt certain of my ability to fight and kill one Indian, but I did not care to engage a greater number, and I struck out for camp in a hurry. Passing the place where I "hung my turkeys up," I shouldered the game, and "made tracks frequently."

When in camp I threw down my turkeys, and got soundly lectured by all hands, as is usual in such cases, for my foolhardiness; after which I reported to Captain Brown that I had heard Indians. Breakfast was soon dispatched, horses saddled and mounted, and we started in the direction of the sounds. After travelling about five miles we came to another old house, which, although long deserted by its owner, had evidently been occupied the previous night. A fire was burning on the hearth, and part of the carcass of a deer was lying on the ground outside; and there were horse-tracks all around the door, as if a party had just mounted and ridden away. Taking their trail, which was broad and plain, we followed at a gallop nearly all day; at times, however, losing the trail, and then, of course, consuming time in finding it again. About noon we passed a herd of cattle, several of which had arrows sticking in their bodies, and were piteously moaning with pain.

During the day we passed several little piles of sticks crossed on the trail. The Indians evidently had one or more prisoners, and the sticks meant that they were to be tortured and burned at the stake. This gave our energies a fresh impetus, and we redoubled our exertions to overtake the party. Encamping for the night we pushed on again, following the trail, on the next day, and at about ten o'clock we found where the Indians had killed a mare, and after taking out her colt, had devoured it—a very common habit of the Comanches when hard pushed by a pursuing party. We hurried along till we came in sight of the hills at the head of the Big Washita river, having ridden at a gallop nearly all day. Toward night we came to a deserted camp which it was evident the Indians had but recently left; meat was still roasting over the fire on their broiling sticks, and a gourd was on the ground filled with water from a spring nearby. The water had not yet become warm, though the sun shone directly upon it.

No shoe tracks were found near to indicate the presence of white persons; all the feet had been *moccasined*, and it was also ascertained that one little child was with the party. We likewise found a strip of calico with a broad hem on it. Near the camp it was evident that a captive had been bound, and cut loose in a hurry to escape. After examining the ground carefully we came to the conclusion that the prisoner, whoever he might be, was, at least, an Indian, as was also the little child. We discovered that the savages had scattered from this camp in different directions, and we found on one of the trails little bits of paper, strewn along at intervals for several hundred yards; and a little further along was a pass, given by Major Leiper to a Reserve Comanche of an unpronounceable name.

Concluding that this was the right trail, we travelled as fast as our now jaded and starved horses could go for another two hours, when night came on, and we encamped on the trail, and rested till morning. We were now on the very headwaters of the Big Washita, about one hundred and fifty miles north of Fort Belknap. Our horses were jaded, and we tired and out of provisions, so that the captain resolved to abandon the pursuit, and return to our old camp on the Little Washita. Travelling leisurely so as to recruit our horses, we arrived at our destination, and found Captain Knowlin and his company anxiously awaiting our arrival.

Having performed the duties assigned to us in that section, we rested two or three days, and took up our line of march for Fort Belknap. Heartily tired of an exclusively meat diet, our lively imaginations conjured up pictures of—bread and butter; for which our stomachs longed with a hunger that could be appeased by bread and butter alone; and this article of diet constituted the principal topic of conversation all the way to Belknap. At Fort Belknap Captain Brown received orders to return to Belton to muster out his men, as they had now accomplished the purpose for which they were mustered in. We had glorious times in fishing and hunting all the way back; travelling all the time just as fancy or caprice dictated, and living off the best of everything which the country afforded. On our arrival at Belton the people gave us a hearty welcome, after which we were honourably discharged; though we had to wait for our pay till it could be brought from Washington City to Austin, which consumed several weeks; after which we received it, at the rate of forty-six dollars per month, in gold.

CHAPTER 4

With the Rangers Again

I now occupied my time in taming wild horses and hunting, having an occasional chase after the Indians, until winter, when I operated with a Minute Company from Burnett county; our duties being merely to guard the frontier from invasion. A Lieut. Hamilton was in command of our company, and there was a *chain* of companies of the same class, extending along the entire frontier, numbering nearly twenty-five men each, under the command of a Lieutenant. They kept up a constant patrol, across the country rendering it exceedingly unsafe for the Indians to venture down on the settlements. Nevertheless, their depredations continued to be of frequent occurrence. The savages would come in by the mountain trails, on the Colorado River, until they would get far down in the settlements, when they would scatter out in small parties of from two to ten, and, by travelling in the dead hours of the night, they would reach points which they considered secure; then, by a preconcerted signal, they would raise havoc in perhaps a dozen different places, at the same time.

This kept the country in a constant fever of excitement, and, as is usual on such occasions, no one knew who to trust. Although the Minute Men were ever on the alert, and zealous in their duty, still the Indians were crafty, and restless in their hostility toward the whites; and, of course, they often succeeded in their purposes; and this gave rise to many complaints against the Rangers; and they were charged with being careless in the discharge of their duties. The two parties referred to in a preceding chapter, continued their contentions without intermission; and while the excitement was at its height, the official term of Governor Runnells expired, and Gen. Sam. Houston was inaugurated in his place. The general was entirely conversant with the condition of affairs, and the first thing he did was to organize a regiment of Rangers, under command of Col. M. T. Johnston, an able officer, and experienced in Indian warfare; and in addition, he had been engaged in the Regulator and Moderator war in Texas, and also in the contest with Mexico, where he had taken part in the storming of Monterrey. He soon enlisted a fine regiment, which was ably officered; and the governor and people naturally expected great success to attend its efforts. Houston's design was to carry the war into the Comanche and Kiowa country.

I enlisted at Waco, under command of Capt. J. M. Smith, who was likewise an experienced soldier, and well qualified to do service in an Indian war. Col. Johnston ordered the different companies to rendezvous at Fort Belknap, on the 1st of March, 1860. Our company travelled up the Brazos River from Waco, where it was recruited, to Fort Belknap, and was the first on the ground.

A few days before we arrived there, a young woman—Miss Murphy—was carried off from Murphy's ranch, near Belknap. So secretly had the affair been managed, that not a trace of her was ever discovered; and all that was known of the presence of the Indians, was, that a few *moccasin* tracks were seen in the vicinity of the house. Miss Murphy had gone to the front yard for wood, while her sister-in-law, a Mrs. Murphy, was cooking in the house, with the door leading to the yard, wide open. The young lady did not return with the wood, and Mrs. Murphy went out to look for her; but failing to see her, at once blew the horn, which soon brought the men to the house; but after the most thorough search, no traces of her could be discovered. The neighbours were aroused, and the search continued, but with no better success than on the previous day; though it was evident that she had been carried off by the Indians. Parties scoured the country far and wide, in the hope of finding some traces of her, but she was never heard of more; at least so long as I was in the State.

We had scarcely pitched our tents at Belknap, before a citizen came into camp with the intelligence that the Indians were depredating on the settlements but three miles distant. We mounted in haste, and were soon off. We were not troubled by delays in putting our army stores in motion, for the reason that we had no commissary department, and nothing for one to do; nor was any time consumed in drawing and cooking rations, for we had none.

We repaired to the place at once, and found that a man named Peabody had been brutally murdered. He was shot with arrows, eight or ten times, and then lanced as often, after which he was scalped.

The murder was committed by nine Comanches, in full view of seven white men, who, had they been worthy of their race—of the name of men even—could have whipped the savages off, and perhaps saved Peabody's life. They alleged a fear that a greater number of Indians were in the vicinity; and so they mounted their horses and left the prisoner to his fate, in full view of his agonized family, and within fifty yards of his own home. Having committed the deed, the Indians mounted and were off, as rapidly as their horses could carry them.

Capt. Smith took prompt measures to secure redress, and inflict vengeance upon the savages. He confiscated all the flour in the neighbourhood, and put all the women to baking bread. The murder was committed just at sunset, and we were there and making preparations for the pursuit by dark; and at daylight the next morning, were off on the trail, which we followed with unceasing energy till stopped by darkness—the Indians, all the time, flying in the direction of the head waters of the Big Washita.

The trail indicated that they were travelling leisurely; and as they took no pains to break the trail, we concluded that they were young warriors. We encamped for the night, and at daylight were again in pursuit, as rapidly as horse flesh could carry us. Our gait, nearly the whole time, was a swift gallop; and from indications, it was plain that the Indians were accelerating or "mending" their pace. At dark, we again encamped on the trail, and near the head of the Big Washita; and we passed the night without any disturbance; and at dawn were off once more in pursuit. But now we came to considerable sign, as if there might be an important village in the vicinity; and following a path that seemed to be extensively travelled, we wound around between two high hills, and into a long, narrow valley, within a short distance of a village containing eighteen lodges.

Everything betokened that the place had been evacuated very recently. A few horses were staked out to graze near one of the lodges, and for that point we charged at full speed; and as we dashed up, we were saluted with the sharp report of several rifles, of no light calibre; after which arrows fell thick and fast. An order was then given to surround the whole place. My horse being somewhat fractious and a good deal braver than I was, dashed right in among the lodges. Seeing myself in a critical position, I drew a box of prairie matches from my pocket, and, lighting them all at once, threw them into one of the dry grass lodges, and in an instant it was in a blaze; and from it the flames spread rapidly, till they reached the one in which the Indians were.

"Seeing myself in a critical position, I drew a box of prairie matches from my pocket, and then, all at once, threw them into one of the grass lodges, and in an instant it was in a blaze."

The savages kept up a pretty good fire for so small a number, until they saw the flames, when all was still as death for a minute or more. Our men ceased firing, to let me have a chance to get out; but my horse continued unmanageable; and though, when the heat became intense, he made a few lunges to escape it, he again wheeled around, gazing at the lurid flame, heedless of rein, voice or spur.

Suddenly the Indians began to show a disposition to come out. They made a racket at the door of the lodge, which they had barricaded, with such lumbering stuff as they could command; and they were now pulling it down. In the meantime, our heavy rifle balls were penetrating the grass walls from every side. Suddenly the Indians raised a piercing whoop, and five of their number charged out. As they showed themselves, we discharged more than a hundred guns upon them, and the whole five fell, either killed outright or mortally wounded; and four more were killed in the lodge.

We now took time to examine the place, and discovered that in many of the wigwams were clothing, buffalo robes, and cooking utensils—evidence that the occupants had but recently decamped. In one of them we captured a large quantity of jerked buffalo meat, which was about the only thing saved from the flames.

As soon as the Indians who dashed out were disposed of, one of the men threw a raw-hide rope over the top of the lodge, so that it caught on some of the projecting poles, and held fast. Instantly a party of men caught it, and pulled the frail structure over; and by kicking the burning grass away, we succeeded, after a severe scorching, in dragging the bodies of those who had remained inside away from the flames. Two of them had been shot dead, and two severely wounded.

We scoured the country for some distance thoroughly, in the hope of discovering other villages; but all the signs went to show that there were no more, and that the inhabitants of the one destroyed had fled before the arrival of the Indians we had been pursuing, who, doubtless, did not belong there, but had only fled to it for safety. It is probable that a party of hunters had seen us long before our arrival, and had raised the alarm; and as our animals were much fatigued we did not pursue their trail as the horses ridden by the Indians were, no doubt, all fresh. We did not recover Peabody's scalp, as it had probably been hidden by the savages, and was consumed by the fire. The Indians killed were all Comanches, but the village had been built and owned by the Wichitas.

We encamped at the spring near the village for a good rest; and

I was soon astonished to find that I was looked upon as a very brave man; and as such I was highly complimented by my officers. At first I was somewhat flattered; but I soon remembered about my horse, and I told them that the credit of the whole affair belonged exclusively to him; as he had carried me where it was exceedingly doubtful that I should have gone with my own free will.

From this place we crossed the divide, and went down the Red Fork of the Brazos. High up on this stream we had a grand buffalo chase. Keeping under cover of a ridge, we deployed as skirmishers, so as to surround as much ground as possible. The wind favoured us, and the buffalos did not discover us until we had marched up over the ridge, and a considerable distance down toward them; when they began to manifest some uneasiness, and the captain at once ordered a charge. As the notes of the bugle rang out the animals raised their great shaggy heads in stupefied wonder at the sudden apparition of three hundred men charging down upon them, yelling, shouting, laughing, and hurrahing like madmen. With a loud, quick snort the nearest ones would whirl on their hind feet, and dash into the herd, spreading panic wherever they went. We soon closed upon them, and the work of destruction commenced; and the rattle of firearms was constant.

The herd of buffalo seemed to roll like black waves over the ground, and extended as far as the eye could reach. The earth was jarred by their heavy, lumbering gait, while the air was filled with dust, and the ear stunned by the rumbling sound. On and on we went, pell-mell, until buffalo, horse, rider—all, brought up with one grand plunge in the Red Fork of the Brazos. The buffalo surging through the swollen stream, and reaching the opposite bank, scrambled up it in the wildest confusion—the strong trampling down the weak or such as were unlucky enough to fall—each only intent upon escape, and only caring for self.

By the time I and my immediate comrades had reached the river, we found that many of the rangers had become almost inextricably mixed up with the buffalo, and a few of them were driven into the water by the struggling mass; but fortunately they all escaped without severe injury, and joined again in the exciting, but dangerous sport. Some of the buffalo bogged down in the quicksand, and were mounted and ridden by a few of the most reckless of the "boys," at the imminent risk of being swamped themselves. The sound of the bugle could just be heard above the din of the chase, calling us to "rally," and we now, for the first time, surveyed the scene behind us. It would be al-

"On and on we went, pell-mell, until buffalo, horse, rider, all, brought up with one grand plunge in the Red Fork of the Brazos."

most useless for me to attempt a description of the ground over which we had passed. The dust hung over the plain in a dense, heavy cloud, but had been lifted sufficiently high to reveal scores of huge carcasses scattered over the earth, while yet other scores were rolling upon the ground in the agonies of mortal wounds; and yet a greater number were staggering and bellowing under the smart of injuries too trifling to bring them down, but sufficient to prevent them from keeping up with their unharmed companions.

Here and there, too, was an unlucky rider, who had been thrown from his horse by accident—perhaps the breaking of a rein, or the parting of a girth; and in the meantime their steeds were flying about, neighing for their company, or lying down gasping for breath. A few unlucky ones were in the melee badly gored by the infuriated bulls, and it became necessary to lead them back to camp; while a few footmen were seen moving around, pistols in hand, dispatching some doughty, but badly-wounded animal.

The killed and wounded amounted to more than five hundred; and when we had fairly rallied, we commenced in earnest to save the meat. We took nothing but the humps and a few tongues, leaving the remainder as a feast for wolves. Those who had lost their horses mounted captured ones, and we were soon off once more for Fort Belknap. On our arrival, we found the remainder of the regiment assembled, except one company, commanded by Captain Ed. Burleson, and which had been in the service for some time, and was at a point one hundred and fifty miles away, without an intervening settlement. This wild region we well knew to be a favourite resort for Comanche and Kiowa hunters, and, therefore, very dangerous for travellers; yet across it, it became necessary to carry a dispatch to Captain Burleson, ordering him to report to Colonel Johnston for duty. I volunteered for the service, and taking five days rations of bread and bacon, I commenced my lonely journey, and on the first day made fifty miles.

During the day I passed over a good deal of fresh sign. There had been a shower of rain in the forenoon, and I crossed trails where the fresh dust was turned up from under the damp soil on the top; but I saw no Indians. I encamped early, as it was a cloudy night, and I could not see to travel. I ate my supper, rested awhile, and then moved to a place about a mile from the road and made my bed in a new place. This is a common practice among both Indians and Rangers. Feeling perfectly secure, I slept till morning, and on awaking, looked to see if my horse was safe, which I soon ascertained was the case; and then I thought of my breakfast.

But judge of my astonishment when I found it was gone! I soon discovered the fragments of my haversack at a considerable distance from the tree, where I had hung it up for safe keeping. It was torn into shreds, and all my good biscuit and bacon eaten, or carried away. The hard bread, however, was scattered around; for although a good article of the kind, it had not proved palatable to my nocturnal visitor; some of it having been chewed up and evidently dropped in disgust. My bacon had been completely cleaned out—had gone the way of all flesh. There was enough sign on the ground to convince me that the robbery had been perpetrated by ten or a dozen "Lobo" wolves; none of the black or grey species being able to reach so high. Imagine my situation and feelings on making the discovery!

A hundred and ten miles from my place of destination, without a bite to eat, and Indians so thick around me that I dare not fire a shot, lest I should attract to me one or more of the straggling bands infesting the country! But there was nothing to be gained by vain regrets, though much time might be lost in that way. The contemptible villains that had robbed me, were, doubtless, at that moment stretched out in some secluded spot taking a comfortable snooze, or felicitating themselves upon the successful termination of their enterprise, and the adroit manner in which it had been executed. The more I studied over it, the madder I got; so I rode off, pondering on numerous schemes of revenge. I resolved to hold the whole community responsible for the acts of the individual, and have ever since took a great amount of solid pleasure in killing a wolf.

I was a day and a night getting to Camp Colorado, where I called upon Lieut. Lee, and related my misfortune. He consoled me with a hearty meal and I rode on. He also tendered my mustang a feed of corn, but the pony, not being used to such coarse diet, refused it in disgust. I had yet twenty-eight miles to ride before I reached Home Creek, where it was supposed I would find Burleson. The route was easily found to the crossing of the creek, but when once there which way to turn I did not know.

About eleven miles from Camp Colorado, I came to a considerable mountain, called Santa Anna's Peak. Staking my pony so that he could graze, I climbed to the summit to take a view of the surrounding country, and see if I could discover smoke indicating a camp. From this point I had a full view of Home Creek, from its source to a point nearly as far down as its mouth, on the Pecan Bayou. While leisurely surveying the landscape before me, I was startled by a slight sound, like the breaking of a twig. Knowing that I stood upon dangerous ground, I held my pistol in my hand; and to cock it was but the work of a moment; and turning around, judge my astonishment at seeing before me a stalwart negro, and distant only about ten steps, with a rifle drawn and nearly ready to fire. There was no mistaking his intention. His eye was a perfect index to his thoughts and his determination. Quick as thought I levelled on him, but before I could speak he addressed me in a very quiet tone:

"Master, don't shoot me."

"Put down your gun, then," I replied, utterly astonished at his coolness and effrontery, and slowly he let the hammer fall and lowered his piece.

"Master," he said piteously, "you isn't gwine to kill me, is ye?"

"What were you about to do to me?" I demanded; "were you not in the act of shooting me?"

"Master," he replied, "I'se a poor black man; my life ain't worth nothin' to you, no how; so jes please let me live a little longer; please don't shoot me."

Again I demanded why he had drawn his gun on me.

"O please, sir, put down de pistol, den I kin talk to you."

I lowered the pistol, keeping a strict eye on his movements. He prefaced his remarks with the very pertinent question:

"Is you from Texas?"

I hardly know what made me deny it, but I replied that I was not. But his next sentence convinced me that I had done well.

"I thought," said he, "you was one of dem fellers from de creek, over dar."

"What fellows? Who are they?" I inquired. He looked at me so calmly, that I saw he was not in the least afraid of me; and after hesitating a little, he asked, in a dubious tone:

"Master, whar did you come from, den?"

I told him quickly I came from Fort Cobb, in the Indian Nation, and this seemed greatly to relieve his mind on some important point, for he said:

"La, master, I thort you was one o' dem fellers from Texas; dey come up in de mountains every few days, huntin' for some of us poor brack folks; dey dun cotch nearly all now and took 'em down in de settlements."

"What is your name, and what are you doing here?" I asked.

"My name Jim, sah, and I lives round de end of de mountain, dar. But, massa, what might I call you?"

I told him my name, and otherwise made myself free with him, when he became very social; and on learning I was originally from Ohio, he made many inquiries about the people, and the country. "I'se always hearn about the north," said he; "and wanted to go dar."

He then told me he had been raised a slave, and he had run off from his master, who lived in Jack County, Texas; and that he had lived in those mountains several years. After talking awhile longer, and finding I had no disposition to molest him in any manner, he invited me to go with him to his cave. Full of curiosity to see more of the strange mortal, I walked with him around the point, over piles of broken rocks, which seemed to have been tumbled down out of the side of the mountain, by an earthquake; he clambered, and I followed, until we turned around the spur, when he stopped before a little hole in the side of a cliff, and pointing to it, said:

"Dar's whar I lib, sah," and he led the way into it.

Stooping down, I followed him into the cave, until he disappeared in the darkness, when I stepped to one side, and placed myself behind a huge rock, that projected from the wall. I thought by doing so, I would have a decided advantage if he was disposed to be tricky. He then called out: "Jis stop a minit, till I strikes a light."

He soon had a large iron lamp burning, which lit up the whole cave; after which, he proceeded to light a fire, and cook me something to eat. He had plenty to live on—flour, bacon, sugar, coffee, and tea. He boasted of this—said he "lived as well as de white folks;" but what was the greatest mystery to me, was the fact that he had a large amount of clothing in his cave—both men's and women's wear. In one place, were several fine coats hanging; and in another, pants, vests, and female apparel. I kept constantly between him and the door, without acting as if I suspected anything. But I could not possibly devise how he came by these articles, and therefore did not like to put myself in his power, lest my coat might soon hang with the rest.

Without seeming to care anything about it, I asked a few questions about his hunting, and the profits it brought him; if he followed trading, and if he bartered any with the Indians. I found he procured his flour and bacon, by selling game to the officers and soldiers, at different posts; and that there were a good many other runaways in the mountains, and that Burleson's men had caught half a dozen of them, and sent them to the settlements. I did not deem it prudent to tell him

I wanted to go to Burleson's camp, or that I knew anything about it. After eating a heavy dinner with him, I bid him a hearty "good bye," and told him I must ride. He inquired very earnestly where I was going, and I told him, without hesitating, to Fort Mason. He accompanied me down the mountain to my horse, and when I had mounted, he shook hands with me kindly, as only a negro can, when he is in earnest, saying:

"Massa, you won't neber tink hard o' old Uncle Jim; 'deed I tink you are one o' dem fellers from Texas."

I put out at a good gait, and got to the crossing of the creek, about an hour before sundown. When there, I had a hard time to determine which way to go, but finally turned up the creek, which happened to be the right course, and I reached Burleson's camp some time after dark, and was warmly welcomed by the captain and his men.

On my way down, I had captured a prairie dog, and put it in my saddle pocket. It was a beautiful little animal, about twice the size of a common fox squirrel, of brownish color, with very bright little eyes, and with ears so diminutive, as to be little more than a curl in the hair. Its feet were shaped like those of a squirrel, with five toes on its front, and four on its hinder feet; and its teeth, too, resembled those of the same animal, but were larger, and stronger; while its tail, except that it was larger, and had coarser hair, was like that of the common ground squirrel. It would have made a fine pet, and been an object of curiosity down in the settlements; but as I could not carry it with me, I killed it.

The region over which I travelled, abounded in game—especially in deer and antelope. On the Clear Fork of the Brazos, I could see immense herds, shading themselves, during the heat of the day. From the top of the table land, on the southwest side of the Clear Fork, I could see more than fifty groups of these animals, at once; and many of them numbered from forty to fifty. It would be altogether safe, to estimate the whole number in sight at once, at five hundred.

I received a terrible fright from half a dozen horned owls, just as I was crossing a little creek, within a short distance of camp. They raised a perfectly demoniac yell over my head, just as I came up out of the creek; and they followed it up, with such a natural laugh, that I put spurs to my horse, and ran a short distance, fearing that I was in the vicinity of a camp of savages, waylaying the ford. After getting some distance away, I turned around, and peering up into the trees, discovered the cause of my alarm to be nothing more dangerous than half a dozen great horned owls, enjoying a social "time," in the cool of the evening.

After a day of rest, in camp, I joined a party in a bear hunt, up Jim Ned Creek, a stream named after Jim Ned, a Caddoe warrior of considerable note, who, as the story goes, is a natural son of Gen. H———y, who is known throughout the west as a daring soldier—gay, and fond of women. He is a man of decided character, large size, and endowed with no ordinary degree of courage. His great resemblance to the general, gives credence to the reputed relationship; but Capt. Beaver, or as he is commonly called, Black Beaver, a full blood Indian, and a very truthful man, who has known Jim Ned, since his birth, says his father was a very black negro, while the mother was a full blooded Indian woman. Nevertheless, Jim Ned is very white, and would pass for a white man in almost any crowd.

But without attempting to determine the vexed question of Jim Ned's parentage, I return to my narrative. Our luck in the hunt, was extraordinary. We had procured good dogs from the settlement, and had rare sport. In three days, we killed five bears, one elk, and a number of deer. We found wild honey in abundance, of which we partook liberally, after which we filled our camp kettles with it, as well as every other available vessel in our possession; some of us even took off our drawers, and, after having washed them in the creek, tied the legs together at the bottom, and filled them with the delicious sweet. We found this decidedly the easiest of all methods of carrying it, as we could hang it astride our horses. We then returned to camp, very tired, badly stung, but full of life.

On our return, we discovered everything in commotion, as the Indians had made their appearance in the neighbourhood, and had been stealing horses; and a party of citizens were in the camp, ready to pilot us to the scene of the disturbances. The captain got his company in the saddle, and went to the spot indicated that night, and next morning early, we struck out on the trail, and had only followed it a few miles, when we came in sight of the Indians, who were only two in number. They had with them four horses—none of them good ones. We raised a yell, and started after them at a full charge. Throwing themselves from their horses, they turned toward the bushes. We run partly around the thicket, and commenced firing into it. Our heavy rifle balls cut the brush and glanced about through it so much, that it ceased to be much protection to them, and they soon found it so.

They then hoisted a white rag on a switch, and we ceased firing.

The captain called on them to come out, which they immediately did, one of them holding his hand over his right ear. On being assured that we did not want to kill them, they regarded themselves as extremely well favoured. They belonged to the tribe of Lipans. The citizens agreed that they would take them to Austin, to be turned over to Gov. Houston. The wounded man said he was "proud, heap proud; white man miss so close."

We returned to camp on Home Creek, where another party was sent out to Pecan Bayou, on a scout; myself among the number. A few miles above Camp Colorado, we found a deserter from the regular service, wandering about in irons. He had a pistol, and plenty of ammunition; but as his irons were riveted, he could not get them off. Luckily our blacksmith was along with us, and he had his rasp with him, by the aid of which, and his shoeing hammer, the manacles were loosed. When set at liberty, the lieutenant told him he might either return to his regiment, or go down to the settlements; and he chose the latter alternative. On the same day, we found a negro woman in the woods, who was taken into cusToddy, to be returned to her owner: but in the night she escaped, through some mysterious agency, although securely tied, and was never seen afterward, by any of the party; and, as catching slaves was not our legitimate business, we made little exertion to find her.

Crossing over on to Jim Ned, we had plenty of sport, killing deer; indeed, our horses were literally loaded down with venison, bear meat, and other game, and we were thinking of anything else, rather than war, when all at once we struck a broad trail, over which a large number of horses had passed. Believing that a drove of animals had strayed off here, from some of the settlements, we followed in the track, with a view of heading them off, and returning them to the settlements. As the tracks were very fresh, we did not anticipate any trouble in overtaking the drove, the first time it stopped to graze. After following the trail for some time, we came in sight of a lone Indian, but nothing else was to be seen. The instant he observed us, he dashed off as rapidly as his horse could carry him, following the course the horses had taken. It was evident that he was a sentinel, and that more savages were ahead; so we started at once in pursuit. It was now apparent that the animals had been stolen, and were being driven off by a large body of Indians. The trail was nearly as plain as a wagon road, and could be travelled with certainty in the night, and we accordingly kept on through the darkness.

Failing to gain on the Indian, we cut our game loose from the saddles, and let it go; and our horses, thus relieved from a heavy burden, ran well; and though we did not gain on the savage, we held our own, and thus prevented him from giving the alarm to his company before we came upon them. It was a tight race, as long as we were on the level prairie; but as soon as we entered the mountains, on the Colorado, he frequently evaded our view, as he was a splendid horseman, and ran his animal with excellent judgment.

His horse was failing, but so were our own; so that we could not take advantage of that circumstance. On our arrival at the top of a mountain we discovered the object of our pursuit—the drove of horses—in the care of about twenty Indians. They had not yet discovered us, when the red imp before us began to yell loud enough to awaken the dead, to say nothing about startling the living. The Indians heard him, and we could distinctly perceive the excitement occasioned; and they at once gave him an answering whoop, and headed the drove for the river; but the horses not being manageable by so small a number of drivers, stampeded, and ran to the right, and nearly parallel to the stream, for some distance; while the Indians, seeing us gain on them rapidly, left their booty and dashed into another gap in the mountains. They had lost time in trying to turn the horses the way they wanted them to go, and we were now close upon them, firing, and yelling like so many madmen.

On we went till we passed the mountains, when we found the Indians had mistaken their route, and ran through the wrong gap, and had unexpectedly found themselves upon the river, with a high bluff before them, and an almost perpendicular mountain on each side, while we were charging close upon their rear; but they hesitated not a moment. Realizing their position, they spurred ahead, and dashed over the bluff into the river. So sudden was their disappearance that some of Burleson's men could not check up in time to save themselves, but went headlong after the savages, who made for the opposite shore as fast as they rose to the surface. After swimming a few strokes, they struck hard bottom and were soon in shallow water, when, giving us a parting whoop, they fled to the woods, and were quickly out of sight.

The river here is very narrow and deep, on the North side. The bluff was about sixteen feet high, and perpendicular above the water. There were three of our party who went over the bluff after the Indians, one of whom we always called Towney—but I have forgotten the names of the others. They all swam ashore on the opposite side; still, as their guns and ammunition were wet, they could accomplish nothing against the long lances of the fugitives, so they wisely followed the river bank down to a ford and recrossed.

The lieutenant then concluded to return and save the horses, as there was no longer any hope of overtaking the Indians in the dark. We soon found the animals quietly grazing, and encamped to wait for the return of the men who had gone in search of a ford, which they found about five miles down the river. We were then forty-five miles from the regular camp; and on the following day discovered a party of citizens who had gone out in search of the horses; but had it not been for us, they would never have seen them again. We then returned, and were soon feasting on all sorts of wild fowl and game, as well as fish, of which we caught thousands.

CHAPTER 5

Another Lonely Ride

After resting my horse two or three days, I set out on my return to Fort Belknap alone, as Burleson was not yet ready to move, and would not be for some time. Out of unadulterated sympathy for my horse, I took no rations for myself, depending solely for my subsistence on my trusty gun. There are two requisites for successful hunting, besides proper equipments and being a dead shot: one is to find the game, and the other is to get within shooting distance. I could not dismount to hunt on foot, nor could I leave my route, lest I should fall in with some roving band of Comanches; and game was scarce on the high table-land over which I was to travel, and as a natural consequence, I went hungry all the way.

On the second day, I became very sick of a fever, which I broke by laying down in a running stream of pure water until I got chilled; and, between hunger and sickness, I was unable to travel fast, and it was two o'clock of the fourth day, before I reached Dobb's ranch, the first settlement on my way, and only thirteen miles from Belknap. I called for dinner, and turned out my horse to graze, and, in the meantime, threw myself down to enjoy a nap, which my exhausted system greatly needed, and which I could now do, conscious of perfect security. I had slept but a few minutes, however, before I was awakened by one of the prettiest girls in Texas. She furnished me with a towel and a basin of water, preparatory to taking my dinner, and after indulging in my ablutions, my appetite attained a keenness which I have seldom felt; and it was with no ordinary degree of satisfaction that I seated myself to a table bountifully spread with warm bread, fresh butter, wild honey, sweet milk, and a score of other dainties, calculated to appease the most ravenous cravings of the stomach.

The young lady sat down immediately opposite me, and after seeing that my plate was well supplied, she began to question me as to where I was from, whither I was going, and to what command I belonged; seeming determined to make me communicative whether I would be or no. Having fasted long, I was not unaware of the danger of partaking too freely of the food set before me; so I measured at a glance just the quantity I would take, and determined not to exceed it; but the girl kept on talking, and detained me till I consumed all the victuals on the table.

Dinner over, I mounted a fresh horse which was furnished me, and started for Belknap. My steed was a half wild Mustang, native to the country, and had been badly spoiled in breaking. I had scarcely touched his back, when he began that species of rearing and plunging, known in Texas as "pitching;" in California as "spiking," and in this country as "bucking." Now my tribulation began. The first half a dozen leaps brought on a pain, and dizziness, and convinced me of my imprudence in eating so heartily, after a fast. To dismount, was to evince cowardice, and the thought was not to be entertained; and, to be thrown, was everlasting disgrace.

The pretty girl was a spectator of my efforts, and I must ride him or die. Great drops of sweat were rolling down my face—the result of pain and sickness, not of exertion. Seeing the case was growing desperate, I drove the spurs again and again into his sides, until, almost frantic with pain, the horse dashed off at the top of his speed, into the woods, and in the direction of Belknap. I arrived there in about an hour, still suffering terribly. It does not injure a man to go three days hungry; I am almost tempted to say, it may do him good, if he is careful to eat sparingly when he once more reaches a land of plenty; but I had made myself a glutton, and must take the consequences.

On arriving in camp, I found that Colonel Johnston had gone to eastern Texas, and that my company commander, Captain Smith, had been elected lieutenant colonel of the regiment, and that Sul. Ross, a son of Captain Ross, sub-agent of the Lower Reserve, had succeeded him as captain. Our first lieutenant was named Lang, and the second lieutenant was Dave Sublett.

The followers of Baylor were not at all pleased that a son of their old enemy should have been elected to an office among the Rangers, although it was not an affair that in the least concerned them. But a feud of the most violent character disturbed the community; and among men of the style of those of Western Texas, hatred almost as inevitably led to personal collision, as it did in Scotland two hundred and fifty years ago. A single incident will illustrate the feeling which prevailed:

Some Indians visited the settlements on the Trinity River, east of Belknap, and commenced at once *"raising Cain,"* as the frontier men occasionally term it, that is, they helped themselves to horses and cattle, burned buildings, destroyed crops, and did all kind of injury which their ingenuity, and a decent regard for the safety of their persons would permit; and Captain Ross was detailed with a body of men, to pursue them, and drive them from the country. We started off on a gallop, and continued it for some time, till we came in sight of a house, when we slackened up to a walk, in order to give the party time to get water; and while at the well, a woman walked out before us, and said:

"You're gwine after the Injuns, are you?"

I was in the advance, and replied politely in the affirmative.

"Gwine after the Comanches?" she inquired.

"Yes, *Madame*," I answered.

"Whose company is this?" she next desired to know.

"The Waco company—Captain Ross," was my response, feeling a conscious pride in our importance.

"I wish the Injuns may scalp the last one o' you," she shouted in a shrill voice.

I bowed politely, and the men all broke out into a laugh, which only increased her indignation; and as long as we were within hearing distance, her voice rang out maledictions upon our heads, and upon the heads of every friend of Captain Ross.

We soon found the intruding Indians, who proved to be a band of Kickapoos; and we were not long in routing and driving them out of the settlements. We did not even get close enough to fire a gun, so fleet, and so cowardly were the savages, who fled, at once, in the direction of Red River; and not caring to weary our horses, with a chase that promised not the remotest chance of success, we returned to camp.

Soon after, however, another company captured fifteen of these same Indians, and were returning with them to camp, when a party of enraged citizens came up, and fired upon the savages, who were mingled among their captors; so that the lives of the latter were in as much danger as those of the former; but luckily, no white men were killed, while two of the Indians were shot down, one dead and the other severely wounded.

This conduct of the citizens so infuriated the Rangers that they turned their captives loose, and told them to run for their lives; then, turning to the citizens, the captain of the party ordered them to leave at once, or he would fire on them; and no second invitation to depart was needed, as the first was looked upon as very nearly approaching the peremptory; at least, it was a "broad hint." By that conduct, these settlers only caused to be let loose upon themselves a dozen or more marauders, who, in future encounters would have a double thirst for vengeance; and, who, but for their rashness, would have been disposed of, either by being sent beyond the limits of the State, or been held as prisoners till the war was ended.

Chapter 6
More Adventures

About the first of May, the regiment, under command of Lieutenant-Colonel Smith, set out from Belknap for Camp Radziminski, an old United States' fortified position, in the Washita mountains. We travelled hastily, stopping during the first night on the Trinity River, and on the second, at the Little Washita, at which latter place, our horses, from some unexplained cause, stampeded. I prevented my pony from escaping, but the lucky ones who did this were few. The entire day was consumed in picking up the fugitives; and by night, only four were missing. Two of these were the property of Col. Smith, and the others of private soldiers. On the following morning, I, with three others, started out to hunt the missing animals, the orders of the colonel being, to follow the trail a few hours, and if we did not see the horses in that time, to give up the pursuit, and go direct to Radziminski, as rapidly as we could.

We, however, followed the trail over one hundred and fifty miles. The horses were trying to get back home; and though turned out of their course frequently, by rivers and mountains, they would seek the first available opportunity to resume it. Sometimes they would wander about so while grazing, that we would be a whole day in striking their trail again. After three or four days, we found two of the animals, which had got wound up in the ropes by which they were tied, and were unable to graze, and hence were nearly starved. We searched the country for the other two horses, but could not find them, when my companions with one accord, voted to return to the command, and let them go; but this I stoutly opposed.

They urged that we had already exceeded our orders, and done better than was expected of so small a party, and that we were in a country celebrated as an Indian hunting-ground, and therefore it would be folly for us to proceed further. I told them to go back, and take the horses, if they wished; but I should go on; that I could strike the trail again, by making a circuit of two or three miles; and that I felt satisfied that it was not more than forty miles to the settlements, in a southwesterly direction, from where we then were; and to tell the colonel that I had determined to continue the pursuit.

About sunset we parted; they commencing a dangerous journey of one hundred and thirty miles, in a straight line, while I held on, in the general course the horses had been travelling. Directly on my route lay considerable of a mountain, which I ascended. The top of it was very level, and I travelled along it for about four miles, when I came upon a small trail. It was now night, but I could readily see by the light of the stars, that a stake rope had been dragged along the path; and this satisfied me that I was on the track of the missing horses. I at once commenced pursuit, until so wearied that I was compelled to lie down to sleep. On the following morning, I rode on, till about ten o'clock, when I came in sight of the settlements, the first house proving to be Murphy's ranch, fourteen miles from Belknap; and here I learned that the horses had passed the place, and been taken up in the town, and advertised as estrays.

Well pleased that my long ride would soon be over, and that I should recover the animals, I made the intervening fourteen miles with great speed, and a light heart; but alas for human foresight and calculations! The horses were gone. One had been ridden away by a Minute Man on a wild goose chase after the Comanches, while the other had been loaned to a mail carrier, and had escaped from him, while staked out to graze. On making inquiry, I learned that a horse answering to the description of the one which had broken loose, had been seen at Rock Creek, eighteen miles distant; it had on spancels, my informant said, and a piece of rope was tied around its neck; and I at once concluded it was the missing animal, and rode out after it. Travelling in the direction of the point indicated, I came to a noted spring, where I expected to find the company encamped who had the other animal, but it had gone.

Being very hungry, I staked my horse to graze, while I could cook some rice, and make a little coffee at the old camp-fire, which had not yet died out; and while busily engaged preparing these articles, I was aroused by a short, quick, snort, and in a moment, the identical animal I had followed so long, came dashing down the hill at a breakneck speed, foaming with sweat and terribly frightened; while close at his heels were five stalwart Indians, on foot, doing their utmost to stop him, and turn him from his course.

The first thing I did, was to send a load of buckshot among the savages, and the next, to tie up the frightened animal, which ran up to mine and stopped; then, changing the saddle from one to the other, I threw out my rice and coffee and left the spot in haste. As I started, two or three guns were discharged at me; but I had no time to stop and inquire the cause. On my return to Belknap, I ate a hearty supper, and was put in charge of the mail for the regiment, which weighed about sixty pounds, and with which I at once left for Camp Radziminski.

The first day out I rode to the crossing of the Big Washita; and at Soldier Creek I formed a mark for an Indian to try his bow—the arrow passing very close to my back. I had noticed for some time the tracks of two Indians, immediately along the wagon road, but had paid little attention to the matter. But discovering the presence of danger, I went back about a mile, and encamped for the night. On the following day I observed that *moccasin* tracks were plenty at the spring where they supposed I would go into camp, from which it is apparent that they believed me verdant in border warfare.

I knew that they were ahead of me, and felt certain of being waylaid; and had made certain that they were in a grove, hardly a mile from the river; and subsequent events evinced that I was not deceived. As I approached the grove, I left the path, and rode through the timber some distance away; and after passing entirely around the grove I again struck the road. After riding some distance, I turned and went back to a good place, and secreted myself in a thicket to wait; I had not been there many minutes when two savages came at a swift run, on foot— one about one hundred yards ahead of the other. When the foremost one was within about sixty yards of me, I fired, the shot taking effect in his right arm and side. He instantly seized the wounded limb in his left hand and bounded down the trail, toward the river, and was soon lost to sight. I followed as rapidly as possible, but they succeeded in crossing the stream, and secreting themselves among the bushes on the other side. Not caring to risk too much I let them go, and went back to the road, well satisfied that the Indian was mortally wounded and would die.

I crossed Red River that day, and for the first time lit a fire to cook; but scarcely had the smoke began to rise, when the wolves commenced gathering from all points of the compass. Being tired and desperately hungry, I put a cup of rice on the fire to boil, and also commenced preparing coffee; but long before the water was hot, the wolves came so unpleasantly near my horses, that they refused to eat, although tired and hungry; but came and stood by the fire where I was.

The wolves kept sneaking up closer and closer, until some were within ten paces, when I rashly concluded to kill one, just for sport; and aiming at a very large, gray one, I fired and he fell in his tracks. No sooner did the others get the scent of blood than they rushed in from all directions upon their fallen companion; and I had barely time to seize my cups and jump on my horse, before they closed in on me from all sides. Once mounted, I felt entirely safe; and I turned and fired a charge of buckshot into the pack that was devouring the dead one; then, wheeling my pony, I rode out from among them.

When at a little distance off I halted my horse and again fired, this time giving them the contents of a six-shooter, well aimed; and every animal that received even the slightest wound, was instantly devoured by the remainder of the pack—sport for me, and I enjoyed it till I was tired, and rode off, leaving the unfortunate wolves to fight it out. I then rode off, keeping in the saddle till nearly morning, when I laid down to sleep in a state of glorious uncertainty as to whether I was on the right or the wrong road. The road forked on the plain, and I did not know whether to turn to the right or the left; but after studying awhile I took the right hand, and laid down to sleep upon my decision.

A little before daylight, I heard a heavy rumbling sound; and on awaking, I saw what appeared to be heavy clouds in the distance, and I at first believed the noise to be thunder; and the reader may well imagine that a drenching on the open plain was not a pleasant thing to contemplate. Presently, however, I concluded the noise seemed to be too suppressed for thunder, and, as I listened, I discovered it grew louder, and was rapidly approaching nearer. Springing to my feet, I saddled one horse, threw the mail-bag across the other and mounted. By this time, I could plainly discern the cause of the noise; on every side save one, I was hemmed in by a herd of buffalo. Hoping they would soon run by, I paused a moment to consider my chances; and in that moment the avenue for egress was closed, and I was compelled to run with the herd. They were travelling nearly in the direction I wanted to go; only gradually bearing a little to the right. By watching opportunities, I worked over to the left, and after keeping them company for about two miles, I succeeded in finding a gap and dashed out, and across a creek, up which the buffalo were running.

Once safe, I stopped to rest my horses and breathe freely, for we had been nearly suffocated with dust. I soon discovered what had started the herd, and was driving it forward with such speed; in the midst of the herd were a number of Indians, spearing and shooting with arrows, as if bent on the extermination of the last buffalo before sunrise.

I was not afraid of being discovered in the midst of such excitement as the savages were enjoying, if I could only keep my horses still; and to keep them quiet, I tickled them on the nose until the party was well out of sight, when I rode off, and in an hour, I found myself at Captain Burleson's camp on Otter Creek, at the foot of one of the Wichita mountains.

The men were delighted with their letters, and they extended to me a hearty welcome; and, after I had rested a little, I was furnished with a guide who piloted me to the colonel's quarters, some miles away. Lieutenant Colonel Smith was in command, and he was delighted to know that I had escaped so well, and congratulated me for persevering so long under discouraging circumstances, and kindly thanked me for recovering his own horse, and offered me a pecuniary reward, but this I refused.

Colonel Smith had been exceedingly annoyed at another stampede, which had occurred on the previous night, in which four hundred beef cattle had escaped. These being his chief reliance for food for his men during the approaching campaign, he naturally felt extremely anxious about the matter; and to add to his perplexity, while I was yet in his tent, an officer rode up and said he had followed the trail about three miles, when it was lost among the buffalo tracks, and that it would, therefore, be impossible to tell with any certainty in what direction to look after the missing animals.

At this point, I recollected seeing a trail cross mine, which I had examined to see if the tracks were those of horses; finding that they were not, I had supposed that a herd of buffalo had passed along there, and had left it, without giving it further attention. I reported this fact to Colonel Smith, who at once agreed with me that it was the trail of the cattle; and at his request I mounted a fresh horse and piloted a company of men to the place. A chase of over fifty miles then ensued, when we came upon the recreant beasts, and returned with them to camp, to the eminent satisfaction of at least one man in the regiment—the beef contractor. I once more was complimented by, and received the thanks of, the colonel, who never withheld praise, when he believed an action merited it.

The colonel was now called away on an official visit to some friendly Indians under the command of Pete Ross, a brother of my captain, and I was selected as one of his escort, with a detail of nineteen others.

While sitting in the tent, a deputation of friendly chiefs arrived to arrange the preliminaries of the campaign against the Kickapoos, and judge of my surprise on seeing among the men the identical one who had been so anxious to convince me that I was a Texan Ranger, while on the road from the Caddo village to Fort Belknap. Before me stood Placido, chief of the Tonchues, who was now on the most friendly terms with the people he so lately dreaded, and he gave me a cordial greeting. His warriors, as well as himself, recognized me instantly as the man they had catechised so severely; "but, now," they said, "we all good friends, and go catch 'um Comanche."

I was greatly pleased with Placido. His name was given him by the Mexicans, on account of his gentle disposition and amiable deportment; and as I may have occasion to speak of him frequently in these pages, I will briefly describe him to the reader. He was about fifty-five years of age, five feet nine inches high, with black, keen eyes, deep chest; he was also exceedingly muscular, but not corpulent. When the interpreter told him I was to be one of the party, he scrutinized me carefully, and, turning to one of his men, said, in broken Mexican, "'*Stah waeno, (esta bueno).*"

Once more the whole party extended their hands, telling me in half a dozen different languages, that we would be good friends.

CHAPTER 7

Kickapoo Campaign

In a short time after this consultation Colonel Smith started in his campaign against the Kickapoos, who had recently been busy at all kinds of depredations on the settlements; but their expeditions had all along been conducted so secretly that they were not even suspected, until we had nearly reached their country. We found them well prepared, and they gave us a warm reception. Just as we were about to leave Camp Radziminski a terrible storm came up, and the noise of the thunder, and the flashes of the lightning caused another stampede among our pack-horses; and just as their speed was at its height, the lightning struck "Old Peg," a vicious pack-mule, ever ready to do mischief in the herd, killing her instantly, and as neatly as a bullet could have dispatched her.

Old Peg had scarcely fallen when a vicious horse, which always kicked and pranced after being loaded, as if to see if its burden was well strapped on, knocked an axe out of a pack, and as it was whirling in the air, kicked at it, and cut his hamstring, so that it was necessary to shoot him. The Indians, and not a few of the white men, seemed to regard this as a bad omen; but I looked upon it in a more practical light, as a special deliverance from unruly animals.

On our journey we had bad grass, bad water, bad fare, and bad luck; the measles broke out in camp, and a large number of the men became infected and helpless; and in this condition we reached the Kickapoo territory.

The tribe had mustered all its warriors, six hundred in number; and it had likewise received reinforcements from the Seminoles and from lawless, marauding bands of Creeks, amounting, in all, to about two thousand men; and this force, instead of awaiting an attack, took the offensive at once. Not anticipating so *warm* and *cordial* a reception at so early a moment, at the hands of so small a tribe, we concluded to decline a meeting; or, in other words, after holding a council of war, we resolved that it would be both politic and prudent to skedaddle; and accordingly we mounted our sick men—some of them so weak they had to be fastened on with surcingles—and started on our retreat. We commenced our retrograde movement at about nine o'clock at night, and in the morning we were at Camp Radziminski once more.

We had but three hundred men in this expedition; but as the Kickapoos had no hope of cutting us off, and fearing that we would be reinforced, they very wisely gave over the pursuit. Indeed, throughout the whole affair the belligerents seemed to be inspired with a mutual fear—each party dreading to come to a direct encounter with the other, which rendered the campaign, on the whole, not a little ludicrous. When we were in the Kickapoo country we dreaded an attack from the enemy; and when the savages came in the vicinity of Radziminski they had a wholesome fear of annihilation there; and consequently the campaign ended with—nobody hurt. Our surgeon and myself once strayed away from the command, and came nearly being captured; but we escaped, and were the only ones in the party who were in danger.

It was daylight, in the morning, and we believed ourselves far enough in advance of the savages to have time to rest a few minutes, and eat our breakfasts. Awhile before this I had been sick of a fever—the result of over-exertion while on a scout—and it had fallen into my lower limbs, causing ulcerations; my feet being so swollen that I could not even wear *moccasins*. We had encamped near a beautiful spring, at the house of a white man with an Indian wife; and I had gone down to fill my canteen, and bathe my fevered limbs; which I did some distance from the fountain itself. But some one of the Rangers—thinking it a good chance to play a trick on me—sent information to the woman that I was washing my feet in the spring; but of this at the time I knew nothing, nor was I informed of it when I reached the camp. Entirely without suspicion, I accordingly returned to the spring for water to make coffee, and on reaching it a very pretty squaw stepped out from a tree nearby, and confronted me. She spoke in a cheerful tone, but there was a wicked look in her eye, and one hand was held behind her. Her glistening eye, and the fact that she concealed one of her hands, appeared strange; but I was considerably more surprised when she addressed me in good English:

"Is your name Pike?"

"No," I answered in an off-hand way, and pushed for the spring.

"What is your name, then?" she demanded, in a suspicious voice.

"Tom Green; but, madam, what do you want?"

"Why, I wanted to see a man named Pike," said she, "who came down here, a few minutes ago, and washed his feet in my spring."

It was now a plain case; somebody had been perpetrating a joke at my expense. But I answered her coolly:

"All right, madam, if you want to see *him*, I will send him down as soon as I go up."

"I wish you would," she said viciously.

Up I went, and addressing a messmate, named Moore, told him there was a woman at the spring, who wanted to see him immediately.

He took his canteen with him, and started down the path, while I crept to the edge of the bluff to see what transpired. There was the squaw, again concealed behind the tree, watching Moore, who was advancing leisurely without the least suspicion; and when he was conveniently near, she stepped out, and demanded:

"Is your name Pike?"

"No," replied he.

"You lie, you son of a gun; didn't I just send a man after you, to tell you to come down here?"

The next instant she produced a big hickory club from the folds of her skirt, and, swinging it high in the air, was about to bring it heavily down on Moore's head, when he sprang quickly aside, and drew his pistol, and shouted:

"Look here woman, if you hit me, I'll be dad shammed if I don't shoot you!"

For a moment the squaw hesitated, and then lowering the club said:

"If your name ain't Pike, what is it?"

"My name is Moore," said he, in a loud, defiant tone.

"Well," said she, "look a-here, I want you to go to camp and tell Pike I want to see him."

"All right," said Moore, glad to get rid of her; "I'll send him down right away;" and up he came, laughing heartily at the joke.

I met him at the top of the hill and motioned for him to keep still; asking at the same time, who next we should send down; but our sport was suddenly spoiled by the order to "saddle up." While this was being done, several of the men went down to the spring to fill their canteens;

and as each filed down the hill, the squaw confronted him, with, "Is your name Pike?" each time only to be disappointed; but requested that "Pike" would be sent down at once.

After having mounted, I rode down to the bluff and called out: "Madam, my name is Pike; what will you have?"

"O you villain," she shouted; "Is that you? just come down here, and I'll show you how to wash your feet in my spring; you dirty villain. Just wait till I get there," she added, in anything but an amiable voice, "and I'll show you," and she started for me; but I raised my hat politely, bowed, and wished her a good day. The last I heard of her was:

"You dirty villain, I'll show you—" and her angry voice died away in the distance.

While in camp at Radziminski, an Indian named Bowlegs, (so called because one of his legs had been broken, and so badly set that it was crooked), came to me with a very long face, and told me of a very grave misfortune which had occurred to him. He had lost his eagle feather and his "big medicine;" and he insisted that I should go out with him to find them. I readily consented, and following his trail for thirty miles, in the direction of the agency, we were successful. I discovered the treasures first, picked them up, and handed them to him; and never, at any other time, did I witness such excessive exhibitions of delight. He danced, and capered, and shouted, like a boy with a holyday ride in prospect.

The feather and the "big medicine," are prized by the Indian above almost all other possessions. The feather is, so to speak, the index to his nobility; and never did Spanish medieval hidalgo cling with greater pride to the banner of his family, than does the Comanche to the wild bird's feathers with which he decks his person. The warrior and his deeds are known by the feather, almost as particularly as they could be by a written chronicle of his achievements. If the quill is painted red, it indicates that the wearer has killed an enemy in battle; if split, it tells you that two warriors have fallen by his hand; and for each additional victim to his prowess, another plume is added; so that you have but to count the feathers, in order to determine, at least, the number of glorious achievements of the warrior. No one is permitted to wear a feather until he has been first to charge up and touch a fallen foe—been first in at the death; for those who thus recklessly throw themselves into the breach, are accounted the bravest; are accounted above the man even, who, at a distance, brought the enemy down by his bullet.

The "big medicine" was a root about an inch and a half long, somewhat resembling *calamus*, and it was bound to the feather by a strip of red flannel, about a foot long and an inch wide, and is worn tied to the scalp lock on the crown of the head; it is regarded as a charm against all the ills "which flesh is heir to;" and especially renders the wearer invulnerable to the bullets and arrows of the enemy. I failed to see it in that light, but took care not to make my doubts manifest.

From this Indian I learned a tradition somewhat after the order of the one concerning the founders of Rome. Crossing a plain on our way back to camp, we saw a very large wolf, which I asked him to shoot with his bow, as he was nearer to it than myself. He, however, peremptorily declined, saying:

"You shoot 'um; me no shoot 'um."

"Why you no shoot 'um?" I inquired. But he only repeated what he had said before, with greater emphasis.

I then became curious to know what superstition prevailed in the tribe to prevent the killing of so mischievous and vicious an animal; and on putting my inquiries, I learned that there is a tradition among the Tonchues, that the first of their tribe was nurtured during his infancy by a she wolf; and that the animal for this reason is regarded as sacred by that tribe. Where do such traditions originate? I leave such things to the antiquarian.

CHAPTER 8

Indian Warfare

About the 20th of May preparations were completed for a grand campaign against the Indians who occupied the country near the head-waters of the Red, South Canadian, North Canadian, Red Fork, Arkansas, and Cimaron Rivers; the invading forces to consist of regulars, rangers, and friendly Indians; and upon the rangers devolved the duty of scouring the great salt plain, or desert, which disfigures so large a portion of the American map; and upon which the unlucky traveller or soldier is required to endure almost every extreme of heat, hunger, and thirst; as there is no protection from the scorching rays of the sun, no means of procuring food, and few fountains of fresh water.

While on this expedition, I was sent out on one occasion with a party of friendly Indians, about thirty in number, under charge of Casa Maria, a famous Caddoe warrior and chief, to the headwaters of the False Washita, and thence north-west, across the divide, between that stream and the Canadian, with a view to reconnoitring and ascertaining if any of the enemy were lurking in the vicinity. We were riding along in regular Indian style, with flankers at every side, and a small guard far in the advance, when suddenly the latter wheeled their horses and waved a scarf or handkerchief, as a token that we were in the presence of danger; and in an instant, flankers and skirmishers came in upon us at a run, while we of the main body halted to ascertain particulars.

The advance guard, on arriving, reported that they had discovered a village of at least a hundred lodges, in the distance; and from all appearances, they felt convinced that we were in the neighbourhood of a superior force. Casa Maria, not content to hear the report, repaired at once to the spot, to view the scene for himself; but before starting, he required his interpreter to ask me if I desired to see our common enemy, for myself, in their houses. I replied in the affirmative, when he turned to his own men, and pointing back to the agency, addressed them in Caddoe; and though I did not understand his language, I judged its tenor, from the fact that the whole party turned for home, on anything else than a snail's gallop. They looked a little disappointed, but the word of the chief was law to them; it was his province to command—their's to obey.

When they had departed, the doughty chief, pistol in hand, made a sign for me to follow him, which I did with eagerness. He led the way, at a charge, riding over the ridge and down to the village, at full speed. On, on, we rode, he appeared determined to storm the village alone. The astounded denizens of the lodges were unprepared for the spectacle; and not understanding the character of their visitors, were stupid with wonder, and gazed in amazement on us, as we almost flew toward them. Riding to a point so near that we could distinguish their features, and they ours, a sudden movement convinced us that they now knew us as we were—hostile warriors. The men at once sprang to their arms, and horses; but before they could mount, we wheeled in a long sweeping circle, at the same time discharging our pistols among them, and then left them, greeting them with a long and loud yell of exultation, and the well known war whoop of the Caddoe.

As we gained the top of the ridge, in another direction from that in which we first made our appearance, and about two miles from the village, we cast a glance rearward, to ascertain what they were doing. We could distinctly see the warriors mounting in hot haste their steeds; and the squaws and boys running to and fro with accoutrements, suitable for immediate chase—everything being in the highest state of excitement. I now wondered what adventures would next fall to our lot, when the chief dismounted, tightened his girth, and motioned me to do likewise, which I did.

Without exhibiting the least excitement, the chief stood his ground, till he saw the Comanches all mounted; then yelling at the top of his voice: "*whita, whita, por los mugers,*" and giving his pursuers a parting war whoop, he struck out in an entirely different direction from that taken by his men. On we flew, across the prairie, till we reached a ridge, which we crossed, after which we turned our course, and ran down a creek in the course taken by his men; and after flying at half speed, for about two hours, we reached a creek which emptied into the Washita, when we slackened our horses to a walk, for ten or fifteen minutes, after which we again started off at full gallop, to a point near the mouth of the creek, where we came upon our late comrades, halted and ready for a fight.

Casa Maria at once deployed his men under cover, after which he sent his horses down into the bed of the stream, at the same time motioning me to go with the horse guard. I shook my head, when he called his interpreter, who informed me that he wanted me to keep at a safe distance, so that I would receive no injury, as he wanted me to ride quick, and tell the white men what I had seen. I told him that I would not go to the rear like a woman, but would bear my part in the impending battle; and that if I was killed, the other white men could do as I had done—come and see for themselves. He then beckoned me to approach him, and told his interpreter to inform me that he desired I should keep by his side.

We were all well concealed, behind bushes, rocks, and trees, lying down as closely to the ground as possible, to await the unsuspecting Comanches, who believed that they had but two men to contend with. Nor did we lie long idle. Soon the enemy, some forty in number, came scouring in, at full speed, closely following the trail we had made, as if by instinct. On they came, till they arrived within rifle range, when Casa Maria drew from his pouch a whistle made from the thigh bone of an eagle, and blew one long, low note, which was followed up by three short, quick, piercing ones; and instantly a volley from Caddoe rifles, greeted the flank of the over confident and unsuspecting Comanches, who broke in every direction—some flying from the field, not to return again.

A portion of the savages however, more resolute than the remainder, soon rallied, and seemed determined to hold us, till reinforcements arrived from the village; and they at once commenced a rapid and well directed fire. But they fought at a disadvantage, as we were thoroughly protected by our position, while they were compelled to stand out upon the open ground. They did not dismount, as is usual; but each warrior rode up within range, discharged his piece, and galloped off to a place of safety, where he reloaded, and returned to discharge it again.

A word of command from our chief, almost instantly changed the whole aspect of the struggle. The men, on hearing it, bounded from their places of concealment, and with guns, pistols, bows, and lances, charged out upon the mounted Comanches. Arrows flew thick and fast for a brief interval; and rapidly we were nearing the foe, and a hand to hand encounter seemed imminent; but before our band had reached the spot where our enemies stood, they wheeled their animals, and fled from the field, utterly foiled and beaten.

Once masters of the field, the whistle of the Caddoe chief was heard again, and instantly his men commenced disposing of the fallen Comanches. There were on the ground, seven killed, and nine wounded; and the dispatching of the latter was at once commenced. All were slain, and their scalps added to the trophies of the victory.

Some of the wounded struggled fiercely with lance and bow, but all were either shot or tomahawked by the infuriated but exulting Caddoes. Some yielded up their lives with stoical firmness, chanting their own death song, though suffering the most intense agony, until the Caddoes would leap upon them, and, with a blow of the tomahawk, end their torture in a bloody death. Others begged piteously that their lives might be spared; but there was no mercy in the breast of the victor for the foe, though fallen and helpless.

As long as the fight lasted, I could shoot and yell with the best of them; but, the struggle over and the success complete, my heart sank within me, and I sickened at the bloody work in which my comrades appeared to take so great a delight. But there was no escape for me; I must stand by and witness it all, without a murmur or a remonstrance. To have interposed an objection would but have added to the magnitude of the tortures inflicted; and, perhaps, brought down upon my own head the vengeance of Casa Maria and his men. That I might, at least, turn away from the scene, I mounted my horse and rode a short distance, as if looking out for Comanches, till the work of slaughter had ended.

Scalping, barbarous as it is, is reduced to an art among the Indians. The victor cuts a clean circle around the top of the head, so that the crown may form the centre, and the diameter of the scalp exceed six inches; then, winding his fingers in the hair, he puts one foot on the neck of the prostrate foe, and with a vigorous pull tears the reeking scalp from the skull. To the dead, this, of course, would not be absolute cruelty; but it is too frequently the case that the process is performed and the scalp severed while yet the mangled victim lives; and there are instances where parties have recovered, and long survived this barbarous mutilation. Occasionally, a warrior is not satisfied with the part of the scalp usually taken, but bares the skull entirely, and carries away in triumph even the ears of his victim.

The scalping concluded and the trophies gathered up and secured, another shrill whistle brought the victors into their saddles, and we began a precipitate retreat to our own village. For several miles we marched in solid column; but an order from the chief scattered the crowd, and every man took the direction which best suited his fancy.

I was now once more alone with the chief. Dismounting, we suffered our wearied steeds to rest and graze for some time, keeping a sharp lookout, the while, to prevent surprise. After the last of his men had disappeared, the chief mounted his horse, at the same time pointing in the direction of the Comanche camp. It was now evident that our enemies had been reinforced, and were returning to the pursuit. A light gray column of dust was rising, the cause of which we were at no loss decipher. We must hasten away or our scalps might soon grace the lodge of the Comanche, as a compensation for the losses they had that day sustained.

We rode rapidly in a southeasterly direction till after night; we came to an elevation which might be denominated either a high hill or a small mountain, near which was a dense thicket. Reaching this, Casa Maria again sounded the whistle, the tones at first being soft and plaintive, but afterward gradually deepening like the screaming of a frightened bird. It was instantly answered from the thicket, when we galloped up, and saw Indians—friends—rise up, like Rhoderic Dhu's clansmen, and greet us.

We laid down to sleep, supperless, and by daylight in the morning were off again for the agency, at which we arrived without accident; and here for the first time, I discovered that half a dozen of the Caddoes were wounded—some of them severely. I remained here only long enough to enable my horse to recruit a little, when I left for Radziminski, to deliver the chief's report to the colonel.

On the following morning, I started back again to the agency, bearing a message from the Colonel to Placido, who was then at that point. On arriving at the Tonchue village, I found everything in a state of deep excitement. A party of wild Indians had invaded their territory with a view to stealing their horses; but, being discovered in time, the intruders were driven off before they had accomplished anything.

A party was just starting in pursuit, and desiring to see the fun, I secured a fresh horse and started with it at full speed. We chased the fugitives some fifteen miles out. They numbered thirteen—eleven Comanches and two Kiowas, all of whom were killed and scalped. The bodies of the slain were carried back by the victorious Tonchues, who made a feast upon them. This may seem strange to one unaccustomed to the manners of this and other southwestern tribes; but, shocking as it is, the custom of eating their enemies slain in battle is almost universal among them.

When I saw the Comanches killed and scalped, I had hoped the affair would, at least, end there; and when I saw the victors carrying off the bodies of the slain, I could not conceive of their motive, for, up to that time, I had not learned that I was among cannibals; but once at the village, I was not long in discerning what was to follow. The bodies had hardly been brought in before the women commenced digging holes in the ground, over which to cook them. The bodies were disembowelled and then cut up, and the pieces put upon stakes over the fire and roasted; after which they were divided out—every member of the tribe, even down to the smallest child, getting a share.

At first I tried to avoid seeing the disgusting spectacle; but when the Indians saw this, they insisted on my presence. During the cooking, a grand war dance was progressing, at which all the achievements of the tribe from the beginning of time, when the little primogenitor of the Tonchues was nurtured at the breast of a she-wolf, down to the victory of that day, were duly paraded, and expatiated upon by improvised song, set to an unearthly music, timed by a monotonous tap, tap, tap, on the little deerskin drum. A pole was erected and the scalps displayed upon it, when the grand scalp dance was commenced. At first, only the warriors who had taken one of these trophies joined in the ceremony; but afterward the old men fell in, and gradually the crowd increased until the entire tribe, save the women, were whirling in circles around the scalp pole.

That portion of the flesh which was not eaten on the ground, was given out, and taken to the various lodges, for future use, and to be set before visitors, as a choice delicacy. As I was sitting beneath the shade of a *mesquit* tree, three or four venerable heads of the village came to me, bearing two large pieces of the meat, which appeared to have been cut from the thigh, and offered them to me to eat. The flesh was of a rusty colour, and had an unearthly, graveyard smell; and this with the sight sickened me. I refused the proffered delicacy politely, but firmly; seeing which, Tocasan, a war chief, and several others of the principal men, who had been in the chase, gathered about, and said very earnestly; "eat it, Cah-hah-ut," which was the name they gave me, "it will make you mighty much brave; mighty much brave."

Seeing that something must be done, I told them I wanted to go to a house near the agency, where I would get some bread and milk to eat with it. But no sooner was I out of their sight, than I buried it, and returned to their dance, which was every moment getting more and more frenzied. They had managed, by some means, to secure a supply of whisky, and their yells and screams, beside other frightful noises, together with their frantic gestures, made them appear more like demons than human beings.

In the midst of their excitement, I left them for the night, and on my return in the morning, found the whole population completely exhausted, stupid, and almost torpid. During the day, however, they sobered off, and on the following morning were ready to join us in a grand circle hunt for wild horses.

This is a peculiar kind of chase; and the only one which ever results in much success. A column of hunters, consisting of two or three hundred men—sometimes even more—is formed in the same order as if on the war path, with an advance guard, and numerous flankers, to look out for horses. As soon as a herd is discovered, the column is notified, by some preconcerted signal, when it instantly halts, and awaits the orders of the chief, who always rides in the direction indicated and reconnoitres, accompanied by four or five of the principal men of the tribe. This done, they ascertain the course of the wind; and taking advantage of that, march their forces toward the herd, keeping at a great distance away, so as not to excite alarm.

At intervals of a mile or so, a band of twenty-five or thirty men will be posted, until the game is entirely surrounded. These squads again deploy, to right and left, as the movements of the herd, or the nature of the ground require. When the circle has been completed, another signal is given, and the ring is contracted as much as it is possible to do, without alarming the herd. As soon as the wild horses scent the hunters, the chase begins. Off go the animals, in the vain hope of escaping the enemy, which they suppose to be approaching only from one side; but no sooner do they approach the circle, than several hunters show themselves, and turn the frightened herd back again; and thus they are kept galloping across, and around the sac formed for their reception, for hours, and until they are so wearied that they are readily taken, by the contracting, and closing up of the circle. Occasionally these horses, over frightened, make a desperate charge upon some single spot in the line by which they are surrounded, and thus make their escape; but this is not usual. And even then, all do not escape, for some of them are sure to be lassoed in the melee.

Our chase was a moderately successful one. We encircled a herd, and worried the horses, till they were nearly exhausted, and then succeeded in obtaining a number. As soon as we had a noose on one of the animals, it was tied and hoppled, and then let loose, in order to create greater confusion in the herd. After securing all the best stock, they were driven home, and turned over to the women and boys, whose duty it is to train them for the saddle, and otherwise render them serviceable to the warriors.

CHAPTER 9

Scouting

Col. Johnston, who had returned to his command, now undertook another expedition against the Kickapoos; and after marching about two hundred miles through the country and exhausting a large number of horses, we succeeded in running them out of the country; and though we had no fight with them, we effectually prevented further depredations on that part of the frontier for some time. The only parties who lost their lives by the expedition were two white men, who were living in a little cabin on the Big Washita River. They doubtless believed us hostile Indians and fled; and mistaking them we charged after and killed both. On learning who our victims were, deep regret pervaded the entire regiment; but it was unavailing, and we could only perform decently the last rites due to the departed. The unfortunate victims of a mistake, were doubtless hunters or trappers, and perfectly innocent of conniving with the Indians, in their depredations upon the frontiers. They were, judging from appearances, but recent settlers in the vicinity.

After our return to Radziminski, the men were allowed to recruit their horses and rest themselves. During the months of July and August scouting parties were sent up each of the forks of Red River, the south and north Canadian, and even to the Colorado and the Brazos. We had, in these scouts, numerous adventures, and some exceedingly hard times, as well as a fair degree of sport. The country over which we travelled is generally barren and almost destitute of water and timber. The few springs and streams are filled with bitter or salt water, which is almost unpalatable. Everywhere rock salt is abundant; the river banks are full of it, and the waters of the streams are so impregnated by contact with it, that a man will hardly sink in in them. As the streams are dry during a portion of the year, thousands of barrels of pure crystallized salt is left in the beds, only awaiting the hand of man to gather and use it.

On the headwaters of the Colorado, we surprised and burned a small village, but took no prisoners. Our horses were jaded, and we could not follow up our successes, or we could have annihilated the savages who inhabited it. As it was, six or seven men and one woman were killed.

The Wichita mountains are located between the Red River on the south, and the Canadian on the north. They are not extraordinarily high—the elevation being only from six to fifteen hundred feet. They are isolated from each other, and do not lie in a chain or range; but each peak rises by itself, from a perfectly level plain. The valleys between the mountains vary in breadth from half a mile to four or five miles; and several small creeks or rivulets are found running through them, whose banks are fringed with a luxuriant growth of cottonwood trees; while other portions of the valleys are covered with the mesquit, a low scraggy bush or tree, peculiar to southern latitudes. It bears a long slim bean, which though pleasant to the taste, is not a fit article of diet.

The most singular thing to me, was that the mountains were composed exclusively of great masses of dark gray sandstone, and only covered with a very slight layer of earth; so slight, indeed, that it could sustain no vegetation save a sickly tuft of moss or grass, with here and there an exceptional locality; while the plain in which they stood, is entirely devoid of rock. In many of these elevations, the layers of stone had a dip of nearly forty-five degrees.

The plain is covered with the best quality of grass, affording pasturage for immense herds of buffalo, antelope, and horses. The mountains and river take their name from a very considerable branch of the Pawnee Indians, called the Wichitas. Although long possessing separate political organizations—if the aborigines can be said to have politics at all—the two branches speak nearly identically the same language, being able to converse with each other fluently—an uncommon thing among savages, after a few years of separation. If the language of the savage is ever refined, that of the Pawnee and Wichita must be; at least it is smooth, soft, and very musical.

In this region, game is exceedingly plenty. Bear, otter, wolves, deer, turkey, etc.; and in addition, poisonous serpents are numerous and large. These last named are great seekers after comfort, and are ever hunting out a good bed to rest in. It is no uncommon thing to find them in the morning in possession of your best blanket; and sometimes your rather too intimate bedfellow. As for tarantulas and centipedes—*they* are innumerable; but they seldom do any harm.

The Indians never kill the tarantula; but when it is found in camp, they carry it away with great care, and let it loose. If urged to destroy one of them they refuse, on the ground that if one is killed, its companions will revenge its death, by biting somebody's horse. The centipede would soon become so numerous that life would not be safe in Texas, if it were not for another species of reptile, the lizard—their active and deadly enemy. I have seen one of these animals attack a centipede as large as itself, kill it, and carry it to the top of a tree, and there devour it at leisure.

On one of our forays toward the headwaters of the Colorado we killed a white woman, and captured another with her child. They were in an Indian village, upon which we charged with great suddenness and violence; and though a portion of the inhabitants made their escape, all who remained were killed, including this woman. On seeing us, she turned the horse on which she was mounted, threw her buffalo robe around her, and covering her head, shouted, "*Americano! Americano!*" But the men did not know her sex, nor understand her words, and in a moment she fell riddled with bullets. The white woman, who was fortunate enough to be captured, was taken down to the settlements, where she was identified as a niece of Captain Parker, an old frontiersman, who was among the earliest pioneers in that region; having built himself a fort, which is still known by his name. He was attacked one night, when this woman was a girl of nine years of age, and the whole family, except the captain and one or two others, supposed to have been killed. His wife was brutally murdered in the presence of her children. There were several families in the fort at the time; and but few of the entire number assembled escaped. The children had all been taken out on the trail a short distance, and, except this one murdered.

Although she could distinctly recollect all the details of the affair, and the form and features of her mother, she had entirely forgotten her native tongue, and we could only communicate with her through an interpreter. She happened to have her youngest child with her, at the time of her capture, which had been named To-ca-san, for one of the war chiefs of the tribe. It was about three years old, and violent in its disposition as a catamount. She informed us that she had one son, who was a good warrior, and also another boy and girl. She informed us that she had never seen a white person over nine years old allowed to live; and that she had been a spectator on numerous occasions when they had been put to death; and that it was uncommon to allow even a child to escape with its life. "Their prisoners," she continued, "are tortured, and then killed and eaten."

On the 15th of August we left Radziminski finally. All the men who had lost their horses, or whose animals were unfit for service, were sent back to Fort Belknap, with quarter rations, but with sufficient ammunition to enable them to subsist off the country. After sending away these, Colonel Johnston found himself with barely one hundred and ten men; and it was with this small force that he proposed to invade the Indian country, and teach the savages to respect the property and power of the white man. The friendly Indians regarded this determination as the freak of a madman; and the chiefs waited upon him in a body, in order to induce him to desist from his undertaking. They represented to him the nature of the country through which he must travel, the scarcity of grass, water, timber, and game. He might possibly find buffalo, but the chances were decidedly against it. They also expatiated on the number, power, and prowess of the Comanches and Kiowas, as well as their desperation; and they advised the colonel to fall back on the settlements, and guard the frontier during the coming winter, and then renew the campaign in the spring.

"You have already done much service," they said; "and your horses are not good, and your young men are tired; let us now go to our own country, and wait for the good grass in the spring; then we will come and help you fight the Comanches." But despite their eloquence the colonel was inexorable; he would make a campaign at once.

Placido represented vividly the hard fate of his command if it advanced; how his men must suffer from hunger and thirst; and how almost inevitable defeat awaited an invasion by so small a party. But he refused to listen to the words of his friend. Discovering this, the chiefs united in firmly, but respectfully informing the colonel that if he undertook the campaign, it must be alone; they would not accompany him, as but one result could attend the expedition.

Colonel Johnston was sorely disappointed at this desertion by his allies. He had relied upon their co-operation; but that reliance had proved delusive. When the friendly Indians had mounted, they parted with every manifestation of deepest friendship; and, for my part, I felt deep regrets at the separation. We had long been together, and were really getting attached to each other. Before leaving, many of them embraced me affectionately; and the Tonchues insisted on my accompanying them, their chief, Placido, desiring me to teach his young men how to read and write. "If you will do this," said he, "I will give you all my ponies when I die;" all his wealth was in these animals, the number owned by him being about four hundred. I informed him that I would go to his village at some other time; but at present I could not accompany him.

"No," they said, "we will never see Cah-hah-ut[1] again."

Six of the Indians, notwithstanding the determination of the main body, determined to remain with us, and share our fortunes. They were, "Jack," a Shawnee; "Black Foot," a Delaware; "Neighbors," a Kechai, and "Yellow Wolf," a Tonchue; "John," a Kiowa, and "John Socie," a Cherokee. These men were faithful to us throughout, and only left the command when discharged by order from the government. They were certainly devoted to us, and were ever ready to take their part in the hardships of the campaign, and endure all the privations incident to it. But these Indians were exceptions to the general rule.

---

1. This word means "good;" and by it I was known among all the friendly Indians.

CHAPTER 10

Col. Johnston's Comanche Campaign

Not deterred by the desertion of our allies, Colonel Johnston determined to set out on the campaign. At first our march was in the direction of Red River; but when near the source of that stream we turned in the direction of the head waters of the False Washita, where we engaged in another hunt for wild horses, which resulted in the capture of a number of fine ponies—just what we most needed, as many of our animals had been worn out by campaigning. Perhaps, however, ours was not altogether a fair game, as we fell in with the herd when nearly run down by the Indians; and hence we had little difficulty in securing our prey.

We saw the savages and horses coming over the prairie at full speed, but they could not see us; and discovering that there was but a small party, we formed in a circle, under cover of a hill, and immediately in front of the horses; and, as the herd passed, we dashed in between them and their pursuers. At the first sight of us, the Indians wheeled and fled. For myself, I noosed a beautiful strawberry roan mare, with a white croup, covered with black spots; but she was fat, and strong, and snapped my lariat, carrying away the larger portion of the rope. I need not here repeat the language I used when she escaped me; suffice it to say, my reflections were not of the most pleasant character, and I am afraid I gave vent to words more expressive than elegant.

During our march, we found an abundance of game as far as Antelope hills, on the South Canadian River, in the Pan Handle of Texas; but after crossing the Canadian, we saw no other wild animals than buffalo; but these were plenty, which indicated that the predictions of the friendly chief would be falsified. Up to this time, we had done

"For myself, I noosed a beautiful strawberry-roan mare, with a white croup covered with black spots; but she was fat and strong, and snapped my lariat, carrying away the larger portion of the rope."

well, and had never lacked for water, though some of it was not of the best quality; and thus encouraged, we pushed on, following the Marcy trail to the famous line of 36° 30', which is the northern boundary of the State of Texas. On crossing the Canadian, we reached a beautiful sweet water creek, where we stopped for a day's hunt; and as buffalo could be seen in every direction, we separated into parties of six or eight, and started on the chase; and, in a few hours, we had the ground strewn with dead and dying animals.

After becoming wearied with the sport, we commenced saving the choicest parts of the meat—the hump steak, shoulder cuts, and loins—which were lashed to our saddles and carried to the camp. When again at our camp, we stretched ropes like a clothes lines, and proceeded to cut up our meat in long, thin strips, and hang it out to dry. This is the universal method among hunters and Indians, of curing buffalo meat—no salt being used. It is exposed to the heat of the sun during the day, and is taken down in the evening, before the dew falls, and put in the mess sacks. For three or four days it requires airing, until the moisture disappears; and in a few days more it may be opened.

From Sweet Water Creek, we crossed over to the valley of the North Canadian—a stream which seems to puzzle geographers immensely. According to some authorities, it is sixty miles longer, and according to others, as much shorter than it really is. Its exact source is in the Texas Pan Handle, in longitude 23 deg. from Washington. It is small, with clear water, and for some distance down it, there is no timber but cotton wood. As we approached it, game became scarcer; and, when once across, all signs of wild animals disappeared. For days, we could not see a crow, or even one of those little brown birds, so plentiful in every prairie region.

We had intended to go from the North Canadian to the Salt Fork of the Arkansas, but missed our reckoning and struck the Red Fork. It was a long, and wearisome march, and we all suffered severely from thirst, and many of the men from hunger. On the Red Fork, we divided up our little stores equally, and turned up Hard Wood Creek, heading directly for Santa Fe. During this march, we suffered greatly from hunger. The stream on which we were is a famous resort for Kiowas, but they had all left it, and gone to a section where game was to be had. All along its banks, there were evidences that but a short time before, there had been a great number of them camped in the vicinity. This is a most singular stream—but eight feet wide, and dry as a floor at its mouth; while three miles up it was fourteen feet wide, with a current of clear, swift running water; and three miles further toward its source, it was the same width, and two feet deep; and after travelling five days more, in the direction of its head waters, it measured thirty yards in width, and was, at least twenty feet deep; and it was yet another day's journey to its head; but whether or not it increased in size all the way, I cannot tell.

We were all out of rations when we left Hard Wood Creek; and as to Captain Fitzhugh's company, it had been out since two days before our arrival at the Red Fork of the Arkansas. After travelling in the direction of Santa Fe for some days, we found so much Indian sign, that after due deliberation, the officers determined to return in the direction of Fort Belknap. The chances of our seeing home looked rather gloomy when we reflected that we had four hundred miles to travel through a region we knew to be destitute of game; the most sanguine reader, I presume, would scarcely venture to say that our prospects were flattering.

From Hard Wood Creek we crossed to the Mesquit, one of the tributaries of the South Canadian; and here we began to feel ourselves safe from an attack by a superior force of savages, as the sign was not plentiful and was very old. On this stream we encamped in a large grove of most beautiful young cottonwoods, near which was a bluff thirty feet high, with a projecting cliff, almost forming a cave. Near the foot of this we found the skeleton of a man and of a huge bear—perhaps a grizzly. The arms of the man had been crushed and the ribs broken; while nearby lay the irons of a rifle with part of the mutilated stock, and a large bowie knife, of the pattern known as the Arkansas tooth-pick.

Judging from appearances, the man had stood on the ground and shot the bear on the level of the cliff; and that the animal, though mortally wounded, had leaped down, and after a desperate struggle, killed the hunter. How long they had lain there was a mere matter for conjecture; but, doubtless, the period might be measured by years. No name was on the gun or knife, and no memorial remained to tell who the unfortunate hunter was; but the surgeon, after examining the bones, pronounced them to belong to a white man.

While on this stream, we had a mule bitten by an enormous rattlesnake, and none of us knew what to do in the matter. As soon, however, as we had reached the camp, Shawnee Jack examined the wound, after which he took a survey of the ground for some distance, till his eye rested on a particular plant, when he took out his bowie knife and dug it up by the roots. The root was a long one, somewhat resembling a small sweet potato, both as to shape and size; and Jack at once bit off a piece, which he commenced chewing till he had rendered it plastic; after which he bound it on the wound, which was a severe one; each fang of the reptile having cut a slit in the hide of the animal, at least five inches long; and a single night, under the influence of this wonderful restorative, sufficed to render the animal entirely sound again.

We were now suffering terribly from hunger; and in every direction our eyes were searching for something to satisfy our craving appetites; but we saw nothing till we reached the South Canadian River, at the mouth of Mesquit Creek. There we came upon a group of low, sandy hills, covered with grape vines,—no other vegetation, however, not even grass being in sight—young and thrifty, and loaded with fruit—the first of the kind I ever saw. This was indeed a God-send to us; the children of Israel never devoured manna more greedily than we did these grapes; and having satisfied our appetites, we carried away as many as we could put in our haversacks and camp kettles. How these vines happened to grow there is a mystery; and why they were so unusually thrifty, considering the soil, is a problem I despair of solving.

Crossing to the South side of the Canadian, we passed over Dry river, which appeared to be the only stream in the country which afforded any water. On the banks of this river we found a small growth of *mesquit* and hackberry bushes; and so famished were a portion of the command, that they actually devoured the dry *mesquit* beans,—which at that time of the year are as hard as hickory wood—with greediness. Of those who were ravenous enough to eat them, I was one. From the valley of Dry River, we crossed a plain to a stream called White Fish Creek, though why so called I am unable to divine, as I do not think there ever was a member of the finny tribe within its waters—if, indeed, it ever had water in it. When we saw it, at least, it was perfectly dry, the bottom being covered with a fine white sand.

On the banks of this creek, we found hack berries and Cheatham berries, of which the rangers partook liberally; but as the latter were not fit to eat, many of the men sickened. On the plain were occasional groups of prickly pears, and on some days we had all we could eat of them; but at other times, they were not to be had, and we were compelled to do entirely without nourishment. Continuing along White Fish Creek, we at length reached Prairie-Dog Fork of Red River.

All along down the creek, I rode on the extreme right of the flankers; my companion on the left, being John Socie, a Cherokee Indian. I had frequently during the day, seen bands of savages watching us, and had notified the colonel of it, through my Cherokee friend, who acted as messenger; and when we encamped for the night, I repeated to that officer what I had observed during the day; and also my suspicions that I had seen an Indian camp, though concerning this I was not willing to make a positive statement. The colonel affected to doubt it, and roundly asserted that there was not a savage within fifty miles of us. I, however, persisted, and told him to prepare for a fight on that, or the following night; but he offered to bet we would not see an Indian between White Fish Creek and Fort Belknap, and there the controversy ended.

By this time, the men had become perfectly careless regarding everything, save the procuring of subsistence; utterly disregarding all the usual precepts taken under ordinary circumstances, during a campaign. Had the Indians attacked us almost any day, with a moderate force, we must have been exterminated; and it is therefore fortunate for us, that they were ignorant of our actual condition. We encamped that night on the north side of the river, on the opposite bank of which was a bluff at least sixty feet high, and fairly sparkling with isinglass. I took a field telescope, and went over on the bluff, to have a view of the sandy country, and particularly that laying to the westward; for it was in that direction, that I believed I had seen the Indian camp, to which I have adverted. It was a long and tiresome walk; and about half way up the mountain I reached a level bench, or steppe, where I found about five hundred small brush shelters, used by a large party of warriors. So recently had they been erected, that the leaves were not yet withered; indeed, they were so fresh, that they appeared to have been cut on that very day. This sign at once aroused me, and admonished me to look out for stragglers; but I saw none.

It was just sunset, when I reached the desired point, and from it I had good a view of the regions around me. The last rays of the sun lit up the country splendidly, in the direction I believed the Indians to be; and on arranging my glasses, the whole of a large village lay in full view. Near them, and grazing, was a large number of horses, with some cattle and sheep.

The camp was at the base of a mountain, and very extensive—a careful estimate placing the number of men, women and children, at fifteen hundred or more. This discovery did not appear much to improve the desperate position in which we found ourselves; and hastening back, I reported what I had seen to the Colonel, who could now no longer doubt the presence of the savages. In obedience to his orders, we did all in our power to make ourselves as safe as possible, and laid down to sleep, fully expecting an attack before morning; but fortunately none came, and as we had nothing to eat, and consequently no cooking, we mounted, and were off at daylight, following the bed of the stream for about twelve miles, where we found a sweet water spring, at which we halted to rest ourselves, and refresh our horses.

That night we killed an old buffalo—so old and poor that it was with difficulty he could manage to walk; and he was the first specimen of game we had seen in a week. Bad as was his meat, we relished it as a luxury; and after eating what we wanted, laid down to sleep, entirely content to take whatever might come. There is a wide difference between a famished man, and one with a full stomach. We put out guards; but what did they care, now that they had plenty of meat, and palatable water? what else did they desire? sleep alone, and—they slept.

The greater portion of the night wore away without anything to disturb its quiet; at about two hours before daylight, and just before the moon went down, Pete Ross was aroused by the clattering of horses' hoofs. Ross sprang to his feet, and awakened his men, just in time to get the first shot. As for the other companies—they needed not to be awakened by their officers; the wild, piercing war whoop sounded in their ears, and each man in an instant had his hand upon his trusty rifle. There was no mistaking the shout—it was the war whoop of the wild Comanche; and no sooner had its echo died away in the distance, than the whole body of warriors charged down upon our horses, and stampeded them; and but for the presence of mind of a few of the rangers, all of them must have escaped. However, about twenty of the men ran in among them, and by constant firing, got up a counter fright, and saved about half our animals.

The savages, having thus obtained possession of a part of our horses, rode away in triumph. Capt. Fitzhugh at once gave orders to his men to mount, and pursue; but before he was off, another party of Comanches raised a demoniac yell, and came down upon us; but discovering that we were prepared to receive them, they retired out of gunshot range; but they kept up such a noise, during the balance of the night, that further sleep was impossible, and we stood by our arms till daylight, by which time the last savage had disappeared.

The first party numbered about sixty, and were splendidly mounted—some of them on fine American horses of great size; the second gang chiefly riding ponies. They were armed with rifles, bows, lances and pistols, which they used promiscuously—some being busily engaged shooting arrows, though at the same time they had six-shooters dangling to their wrists and fastened by a string. They were for the most part naked, except that they wore breech clouts, though some sported leggins, and all had head dresses and moccasins. A few only were in full dress.

The Comanche people wore the buffalo scalp, while most of the stampede party sported Kiowa feather caps, some of which fell into our hands. They were very nicely made of long white plumes, like swan feathers, and beautifully coloured at the tips with red, yellow and black. The quill part is sowed to a close fitting skull cap made of buckskin, and they are set so close together that when it is drawn over the head the plumes stand out in every direction, giving to the wearer a terribly hideous appearance. The buffalo scalp is worn with horns, and it is so arranged that these protrude from the top of the head, they being scraped so thin that they are very light. The skin of the nose is cut off above the eyes, while that of the neck and hump hangs down the back, the whole being softly dressed with the hair on; and as an additional ornament it is often artistically beaded. The faces of the savages were painted in the most hideous style; black, red, yellow and white being the prevailing colours.

Part of the time our struggle was a hand to hand fight, and the savages succeeded in carrying off seven of our men, and all their own killed and wounded; so that it was impossible for us to ascertain their loss, though it must have been severe, notwithstanding it was a night struggle and the moon was low. We judged from appearance that there were about seven hundred Indians altogether, and this was perhaps rather below than above the truth.

Our loss in the fight was seven men, forty-six horses, and seven pack mules. It would have been useless for us to have attempted to follow up the savages in the dark as soon as the fight had closed, and by morning the marauders were far away; and long before we could overtake them, we knew we would be surrounded, and "wiped out" by superior numbers. Nevertheless, the colonel did reconnoitre for some ten miles, but learned nothing, except that was an unhealthy locality for Texas Rangers.

We now destroyed all our baggage and cooking utensils—everything save what was absolutely necessary to preserve life, and started for Belknap. Tents, saddles, pack saddles, everything that would burn was committed to the flames; while kettles, plates and pans were broken, and our axes buried in the quicksand. As many of our men were now without horses, we were compelled to adapt ourselves to circumstances. By the order of march, the footmen moved first, and then the cavalry close upon them; and in this manner we made our way across an immense plain, which seemed to be one solid city of prairie dogs. A few of these animals were killed and eaten; but our ammunition was nearly exhausted, and consequently no shot was fired, unless under the most pressing circumstances.

This section was almost entirely destitute of water, and we suffered intensely from thirst. Indeed the whole plain was one broad, barren waste; and over it at least one hundred miles of our journey lay. The sufferings of the men were so great, that on the second day after the disaster, the command was threatened with open mutiny, the soldiers demanding to be allowed to scatter; and it required all the address of the officers to prevent them from dispersing over the plain in search of water and food. Major Fitzhugh threw himself down and begged that someone would shoot him and thus put an end to his misery; while Captain Wood sank down exhausted, and urged us to go on and leave him to his fate.

How different the conduct of men when in like trying circumstances! Major Fitzhugh gave way to despair, while his brother Gabriel, suffering equally, only increased in resolution as difficulties thickened around us. Captain Wood was a large muscular man, yet he sank down, while others of far more slender mould marched onward with resolute and rapid step.

We had not gone far out on the plain before we discovered that we would be unable to traverse it for lack of water; and we were once more compelled to seek the banks of Red River. Here water would be plenty, but the route over which we were to travel was covered for miles with sharp, flinty rocks, and pieces of isinglass, and in addition was extremely hilly; and our feet would suffer fearfully from the travel on the stones and sand, while our eyes were inflamed by the reflected rays of the sun. But we had no choice; we could not die from thirst.

Before we had reached the river, I was almost famished for water; and coming upon a bluff of salt-rock, at least nine feet thick, beneath which was a sort of cavern, filled with cold brine, I plunged into it, clothes and all, and was enjoying a bath, when Colonel Johnston rode up to me and directed me to go in a southerly direction till I found water, and then to fire a signal gun; and as a companion I had John Socie, the trusty Cherokee, with a horse and several canteens, to bring back water to the famished men. About seven miles from where I left the colonel, I came to a creek on the south side of Red River; and when I reached it, my thirst was raging to such a degree that I jumped into the water, drinking my fill, and then rolled in the cooling wave with as perfect an enjoyment as physical pleasure can afford.

After I had taken time to collect myself, I discovered that I had been drinking bitter water; but hoping that further out into the stream it would be better, I waded in, but found that there it was salt. This was discouraging; but on remembering the condition of my companions, and the necessity of relief, I started to swim over the stream, hoping to find a spring on the other side. As I proceeded, I continued to taste the water for the double purpose of ascertaining its quality and of cooling my parched tongue; and, to my surprise and gratification, when I reached the middle of the creek, I found that it was sweet. Instantly I returned to the shore and commenced firing my gun, as a signal for the exhausted command to make one more effort to rally. I discharged my piece a number of times and, at length, had the satisfaction of hearing three shots in reply, and I knew that the colonel had heard me; and feeling assured that the command would come up as rapidly as possible, I commenced exploring the stream to find out where the sweet water came from, and discovered that it flowed from a spring, a mile and a half above. Here we again discharged our pieces, and again received a reply, but it was a great way off.

I at once filled all the canteens with us, and sent John back on his horse, to relieve the command; and on his arrival, the precious treasure was distributed sparingly among those who suffered most, or sent back to those who had fallen out exhausted, on the trail. As I had nothing to do during John's absence, I laid down and took a sound nap; and was only awakened by the sound of hoofs, when he returned to the spring, which he did as speedily as possible.

From him I learned that during the morning an open mutiny had occurred in camp; and that it would have proved successful but for the eloquent words of Lieutenant Colonel Smith, who appealed to the men not to abandon their companions who were unable to travel, but stand by them till we reached another watering place, when they could once more be refreshed; and the mules and horses could be sent after those who had fallen out. This appeal, touching as it was, however, was but partially successful, till the sound of my signal gun re-inspired all as if by magic; and they set out with renewed hope, if not with increased vigour. Some of those who had thrown themselves down in despair, at once aroused themselves from their lethargy, and stepped off at a lively gait in the direction of the crystal treasure.

Fully convinced that they could not now miss the spring, the Indian and myself started out on a hunt. We were both much refreshed by water and rest; and we stepped off at a lively pace, and after wandering about for some time, we espied a deer grazing, or, rather, licking salt. It was in the midst of an open prairie, so that it would be difficult to approach it. But, stealing around a little to the leeward, we kept our eyes fixed steadily upon it, and advanced rapidly, with long and hasty strides, till it gave indications that it suspected the presence of an enemy, when we halted, standing upright, and rigidly still. After gazing around for a moment, the animal appeared to dismiss its apprehensions, and put down its head again and commenced licking the salt.

Once more we began advancing, till we were almost within range, when it gave its tail a nervous twitch, causing us to stop again. It viewed us for a moment, but manifested no alarm, and again resumed its former position. On we glided, and this time we got within a short gunshot range, and Socie discharged his piece at the deer, which bounded up in the air, and then starting ran almost directly toward us, until I had time to give it another rifle ball accompanied by three buckshot, which brought it down. We now discovered that John's bullet had passed through its lungs, and that it had been mortally wounded, though it might have given us a long chase but for the contents of my piece.

We now sat down to rest and get cool after our long tramp, and to devise means to get our prize to camp. The animal was a large, fat doe, and would weigh at least an hundred pounds. As I was the stronger man, I proposed to John that he should carry my gun and pistols, and I would carry the deer. He had suggested that we leave half of it; but this I refused to do, when I recollected the condition of our men; so he acceded to my proposition, and helped me to shoulder the deer.

At the spring, we found all the men assembled who were able to walk; and, in the distance, we observed the pack-mules coming in with the stragglers. I never before saw any one enjoy anything so intensely as did these men the prospect of a dish of venison. The sight of the dead carcass called out the wildest expressions of joy from the famished rangers; and not many minutes elapsed, before the skin was off, and I was called upon to divide the flesh. Each man was allowed a small slice: the largest and best being reserved for those who were most nearly famished. Many a tear of joy was shed over these scanty morsels; and more than one rough, stalwart ranger rushed forward to embrace me, and overwhelm me with heartfelt thanks; and not a few poured forth praise to Heaven for our deliverance.

We did not leave the place that day; and while sleeping that night, the Indians made another attack upon us; but no one received injury, nor were any of our animals stolen. The savages were readily driven off, and we saw them no more.

Being now comparatively reinvigorated, we again attempted to cross the plain which had baffled us before. Following this creek to its source, we came to an immense prairie dog town, where not a leaf of grass or growing thing was to be seen—all having been devoured by the buffalo. While exploring the creek, we discovered whence arose the varieties of water within it. The shores were of gypsum, imparting to it a bitter taste near the edge; on its banks was a salt bluff, which rendered it brackish, as the water washed around it; while on the left bank the sweet spring poured out a swift stream, which, on account of the peculiar shape of the bend, kept out in the middle of the creek.

We were three days crossing the plain, and our only subsistence was a few prickly pears of stinted growth. When one of these plants was found, the ravenous appetites of the men would not even permit them to scrape off the thorns with which they are covered; but all was devoured together. Many of them suffered severely from this cause; the lips and tongue being penetrated, causing them to swell badly, and be extremely painful.

After three days weary marching and on the morning of the fourth, we suddenly came upon the verge of the desert, and but a short distance was travelled before we were in the midst of one of the most fertile and luxuriant spots in the State. Grass was high, and as we soon found a ravine in which water was plenty we hitched our horses to graze for a couple of hours. The animals being greatly refreshed, we pushed on, and had only gone a short distance when we came suddenly upon an immense herd of buffalo. We at once dismounted, and made all the necessary preparations for a grand "still hunt." Our preliminaries were arranged under cover; the regiment being divided off into two parties, one of which was under command of the colonel himself, the direction of the other being left to the Indians who were with us.

The colonel's party kept in the low ground, while the other filed down a ridge in full view of the herd, but on the windward side; and in this manner we advanced, till nearly within gunshot of the animals. Suddenly we wheeled to the right, down into a deep ravine, and stooping low, crawled four or five hundred yards, and were almost in the midst of them, when, at a given signal, each man marked his meat and brought it down. After the first discharge, the herd commenced a precipitate flight; but the men, determined to fast no more, drew their revolvers and continued firing till the herd had escaped beyond range. Twenty odd of the buffalo were shot dead in their tracks, and many more wounded. We were, however, not after sport, but meat; and leaving those which were crippled to do as best they could, we fell to cutting up the dead, and devouring their flesh raw.

Three or four of us rushed upon one cow, and began cutting out pieces of meat from as many different parts of the body, although the animal was not yet dead, but struggling violently. Capt. Wood sliced out one hump steak, Shawnee Jack cutting out the other; while Neighbors ran his knife into that delicious piece of half fat, half lean, that lies behind the shoulder blade, just under the back part of the hump. For my part, I knew that that meat would require cooking, and I was too ravenous to await so slow a process, and as I looked upon buffalo tallow as a dainty, I plunged my bowie knife into her side, and thrusting my arm through the whole, wound my fingers into the caul fat, and tore it out and ate it while it was yet warm. I am aware the reader will decide that this was barbarous; but let it be borne in mind, that we were famishing. So hungry was I, that this huge flake of fat, dripping with blood, seemed like the sweetest morsel I ever tasted.

Our hunger slightly appeased, we returned to the ravine in which the water was so plentiful, staked our horses to graze, and at once commenced gathering in our meat, cooking, and eating all the time, till our appetites were entirely satisfied. One thing that marred the delicacy of the meat, was the fact that we were without salt. While crossing the desert, mountains of the article reared their heads around us, but we were without meat; now meat lay in profusion about us, but we were without salt.

Ourselves and horses rested, we resumed our march, and after travelling about five miles, reached the Big Washita River. Here we halted, for a rest of five days, which we spent in hunting. We had jerked meat for bread, and fresh meat for beef; feasted continually on elk, deer, antelope, and wild turkey. During these five days of carousal, the sufferings on the desert were forgotten; and at the end of that time, fully restored to our wonted vigour, we resumed our march.

The direct route would have taken us across another desert; but we had had experience enough on them, and we therefore determined to follow the watercourses, though they were ever so circuitous. We accordingly kept down the Big Washita, till we reached the point where the Belknap and Radziminski roads cross, when we left it, and started direct for our place of destination, distant seventy-five miles. Our route lay through a good country, with plenty of game, and we fared, like the rich man—sumptuously every day—but only on meat; and therefore the reader may imagine our joy, on reaching the Little Washita, at meeting a wagon loaded with flour and bacon, with two ovens and two skillets. What visions of bread once more arose before us! and how soon we were at work, kneading the dough!

Our readers who are initiated into the mysteries of cooking, may form some idea of the bread we made, under all the disadvantages that surrounded us; but it was bread, and was a feast to us. Weeks had intervened since we had tasted aught but flesh; and now we baked and ate, and ate and baked, till all were fit subjects for the hospital, and some came near finding the graveyard. Orders to march next day, found not a man free from colic, or dysentery; though a few were able to travel, and they travelled. Every mile or so, a man would drop out; and when we reached the end of our day's journey, of twenty-five miles, there were but few men with us; yet the stragglers finally all came in and reported, though it is wonderful that some did not die by the wayside.

The next day was one long to be remembered by every ranger, as it was the last of that ill-started campaign. Dirty, ragged, long haired, unshaven, and generally barefooted, we reached Belknap on the 30th of October, 1860; and immediately we were mustered out, and paid in scrip, which is now worth less than nothing; but which, had not the state gone into rebellion, would have ultimately secured us fifty-two dollars a month in gold.

CHAPTER 11

Knights of the Golden Circle

Having been honourably discharged, the rangers began to scatter to their homes. Many had friends in the vicinity, who came after them with wagons; refusing to let them ride their war ponies, but leading these home in triumph, decked with flowers and ribbons. Parting among the men, rough as they were, gave rise to many affecting scenes. Hardy warriors wept like children, as they separated from the companions of their hardships and dangers. Truly, it might have been said of us that we were a band of brothers then; but how soon—such is human nature—to become deadly enemies!

I had enlisted at Waco, two hundred miles away, and had no means of reaching that place except on foot; and learning this, Colonel Smith tendered me a horse, but he was wild, having only been caught that spring, when we made our hunt up the Canadian. He was remarkably fleet on foot when in the wild herd; no less than sixty horses having been run after him—first all at a dash. In the race we had roped all the mares, when he came back to fight us, trying first to drive the mares, and then the men, away. Failing in both of these purposes, he dashed around and around in a circle, always eluding the rope, though thrown by our best horsemen; and in this way, he baffled us till our own horses were worn out; when, finally, an Indian, named Bob, shot him just between the last two short ribs, and let the ball range forward into the stomach—a process known among the savages as "creasing," and is frequently employed with success; and it is a far safer way than shooting them in the neck, as is sometimes done. Nevertheless, it is a barbarous proceeding, and could only be adopted by those devoid of every quality of mercy.

Such was the animal tendered me, and the reader will not be at a loss to conjecture that riding it was not the most pleasant thing in the world. It had thoroughly recovered from the gunshot wound, and was well nigh as wild as when first seen on the prairie; and was, withal, the most vicious beast I ever mounted, when we set out; but, strange as it may seem, by the time we reached our journey's end it was completely subdued, both to ride and work in harness—was as docile as it had been wild.

Soon after we arrived at Belknap, during the spring of 1860, a man visited us, who introduced himself as Captain Davis; but how he obtained the title was, and is, a mystery. He informed us that he was a member of the Knights of the Golden Circle, and that he was fully authorized to receive and initiate men into the order, from his superiors; and that when fully initiated, the mysteries and objects of the institution would be explained; that some of the objects must now be kept secret; but there was one that he could reveal; it was the intention to raise a force of twelve thousand men to invade Mexico, under command of General Sam.

Houston, the then Governor of Texas; and that they were to be paid by English capitalists at the rate of eighteen dollars per month; and that, after the conquest, the States of Nueva Leon, Chihuahua, Coahuila, and Tamaulipas were to be annexed to the United States; that Gen. Houston was not taking any public part in the matter, for State reasons; but that, in a short time, he would throw off all concealment, and declare his purpose to the world. British subjects, Captain Davis declared, were to pay the general a fabulous sum for accomplishing the work, and then settle an annuity upon his wife. He said that though all the details had not yet been arranged, they were being rapidly consummated.

He explained to us that the Knights were organized with three degrees—the military, the financial, and the legislative. The first of these was intended to be popular—to catch the masses of the people; and as men should not be made to pay too extravagantly for the privilege of serving someone else, the initiation fee to this degree was but one dollar. To get into the financial—ominous name—more money was required, and the initiation fee was put at five dollars. To become a third, or legislative-degree member, influence, and not money, was requisite. A man odious to the Knights could not have bought a seat in it; an influential politician could have obtained one at a mere nominal price—perhaps for nothing. Members of the first degree were not allowed to know what was done in the second: and those of the second were kept in ignorance of the transactions in the third; and as everyone was sworn to do the bidding of his superior, and each degree to obey the directions of those above it, the despotism was complete. It was the province of the few to command; of the masses to obey.

This was the feature to which I objected. I was rather pleased with some things—particularly the prospect of adventure; but I could never take an oath to do an act the nature of which I knew nothing; nor could I swear to obey irresponsible men, who proposed to do anything unlawful. If the object was legitimate, it occurred to me, why this secrecy? and, I believe subsequent events have proven that my objections were well taken; indeed, a few months sufficed to satisfy me upon that subject, and, I think, to satisfy all the world.

The captain was a ready talker, and well calculated to seduce the unwary into his schemes; and nearly all the rangers were induced to become members of the order, after which he left to enlighten the people of other sections. He was exceedingly lavish in his promises; to become a knight was to secure perpetual fame at once; and few of the rangers who joined but believed that the lowest position which would fall to their lot would be that of a field officer. "All promotions," he said, "were to be made from the ranks;" (an old story, every soldier knows), and all the great estates in Mexico were to be confiscated to secure fortunes to the adventurers. Immense tracts of land were to be granted to members of the order; the mines in Sonora were to be parcelled out, and every possessor to be made a Crœsus at once; and a hundred other glittering promises were made, which, under any ordinary circumstances, would have excited men of a wild, roving disposition; but in this case, success in obtaining enlistments was chiefly the result of other causes.

Mexican depredations on the Rio Grande had been frequent; and many a ranger was longing to retaliate upon the perfidious perpetrators in Tamaulipas and Nueva Leon; and they looked upon this as an excellent opportunity to join in a scheme which promised them revenge—far sweeter to the pioneer of western Texas than the wealth of an Astor or a Vanderbilt.

But very soon the attention of the Texans was turned to other enterprises than the invasion of Mexico, and the Knights had other foes than Spanish mongrels to fight. When I reached Waco, the most intense political excitement I ever witnessed was prevailing. Mr. Lincoln had just been elected president, and orators were busy on every street corner "firing the southern heart," which they fully succeeded in doing, though it has since pretty completely burned out.

I heard nothing now, but clamour about "Northern aggression," and "Southern rights," wherever I went. The State should secede at once; the politicians willed it, and the governor must obey. The cry was "secede, secede!" break up all connection with the Federal Union, by fair means or by foul—only secede. Of course I was at once questioned as to my views, and supposing there would be freedom of expression, I spoke my mind without reservation; but they did not look upon the matter in that light, and they plainly intimated that I could choose between conversion to the views of the secessionists and exile. I, however, refused to be converted, and was at once denounced as a Tory, a Lincolnite, and an abolitionist; and it was confidently expected that these epithets would enlighten my obtuse intellect and arouse my *patriotism?*

This procedure was persisted in from the time I was mustered out, in November, 1860, till after the first battle of Bull Run, in July, 1861, when I left the State; and that, too, in the face of the fact that the greater part of this time was consumed in protecting the homes and fire-sides of my maligners from the depredations of the wild Comanches. It may be chivalry thus to avail one's self of services so onerous and dangerous, and then vilify him who accomplished them; but it does not agree with my idea of the meaning of that term.

For a time Gov. Houston resisted the wild fanaticism which prevailed; but the current was too strong; reason was hushed; force and fraud were the order of the day; and chivalry and mob violence ruled the hour and defied the law. A convention was called and candidates were out early, "defining their positions," and soliciting the suffrages of the people.

In McClennan county, where I resided, the candidate of the secessionists was an ambitious and unscrupulous lawyer, named Coke, while the Unionists supported Lewis Moore, an old and highly respected citizen; public spirited and unselfish, and only interested in developing the resources of the State and nation. He had taken a prominent part in the Texan revolution, and in all the border wars, and in the Moderator and Regulator struggle in 1836-8. Election day came, and Coke received 196 votes, to 94 for Moore—an exceedingly light poll—but only light because no man ventured to tender his ballot without being prepared to defend it with the pistol and bowie knife. I went to the polls unarmed; but I soon found that I was alone in this respect; but I ventured up and tendered my vote. A Mr. Wm. Chamberlain was receiving the tickets, and a Major Downing was acting as judge;

and when the former observed that my ballot contained the name of Lewis Moore, his countenance darkened, and he asked me how I came to tender my vote there.

"You have not been in this country long enough, sir," said he.

"I have, sir," was my reply, but it was made in a quiet tone, and entirely different from that in which he addressed me.

"But you have been constantly away, running around after the Indians," he continued; "how is it you wish to vote here?"

"Because," was my response, "I am registered in the service for this place."

"But you can't be allowed to vote, sir," he persisted.

I began at once to explain my view of the law; that I was a ranger, and had served the people, and felt that I had a right to vote at any polls in the State, when he stopped me, saying:

"It is useless to multiply words; you can't vote."

I then left the court-house, went to the hotel, and got my pistols—a splendid pair of navy revolvers, and returned immediately; and seeing my movements, a number of Union men followed me, crowding the room in which the election was held. Nearly all of them were old, gray haired veterans, who had devoted their lives to the service of the State, and were as incorruptible patriots as ever trod on American soil.

Laying my ballot on the table, I addressed Mr. Chamberlin with:

"Sir, I have come to vote."

He looked at me, hesitated a moment, glanced at my hand, which was on my pistol, and the crowd of Union men around me, the countenances of every one of whom evinced a fixed determination the meaning of which he could not mistake, and then turned to the judges, but said not a word.

"Put that ticket in the box, and record my name," said I, calmly, but firmly.

He did not need another bidding, but slowly dropped the ticket in the box, took up his pen, and was about to record my name, when the Major said:

"The law requires a vote to be sworn in, after it has been challenged."

"Very well, sir," said I; "if the law requires it, I will be sworn."

He then produced a Bible, and holding it out to me, I laid my left hand on it, and the oath was administered, after which the book was held up toward my mouth, but I stepped back.

"Do you refuse to kiss the book?" said the judge.

"Yes, sir," I replied.

"For what reason," he continued.

"Because the law does not require it," was my response.

Chamberlin then registered my name, and I walked out of the court-house.

This was not an isolated instance of the persecution of Union voters. The polls were at length closed, and Coke coolly declared elected, in spite of the smallness of the vote, though this was one of the most populous counties in Central Texas; and in defiance of the fact that a large majority of the people were opposed to secession. But the malcontents were demonstrative, and had secretly organized and armed themselves, and had the control of the polls; and no Union man approached but felt that his life was jeopardized by the act.

There was a remarkable difference between the appearance of the two parties. The secessionists were mostly young men, who were both ambitious and fanatical, and who had been led astray by artful demagogues, who had "*an axe to grind.*" They were noisy, and many of them, before the sun had reached its meridian were drunk. They were chiefly of that class of floaters, who have no interest at stake, and whose dissolute habits are the bane of the society in which they flourish.

The Unionists, on the other hand, were generally venerable men who had done much service during the many wars in which the State had been involved. They had fought to render Texas independent, and had given their voice for her annexation to the Union; and they strenuously resisted a faction which proposed to undo the work which had cost them so much. They possessed property and character, and were not to be swayed by every demagogue who sought preferment and office. Such was the condition of affairs as far as my observation extended; such, I learned, was the situation throughout the State on that eventful day.

CHAPTER 12

Tyranny and Perfidy of the Secessionists

Soon after it became known that the secessionists had carried the State at the election, the commanders of the various United States posts commenced surrendering to the State troops. I was present at the capitulation of Camp Colorado at the request of a number of Union men, who desired to obtain accurate information regarding the nature of the proceeding. The insurgent forces were under the command of Henry M'Culloch, who, knowing that I had seen service, pledged me a captain's commission, if I would join the "Confederate" army; and had I done so, I have every reason to believe he would have made his promise good; but I refused his offer firmly.

After I had witnessed the capitulation, I returned to Waco. The Ordinance of Secession had been passed and referred to the people, and the whole State was in a blaze of excitement. Arbitrary arrests, broils, murder, and hanging were the order of the day; and under the pressure large numbers of the Union men were giving way, and the secessionists were receiving daily accessions to their strength. The people were either deceived into secession, lied into it, or driven into it.

Every species of deception was practiced that the ingenuity of crafty politicians or a licentious press could invent. The motives of the Northern people were misrepresented, and Union men, both North and South, outrageously belied. One week the secession orators would herald to excited audiences that independence could be consummated without any war at all; simply by every man voting a secession ticket and showing to the North that the South was thoroughly united; they would proclaim that the North was utterly demoralized and powerless to coerce the seceding States into obedience; nay, that so divided by contending factions were the people of that section, that they were not even capable of preserving their own integrity; that even the Northern States could not maintain a union among themselves, much less impose one upon the seceding States.

The next week the cry would be changed, and the Northern States would be represented as thoroughly united, and more unjust and defiant than ever they were before; that there were no people in the North that sympathized with the South, or who were willing to see that section get justice and equal rights. That every man in the free States was a practical abolitionist, and nothing would satisfy their rapacity but the immediate and unconditional surrender of slavery; and even that might not avail; and that it was more than likely a concession on that subject would invite aggression on another. Southern men were appealed to in the most impassioned language not to submit to these demands or compromise, but to rouse themselves to view matters of State in their true light, and to prepare for a contest that was inevitable.

Every proposition of the North was treated with disdain; even the President was hung in effigy, and treated with every indignity, simply because he was a Northern man, and was elected by free State votes, when they well knew that he would be bound by the same oath to maintain the Constitution that had bound all the Presidents of Southern birth. The sentiments of known Union men were wilfully misrepresented, and, thus distorted, heralded to the people, in order to infuriate them against individuals who professed loyal sentiments. For instance, General Houston would make a speech in Galveston, and take the most sincere and unqualified Union ground, and forthwith the fiends of secession would dispatch garbled extracts of it to every paper in the State that advocated secession, which, in turn, would give it, with the comments of its unprincipled editors, to the excited public. Sometimes they would manufacture and publish speeches for Houston and other patriots which they never delivered; and these were scattered broadcast to the mob, representing them as being at length thoroughly convinced that secession was the only means by which the Southern people could maintain their liberties and their institutions.

If he made a Union speech in Austin or Waco, denouncing the secession leaders, and charging them with seeking to overthrow the last vestige of personal liberty and constitutional government, and avowing the most vindictive hostility to all men professing secession principles, and professing undying devotion to the Union, at all hazards, no sooner would the words fall from his lips, than his discourse would be garbled to suit the cause of secession, and scattered all through the country. On one occasion, I remember, after forged speeches had been published over and over, and attributed to Houston, his friends in Waco wrote a letter and requested him to come out and deliver another address, and contradict them, but the old patriot answered despondingly that it was useless; he had tried it, and as fast as he contradicted one lie, they would publish another, and he would prefer to keep silent. But why enlarge upon facts patent to the world? Secession was born in sin and cradled in iniquity, and no man who is not lost to every feeling of patriotism, nay, who does not wear within himself the heart of a fiend, will presume to defend it.

But despite of frauds, despite of lying and forging, the Germans in the vicinity of San Antonio, and the settlers in the northern section of the State remained true to the Union; and as the secessionists had determined to secure uniformity, force was resorted to, and bayonets supplanted arguments and deception. The first attempt was upon the Germans, and the headquarters of the southwestern military district was removed to San Antonio, and ten or twelve thousand desperadoes were sent thither to overawe all who remained loyal to the old government; and this process was found to succeed admirably; for in the presence of such a force, unarmed, unorganized citizens are usually constrained to keep silence. The houses of all the settlers were searched, and when arms were found, they were confiscated; and a most perfect military despotism was thus established over a disarmed populace.

Next, it was important to the insurgents that the people of northern Texas should be subjugated; and the work was intrusted to the notorious Ben. McCulloch, who made his headquarters at Dallas, and had at his command some fifteen hundred men; and this force was soon increased by the arrival of reinforcements, to ten thousand; and having used his army in coercing Union citizens into secession, till he was satisfied, he marched it to Fort Smith, Arkansas.

Outside of the districts patrolled by the armies, the work of converting Unionists by force was adopted by irresponsible bodies of citizens. Vigilance committees were organized in every town and village, and their motto was: "No mercy to traitors," meaning those who were true to their country and the old flag. In Waco, one of these committees waited upon several old and esteemed citizens, giving them their choice, either to cease their opposition to the rebellion, or leave the country. They publicly proclaimed their determination to hang every "Lincolnite" in the country who refused, to use their classic language, to "dry up," at their bidding; and their threats were by no means idle ones.

One night they visited a hotel, and seized one of the guests—a young man from New York, named Wilkinson—and in the dead hours of the night took him to the court-house, and there tried him before a self-constituted committee; and he only escaped hanging by three votes, although there were no charges against him other than that he had asked a man to go with him to New York, and had demanded of certain merchants that they should secure the firm, in whose interest he was then acting, certain debts that they had contracted.

Soon afterward, they arrested Dr. Larnard, son of Major Larnard, paymaster in the United States' Army. He was widely known as a worthy citizen of McClennan county, and highly respected. The crime with which he was charged, was that of allowing his negroes to give a party to the negroes belonging to some of his neighbours; and his sentence was, that he should not be allowed to go beyond the limits of the county for a year; and he was admonished that if he did so, the fact would be discovered, and he would instantly be hung.

The despotism of the secessionists had now become so intolerable, that Union men were everywhere fleeing from the State, as the only means of saving their lives. Not desiring to leave yet, but at the same time anxious to avoid trouble, I shouldered my gun and mounted my horse, and started for a hunt on the Pecan Bayou and Jim Ned Creek. While on my way, I stopped at Cora, a little town in Comanche county, on the day that the ordinance of secession was submitted to the people, which was on the 23rd of February, 1861; and while hitching my horse, an officer came out and proclaimed the polls opened; and immediately the parties who had been standing around, and numbering from eight to ten, went up and cast their ballots—all going for secession. They were all armed, and at first I supposed they were rangers but I was mistaken. I walked into the court-house, and when the men to whom I have referred, had finished casting their ballots, the clerk turned around and addressed me:

"Do you want to vote, young man?"

I answered in the affirmative.

"How do you want to vote?" he next inquired.

"Against secession," I promptly responded.

"Where do you live?" he asked.

"In Waco."

"Then, why didn't you vote there?"

Without giving me time to answer, one of the armed men came up and addressed me with,

"You was afraid to vote there, was you?"

"If I was afraid to vote there, I am not afraid to vote here," I said, imitating his tone and manner as much as possible.

"How is it that you want to vote here?" asked the clerk.

"Because I am a ranger, and by law have a right to vote anywhere at a State election," I answered.

When they found I was in the frontier service, there was no further parley, and my vote was taken, and my name registered. But when I started for my horse, I was followed by the armed crowd; and as I mounted they seemed inclined to enter into a conversation. But knowing that any further parley with them would only result in a collision or a dishonourable retreat, I put spurs to my horse, and left. As I was going out of the town I heard a voice shout: "O yes! O yes! the polls of the election are now closed." The law required that they should be kept open from 6 a. m. to 6 p. m.; but these had not been kept open more than forty minutes—perhaps not that long.

Chapter 13

Out in the Wilderness

This was the last village I had to pass, and I was soon far away in the solitudes of the wilderness, where political contests are unknown. Game was plentiful. Far out on the Jim Ned Creek I found a new settlement, made since my last visit to that part of the country. It was built by a man named Hunter, who was a hunter by occupation; and he invited me to make my home with him while I remained in that section; remarking, at the same time, that as the Indians were pretty thick, we had better hunt together; and I accepted his hospitality.

His family consisted of a wife, two daughters, and a son-in-law; one of the ladies being single. One evening, as I was returning to the house, after a lonely day's tramp through the woods, I chanced to meet the younger of the two daughters, nearly two miles from the house, carrying with her a rifle and a pistol. She asked me if I had seen her cows, but I regret to say that I had not. I then asked her if she had any idea how far she was from home; and she answered correctly, and with perfect coolness, regardless of the danger from the savages who continually infested the neighbourhood. Nor did she seem in the least disturbed when I informed her that I had seen at least a half a dozen that day; but she quietly inquired:

"What sort of a hide is that you've got?"

It was the skin of a panther nine and a half feet long. She examined it closely, but expressed neither surprise nor fear when I told her that I had killed it within a quarter of a mile of the spot where she then stood. I then went with her till she found her cows, when I drove them home; and frequently, after that, we went cow hunting together. She always carried her rifle with her, and could bring down a deer, at a distance of a hundred yards, as well as a man could do it. She had never yet been attacked by Indians in her lonely rambles, and if she had been, more than one would have been required to get off safely. She had been at a neighbour's house, some time before, when it was hemmed in by savages, and besieged for several hours. There were several men in the house to defend it, but she was the only female, save the wife of the owner of the cabin. The men were only there by chance; they were hunters, and being pressed by Indians, took refuge in the house, otherwise she and the lady owner would have been there alone.

During the attack Miss Hunter moulded bullets for the men, and rendered every assistance in her power, keeping perfectly calm and collected all the time, though she full well knew the terrible doom that awaited her if the savages succeeded in carrying the house by storm, or in setting it on fire.

We could often kill deer by standing in the door of the old man's house; and his dogs almost nightly had a row with a catamount, or some other wild animal which was essaying to carry off his pigs or chickens from his very door.

I remained with Mr. Hunter several weeks, when having accumulated all the peltries my horse could carry, I started on my return to the settlements, after giving the family with which I had lived so pleasantly an affectionate good bye. I had been so kindly treated that I was loath to leave, and his wife urged me now that as I had killed their winter's meat, I ought to remain and help eat it; but I could not entirely make up my mind to do so, and we parted.

On the way back to Waco I witnessed a very singular contest. On reaching the edge of the settlements, I encamped one night beneath a very large live oak tree, and in the morning, just as I was getting ready to start, I espied a very large pack of wolves chasing a young heifer across the prairie. There must have been nearly a hundred of these animals in the pack, and when I discovered them she was getting extremely wearied, and, indeed, nearly exhausted. Nearby was a herd of about one hundred and fifty cattle, of all sizes, beside young calves, and for these the heifer made direct for the herd, bellowing at every jump. No sooner did the herd discover her distress than the old cattle commenced snorting, and soon ran together in a huddle, with their heads outward, and making a complete circle, enclosing the calves.

The heifer at length reached the flock, and after running twice around the circle found a position in it, when she at once assumed a defiant attitude. The wolves followed her till she reached a place of security; and so many were there of them that they became scattered into a complete circle, entirely enclosing the cows. The cattle stood eyeing the intruders for a time, and then raised a loud snort, and simultaneously charged upon the wolves and drove them flying over the prairie for several hundred yards.

It was amusing to see the change in the deportment of the wolves. A few minutes before they were pursuing their victim at a furious rate, with ears and tails erect, the hair of their necks on end, tongues lapping for blood, and eyes aglare with rage; but now they were flying with ears drooping, tails between their legs, and piteous looks—a perfect photograph of fright personified. The wolves were scattered in every direction, and some of them were still running, though many had taken courage to halt and reconnoitre, when I concluded to take a hand in the *imbroglio*, and therefore commenced shooting at the animals, and those that were nearest me doubtless felt the effects of my shot, for several fled to a high hill not far off, while those at a distance turned around to see what new enemy had presented himself.

After I fired my pistols off, I very foolishly neglected to reload them, though I continued howling like a wolf to call them up so I could fire into them again if I so desired. Before I was aware of it five very large gray ones bounded up from behind me, full of fight. I did not want to break my pistols, so I picked up a large bone that lay at the root of the tree, and began to fight my assailants with great vigour, believing I could soon run them off, "but they didn't run worth a cent," but would stand sideways to me, then springing straight up into the air and turning their heads around, snap at me.

Their jaws would snap like a steel trap when they closed, and every time I hit one over the head his eyes would almost blaze with rage. I struck and kicked them several times, but finding that they were not disposed to retreat, I thought perhaps it might be prudent for me to do so, and walking backward, I made for my pony, and when near enough, mounted with a spring and dashed off some distance and loaded my pistols. The wolves did not attempt to pursue nor did I fire at them again; for so large a pack had they endeavoured to do so, might have pulled my horse down and torn both it and me into fragments, and devoured us. Another incentive to a retreat was the fact that the smell of my peltries had already begun to attract their attention, and even if I did not annoy them by any more firing, I was by no means safe; and I therefore made the best of my way to Waco.

"The cattle stood eyeing the intruders for a time, and then raised a loud snort, and simultaneously charged upon the wolves and drove them flying over the prairie for several hundred yards."

CHAPTER 14

Farewell to Dixie

When I arrived at Waco I found the wildest excitement everywhere prevailing. A large number of Union men had been arrested, and several hanged. Neither the property nor the life of the loyal people was safe. A number of men for no other offense than refusing to openly commit themselves to secession, were rendered homeless by the torch of the incendiary; and like the leper, no one would give them shelter. A draft was imperiously called for, for already it was discovered that however much the Southern heart was fired, the number of volunteers the exigency demanded, was not forthcoming. Draft, draft, draft; every where the word was repeated; nothing would satisfy the rebels but a resort to conscription; but they knew less of the unpleasant character of that bitter operation than they did three years after, or they might have hesitated before demanding a resort to the wheel of fortune.

Soon after my return, a ranger, named Michael Somerville, an Alabamian, and a friend of mine, quietly informed me that the vigilance committee had my case under consideration, and had been discussing the propriety of hanging me, and that the subject had been broached to the rangers, but it was soon discovered that I had entirely too many friends to permit them to molest me seriously. It was then resolved to draft me; and to this my friends offered no objection. About the last of July, 1861, an order for a conscription in McClennan county was received at Waco. The document came in on the mail stage from Austin about nine o'clock at night, and on the following morning, after eating an unusually early breakfast, I mounted my pony and was off for the north.

The first place aimed for was Jefferson, at the head of Soda Lake, a place of some commercial importance; and on reaching it, I found the excitement there as wild as at Waco. Already large quantities of stores were being accumulated there, to be used in the pending campaign, and the streets continually echoed to the sound of the drum, as company after company of the Johnnies passed through them. From Jefferson I started to the north western corner of Louisiana, where the State joins both Texas and Arkansas. While travelling along one day, I heard some guns firing a short distance to my left, but supposing it to be a company of troops discharging a volley at a target, I paid no attention to the matter.

But presently two men rode hurriedly past, and from what I could gather of their conversation, I was led to believe that some horrid transaction had just taken place. Desirous of knowing something of its nature, I rode rapidly along, and soon overtook the two men and entered into a conversation with them, and asked them, in a careless manner, what the firing meant; and in response, one of them gave me the details of a most horrible murder which had just been committed. A house stood near the corner of the State, to which I have already adverted, owned by a prominent Union man, whose name I cannot now give, it having slipped my memory; and it appears that he had given offense to a Captain Jolly, who was an aspirant for a commission in the rebel army; and that as a method of revenging himself, Captain Jolly had led twenty-four men to the house, and in cold blood, he and his party shot down and killed four men and wounded two more; and that they had likewise killed a negro woman. My companions manifested the utmost abhorrence at the deed, and soon gave me to understand that they, themselves, were Union men.

As I travelled through Arkansas, I passed myself off as a nephew of Albert Pike, who was at that time a brigadier general in the rebel service; replying, when questioned, that I was going to Little Rock to see the general, and enter the service. Of course I had to play the part of a secessionist all this time; had I done otherwise, my life would have paid the forfeit. But once in Little Rock, I had played my game out, and I had not the remotest idea how I was next to proceed; but knowing that delay was dangerous, I at once set about contriving a way of escape, and finally got off.

Near the town of Arkadelphia, I overtook a preacher on the road, and we immediately entered into a conversation on the political situation, and I was not long in ascertaining that his sympathies were with the Union cause; I then told him frankly, that I was a Union man, and I inquired of him how persons of that political faith were treated in that region. He appeared frightened at my frankness; and as we were near the town, he advised me not to go through it, but take a byway that led around it, and into my road again some distance beyond the place. He then stated that at least twenty men had been hung in that vicinity, for their devotion to the old government.

I politely declined to accept his advice, as to making a circuit of the town, but told him I would ride through to see the sights; and on arriving in front of the hotel, I dismounted, threw myself "around a drink," and then mounted again; but did not ride off immediately, as I had entered into an interesting conversation with the clergyman. But I had not been there long, when I was surrounded by a large crowd of soldiers, who at once set to questioning me, as to what was the news, where I was going, where I was from, etc.; and to all of these, my answers were so different from the tenor of our private conversation, that the reverend gentleman must have pronounced me, in his mind, as a rival of Baron Munchausen, with a fair prospect of eclipsing his fame. Nevertheless, he seemed pleased at the sudden political summersault I had turned, and he doubtless fully appreciated my motives for becoming so readily a convert to secession.

While riding along with my clerical friend, I was warned of a "little log grocery on the hill," where, my informant said, about a dozen men, mostly strangers, had been set upon and killed, by secessionists, since the political excitement had commenced. It was located in a dense, piny woods, and frequented by the lowest class of men in the country; but this admonition instead of rendering me cautious, only excited me, and started within me a desire to "see the sights;" and I therefore rode directly up to the grocery, which, on my arrival, contained no man except the keeper. I at once dismounted, and entered, determined to see what the place was like.

The landlord of the place was a very clever man—all grocery keepers are, you know, on the same principle that the cat is, while you stroke it the way the fur lays—and at once entered into a conversation with me about the state of the country, and *our* prospects of whipping the Yankees; and of course, according to our figures, it would be easily accomplished. When he learned that I was a nephew of Albert Pike, he was glad to see me, and insisted on my remaining with him, which I did, from the time of my arrival, at noon, till ten o'clock the next day.

During the afternoon, a party of men collected around the place to drink, talk politics, and curse the Yankees; and of course I bore my part, and if some of my Yankee friends could have heard me "set them up," they would have been astonished at my hypocrisy, if not edified by my discourse. At supper, my new found friend shut up the grocery, and took me home with him to supper, and I was introduced to his wife and brother, as a nephew of Albert Pike. His wife prepared for me a splendid meal, while he took me around and showed me his place, stock, crops, and niggers, all of which, of course, I admired. While we were eating supper, his brother came in, and called him out, and the two stood whispering together for some time in an excited manner, at the same time, as I thought, casting suspicious glances at me; after which the elder brother went away abruptly. What now, I wondered; was there some scheme on foot against me? They eyed me several times exceedingly closely; and I asked myself: could there be any suspicion against me? I had certainly not been indiscreet? then what could that hurried manner, and those sidelong glances portend?

I began to think I had been followed from Texas by some vindictive rebel, who wanted to prevent my going north, when the mystery was suddenly solved, without my being compelled to ask any questions. The man, whose name was White, informed me that his brother had just been in to invite us over to a dance. His daughter was married a few days since, and they had been dancing ever since. This was the third night, and the party would break up in the morning. What a weight of anxiety that declaration, which I saw was made in good faith, removed from my mind! I tried to beg off, as I needed rest; but it was of no use; his brother, he said, would accept no refusal; and without more ado, I went.

We had a walk of about two miles through a gloomy swamp, when we began to hear the sound of a violin breaking the stillness of the night; and also the sound of shuffling feet, keeping time to the music, together with the heavy rattling of a puncheon floor; and very soon after, we emerged from among the bushes into a little clearing, where was a large double log-cabin: with lights streaming out through every crevice; and into this we entered without ceremony. Forty or fifty stalwart men—real sons of the forest—were there, with checkered coats and what had been linen standing collars on heavy cotton shirts with no bosoms; but, alas! exercise in a hot climate in midsummer generates sweat, and sweat will tell upon standing collars; and theirs were clinging to the neck like wet rags; they likewise had on striped home-made pants, and very heavy cowhide boots.

Some of the girls were truly handsome. I never was much of a critic of ladies' clothing, and, therefore, I will not here undertake to describe the outline, except to say that the dresses were of very costly material, and made after the very latest of rustic fashion, and each one was highly pleased with her appearance.

On a kitchen table sat a very big, and, certainly, a very black negro, playing the violin, and calling off, in mellifluous sing-song tones, tuning his voice to the music of his instrument, perfectly. There were two *cotillions* on the floor, whirling and twirling, in the giddy mazes of the dance, to the voluptuously measured cadence of the *Arkansas Traveller*, (who has not heard it?). The music is familiar to almost every ear, but, alas! how few there are who have been so favoured by Divine Providence and propitious circumstances as to have seen the *Arkansas Traveller* danced by natives to the *manor* "born"—no other people know the *manner* of its performance, as do the people of Arkansas; and no other musician can render the piece on the violin or banjo like a Arkansas plantation darkey. By the side of the fiddler sat a veteran banjo picker, who added much to the effect of the music; and, as the fiddler called off the figures of the dance, this old darkey would recite the dialogue of the *Arkansas Traveller*, keeping perfect time to the music. For the benefit of the reader who has never had the pleasure of seeing it performed, I will endeavour to convey an idea of it, although one can give but a faint conception, on paper: the thing must be seen and heard to be appreciated.

The scene represents a belated traveller in Arkansas, in an "airly day." I suppose, reader, when your "dad" and mine were boys, or, perhaps, earlier, he halts before a dilapidated cabin, to see if he can get to stay all night. It is a miserable squalid place. The rain is pouring down in torrents, and the old man of the house is perched on a whisky barrel in the only dry corner, playing the first part of a tune. The children are huddled around the fire, peering curiously at the stranger, while the old woman, with one arm *akimbo*, is stirring a pot of mush over the fire, holding her dress back between her knees, to keep it from burning. The roof of the cabin is partly demolished; a couple of pigs ruminating about on the ground-floor, and chickens, with dripping feathers, roosting on the timbers over head. This is the state of affairs when the story opens; the reader can gather the remainder as the old banjo player recites it.

"Balance all," shouts the fiddler; when the old banjo picker starts off with:

"*Hello, ole man, kin I get ter stay here all nite, rad di di da di di da da da.*"

"There were two cotillions on the floor, whirling and twirling in the giddy mazes of the dance, to the voluptuously measured cadence of the *Arkansas Traveller*."

"First and third couple, forward and back," yells the fiddler.

"*Yer kin get ter go ter de ole boy, I guess,*" breaks in the banjo picker, keeping time with the dancers' feet.

"First lady balance second gemman."

"*I say, ole man, whar doe dis road go to, rad di di da di di da da?*"

"Swing," yells the fiddler, and old white head goes on with:

"*I ben a livin' here about forty years an' it aint gone no whar yit, ra di di da di di da da da,*" etc.

"*How far is it to de forks ob de road? rad di di da,*" etc.

"*Ef yer done kep on, yer done ben dar by dis time,*" then again chimed in his *rad di di da di di da da da.*

"*I say ole man, is ye gwine ter let me stay all nite? rad di di da da.*"

At the next break in the music, he answers:

"*Aint got nuffin to eat, stranger, yer better go on ter de nex house, rad di di da da,*" etc.

"*How far is it, ole man, to de nex house? ra di di da da,*" etc.

A pause then ensues, when he continues:

"'*Bout nineteen miles, I guess, rad di di da,*" etc.

"*Ole man, dats too fur ter ride ter nite in de rain.*"

He then paused, in order not to speak his part, when the other called off, but after the call, chimed in again:

"*I can't help dat, yer know, rad di di da da.*"

After a moment's reflection, the traveller seems to resolve on a new course of tactics, and begins with:

"*I say, ole man, why don't yer put a new roof on yer house? rad di di da di di da da.*"

"*Oh, er's a rainen too hard.*"

"*Why don't yer put de roof on when it aint a rainen? rad di di da,*" etc.

"*Oh, when er don't rain, er don't need it, rad di di da di di da.*"

The old fellow keeps on playing, while the traveller again reflects a moment; one thing is certain, it is raining too hard to proceed, and he must stop; and a happy idea suggests itself. Hitherto the man with the fiddle had only played one part of the tune, and it seemed to be a favourite air; and the traveller, who is himself a master violinist and composer, says:

"*I say, ole man,*" (the reader will remember I give it as the darkey recited it), "*why don't yer play de rest ob dat piece? rad di di da di di da da.*"

All this time the dance is progressing, and the young folks "spreading" themselves, and full of glee, at the recitation, while the violinist almost excels himself.

"Don't know no more; does you know it all? *rad di di da.*"

"Sartinly, I does." Instantly the old man springs from the whisky barrel, invites the traveller to dismount, orders one of his own little urchins to put the traveller's horse in the stable, tells his wife to get supper, assures the traveller that his son will soon be back from mill; has a chicken taken down and killed for supper, has a jug of whisky brought in from the smoke-house, and assures the traveller that they are not so nearly starved out as he had a moment before supposed; then mounting his guest on the whisky barrel, gives him the fiddle, and calls for the balance of the tune, which was played with a gusto, and christened the "Arkansas Traveller," since so popular among violinists.

The dance was exceedingly amusing. The girls moved very lightly and with considerable grace; but the men made a tremendous lumbering over the loose puncheon floor. When it came to the "balance all," the heeling and toeing of those heavy boots, was positively horrifying; but the "swing" was rendered with such a hearty good will, and the girls seemed to enjoy it so well, that I almost wished I was a dancer myself.

The bride showed us to the supper room, where we found a table loaded with every luxury which the State could afford. We did justice to the viands, and then went back to the dance. The bride was anxious to dance with me; at least her uncle told me so; and I felt considerably abashed, when I told him I could not dance. Not to be able to dance, in Arkansas, is as bad as to be no horseman, in Texas. The bride went through one set with her uncle, who appeared to be about the best dancer in the house. The girls all seemed to vie with her, which made me conclude that they wished themselves in her place; while the lady herself acted and looked as pretty as she knew how.

The fiddler threw all his powers into his playing and his stentorian voice; and the men heeled and toed with a hearty goodwill, and the puncheons rattled beneath their measured, swinging tread. It was a complete and graphic picture of good old fashioned social life. Indeed, the dancers exerted themselves so long, and well, that the puncheons seemed to take up their spirit, and appeared as if endeavouring to extemporize a hornpipe on their own hook. I had often heard the old story of the man in Arkansas who gathered up half a bushel of toe nails on his floor, after a dance; and I was scarcely inclined to doubt its truth, after what I witnessed on that night.

We enjoyed ourselves hugely, till after twelve o'clock, when we went back to my friend's house. When I was about to start, on the following day, he insisted that I should remain longer with him; but I urged the pressing state of affairs, telling him that we Southerners must take the field, as quickly as possible, if we would prevent the country from being overrun by the Yankee vandals of the North. Excuse me, reader, but I was talking at a mark then.

When I arrived at Little Rock, I found the town full of soldiers, who had come in response to the first call of the governor for three thousand men; and these were the same troops who fought at Wilson's Creek, a short time after. While at Little Rock, I was attacked by bilious fever, and was sick for ten days. I stopped at a hotel kept by Capt. Lee, who was a violent secessionist. My story about being a nephew of Albert Pike, was of great service to me; and I was enabled to keep up appearances, without being detected, by the fact that he and his sons were all out in the Indian Nation, recruiting savages for the rebel service.

When I got well, and was able to leave, I found myself guard bound. The town was under military law, and every road was picketed, so that escape was next to impossible. I had been compelled to sell my horse to pay expenses while sick, getting but fifteen dollars for an animal worth at least one hundred; and I was walking along the levee a little disconsolate, when I saw a little steamboat called the William Henry, and I immediately went on board of her. Looking around, I saw the carpenter at work on the bow, and I stepped up to him, and inquired if he wanted any help, telling him I would assist him down to Napoleon, for my fare. To this proposition he readily assented; remarking that he always liked to have help when there was work to do.

While I was talking to him he stuck the foot adze into his foot, and cut the big toe almost loose from his left foot. The blood flowed profusely, and I at once set myself to work and bandaged up the wound, in the presence of the captain and mate, and he was sent to the hospital immediately. As soon as this was done, the captain turned to me and said:

"Young man, are you a ship carpenter?"

"They call me one," I replied.

"Do you want to ship?" was his next question.

"Yes, for a while," was my response.

"Then go to work," said he, "and I'll give you fifty-five dollars a month, and fare in the cabin."

"I'll do it," was my response, "as long as I like the boat; and I'll tell you how I like it at Napoleon."

He was satisfied, and turned away, while I went on shore for my outfit. At the tavern, I found no one but a *negro clerk*, to whom I paid my bill; and, as he had too much manners to be inquisitive, I left the house without being reported to the police—the hotels being required to report all arrivals and departures to the military authorities. Once more on the boat, she soon shoved out, and I began to feel tolerably safe. I found there would be plenty of work all the time, but as I had never been a carpenter—never having worked a stroke on either house or boat in my life, I was a little afraid I should not be able to sustain myself in that capacity. "A still tongue makes a wise head," was my motto then; for I did not know the technical terms used by carpenters or boatsmen. I did not know even all the names of the tools furnished me to work with; so it was manifestly to my interest to preserve silence.

I went to work, however with confidence, and energy; resolved, if they found out how little I knew, it should be by observation, and not from anything I might say. The work must have been creditably done, for I heard the captain boast to the pilot that I was the best "chip" he ever had. My greatest horror was a recruiting officer, named Harrison, who come down to see me. He was a reckless man, a planter, who seemed to care little for money, and I may add, for anything else. He said he wanted to raise a company of guerrillas, for the purpose of "carrying the war into Africa;" and that he wanted young men who were not afraid to follow him, and that he intended to go right into the Northern States.

This boast may be a little amusing, but Mr. Harrison was not the only one who at that time indulged in such hallucinations, and who entertained such wild hopes. He intended, he said, when he got into the Northern States, to "go for all that was in sight, and let the tail go with the hide." I told him he was just the man to suit me, but I was engaged on the boat, and could not quit her. His was the sort of service I liked, but I could not go into it now, at least until the captain could get another "chip;" but in the event that I enlisted, I would have a preference for his company; and to make him believe I was serious, I took his address. He was one of the men who accompanied Lopez to Cuba, and said he had been in two fights on that island in an hour and a quarter. He was satisfied to take my name as I gave it—Mr. Fitzhugh. He would stand and talk to me and the other boat hands by the hour, and often puzzled me by his sudden and almost inexplicable questions.

At Napoleon I sawed out five large hatches in the boat, so that freight could be stowed very rapidly in the hull; and after this had been done, the men began to load her throughout with military stores. The boxes were handled very carelessly, and would frequently split open, when I would be called upon to nail them up. They were filled with harness of all kinds. Besides these the boat took on a large quantity of ammunition for musketry and artillery, and also a full battery of guns, and sixty-five government wagons; all consigned to Fort Scott, Arkansas, for the use of Ben McCulloch's army.

The next morning a large boat—the *Mary Kean*—came alongside, and I told the captain I was too weak to work, and would consequently go up to Memphis on her. He did not like to have me leave him, but seeing that I was really not in good health, he offered no objection. The best of the joke was, I told him I wanted to go into the service, and that, by confederate law, he dare not dissuade me from going. On board the Kean I found a great number of rebel officers, strutting about in new uniforms and gauntlet gloves, with all the dignity of princes of high degree. I took one look in the cabin, and that was enough for me; and I instantly put down on deck, and stowed my humble self away on a lot of coffee-sacks.

The fever had returned on me, and I was suffering terribly. At Memphis I stopped at the "Woodruff House," a neat little tavern, kept by a woman named Smith, whose husband was in the rebel army, and was stationed at that time at Fort Pillow. At this house I remained sick a week, and when well enough to go out, I found myself once more guard-bound, with a duller chance of making my escape than at Little Rock.

The first thing I did was to visit all the depots, at each one of which I found a provost guard stationed, who inspected the passes of passengers. I made a careless inquiry, and found that every road leading from the city was picketed. It was at the time when Tennesseans were moving their troops through Memphis into Missouri, a great part of which were at Wilson's Creek.

The provost marshal's office was kept by Col. C. H. Morgan, a man, by the by, who very much resembled the notorious John H.; and to him I went, telling him that I wanted to go to Bourbon County, Kentucky, where my parents lived.

"Well, sir," said he, "you must bring with you two respectable witnesses, whom I know, to testify that you are a good Southern man."

I replied that it would be useless to try to do that, as I was an utter stranger in the city, and that no one knew any more of me than he did; and he at once informed me that I could not leave the city. At this I got angry, and told him I would go without a pass, and he replied that he would have me arrested. I at once moved for the door, and as he had no guard, he could not stop me. I told him that I did not think his recommendation would be of much value to me or any other honest man, and then made tracks.

This was in the evening, and that night I sold my Mexican saddle and other equipments, which had belonged to my horse, so that I was without baggage, except a pair of saddlebags, to carry; and I resolved at once to get out of Memphis at all hazards.

Next morning, as I was standing in the door, I saw a great crowd about the market-house, which was only a short distance from the tavern; and when I first observed them, they were just about scattering to go home. There were a great many country wagons there, which had come with produce; and these were about to leave the city, and it occurred to me that the opportune moment for escape had arrived. I hurried off, and paid my bill, and then walked to the market-house, and hailed a countryman, asking him to let me ride in his wagon. He did so cheerfully, and when in I asked to be permitted to drive, to which he agreed; and taking off my ranger blouse, I threw it in the wagon, and we drove out. There were provost guards on duty in the streets, arresting every suspicious person; and there were pickets at the end of each street, but they did not stop us, as they evidently supposed we were both farmers; and on we rattled through two camps of five thousand men each, and finally reaching a point about six miles from the town, I parted from my friend, and took the road for Nashville on foot.

At Summerville I was stopped by a crowd of men who were very anxious to know who I was, where I was from, where I was going, what I had been doing, and what I was going to do, and so on; and they also appeared exceedingly anxious to ascertain my political opinions. Of course I was secesh. I had been warned before I got to town that I had better go around it, as no one was allowed to pass through it, unless they were well known rebels. Nothing daunted, however, I halted in the village, and sure enough, was overhauled and placed in the hands of the vigilance committee.

On learning that I had been a ranger, one of them, a Mr. Reeves, inquired if I knew any man of his name in Texas.

"Calvin Reeves?" I asked.

"Yes; and he is my brother," was the response. He then asked me a great number of questions, which I answered without hesitation, and so truthfully, that my account corresponded exactly with that which Reeves had given himself. We had both been in Johnston's regiment, and our narratives corresponded exactly. The examination lasted from twelve o'clock till dark, after which they professed themselves satisfied that all was right and released me, telling me that I could go on. But I had not proceeded more than a hundred yards before I was called back, and one of them said to me:

"You say you are going home?"

"Yes, sir;" I replied.

"You live in Paris, Bourbon County, Kentucky?"

"Yes, sir."

"And you intend to fight for the south, do you?" my questioner persisted.

"I will if I know myself," said I.

"You think you will stick to your principles, when you get there?" he said.

"Yes, sir, I feel very confident of that," I answered.

"You know," he continued, "that a good many Kentuckians are a little tender-footed now; they don't like to come out against the Union, and they don't like to go with the abolitionists; and I am afraid when you get back there, you will let them talk you out of your principles."

"I am not so easily converted as that comes to," said I, jocularly.

"Well, how is it," he asked, "that you are on foot?"

"Because," was the reply, "I am unable to ride."

"Well, then," said he, "we will help you;" and they accordingly made up a purse of eight dollars and seventy-five cents and gave it to me.

"Now," said one, "you go over to the tavern and stay all night."

I arose to comply, and was thanking them for their kind interest in my welfare, when a stout looking man, who had sat in a group of three or four others, apart from the near ones, rose and remarked:

"Young man, I think you had better go with me; I will give you accommodations for the night."

He then led the way, and I followed him home, and he gave me a very good supper, after which I retired at once. All this time I was wondering what made him take such an interest in me. After I was in bed, Reeves and a lawyer visited me, who said they had called to have some further talk about Calvin Reeves and his doings in Texas; and it was not until I had told them a second time all my acquaintance and experience with him that I discovered they were comparing my statement with his.

"Why," I asked, "have you not seen him yet? He left Texas some time since, to come home."

"O yes," they replied, "he has been at home, but has now gone off to fight the Yankees."

They bowed themselves out about midnight, after having talked me nearly to sleep several times. The most of the conversation was about politics, and I excused my ignorance on the different topics advanced, by telling them I had just got in off the plains, and was not posted; but taking good care to be just secesh enough to give confidence, and not strong enough to arouse suspicion.

When they had gone, I began to flatter myself that I was done with them; and that now all were satisfied and I should be troubled no more. Next morning I met my host at the breakfast table, and found him dressed for a journey. He then began a conversation by remarking:

"My name is John D. Stanley; I am sheriff of this county, and am going down the road with you as far as La Grange. It is nearly car time now."

He then added that a man had been killed at La Grange, and he was going down to see about it. We went to the cars together and occupied the same seat; and on our journey he kept up a continued questioning; but I was not to be thrown off my guard. He, however, only went as far as Warsaw with me, and then returned to Summerville, while I took the train to Nashville. His story about the murder, was, doubtless, a hoax, or he would have gone on with me to La Grange.

Nashville was the only civil place I had been in yet; and there was less of bitterness than I had seen elsewhere.

At this place I was met by my father, to whom I had written, requesting him to meet me there. His journey was made at the imminent risk of arrest and incarceration in prison; but fortunately he had a commission from Governor Magoffin, of Kentucky, on which he got through. As King Isham G. Harris remarked:

"Col. P——, that is a better pass than I can give you;" and I believed him when he said it, for at that time Gov. Magoffin's name would pass a man in either section, and Harris' would not.

In due time we arrived at Portsmouth, Ohio, where my father was publishing a paper at that time; and the reader may imagine my joy at again meeting my mother and sister in a land of freedom; though my joy was marred by the fact that my youngest brother was lying at the point of death. Three weeks after I returned, he expired, dying a Christian's death, full of hope in eternal life.

CHAPTER 15

In the Union Service

I had intended on arriving at home to enlist in the Union army, and under the old starry banner at once, but deferred the matter on account of my brother's sickness; but within a few days after his death I enlisted at Portsmouth to join Fremont's bodyguard, but eventually went into the 4th Ohio Cavalry, commanded by Colonel John Kennett. I was sworn into the service by Lieutenant S. K. Williams, and was sworn into the 4th Cavalry again by Captain O. P. Robie, of Company A, at Cincinnati, and on the 16th of September, 1861, found myself at Camp Gurley, undergoing lessons in the intricacies of the cavalry drill under Sergeant Charles D. Henry, of Company A.

We drew horses soon after I arrived in camp, and after a few weeks of preparation in tactics and the usual amount of soldier pranks in the neighbourhood, we moved to Camp Dennison, when on the 20th day of November we were finally mustered into the service. We remained at Camp Dennison till the latter part of winter, or the first of spring, when we were ordered into Kentucky. I was exceedingly sick of the idleness of camp life, and hailed marching orders with delight, as did all the boys, who, like myself, delighted in a roving life.

I do not recollect the day of the month on which we left Ohio, but we at once proceeded to Louisville, stopping a brief period at Camp Kennett, near Jeffersonville, and in due course of time found ourselves on the mud-bound shores of Bacon Creek. This historic stream derives its name from a circumstance connected with the early settlement of Kentucky; a lot of hunters having encamped upon it to bacon their bear meat. This fact I learned from the "oldest inhabitant," and considering the circumstances and the customs of pioneers, I have no doubt of its correctness.

At this time we were under command of General O. M. Mitchell, and it is perhaps unnecessary here to add that men under so energetic a commander were never idle. We scouted the country thoroughly in every direction, but did not meet the enemy at any point willing to give us battle, and hence we had no fighting in Kentucky. During our trip down Green River, we all suffered severely from cold and exposure, but the rebels always retired before us; and perhaps they were right.

On leaving Bacon Creek, we marched on Bowling Green, General Mitchell being, as was usual with him, in great haste to follow up the flying enemy; and such was his energy, and so well appointed was everything in his army, that the obstructions in the roads, upon which the rebels had wasted so much labour, scarcely formed an impediment to his march. He had a regiment of pioneers from Michigan who were the best working men I ever saw, and they cleared the way for the advance with a rapidity almost unparalleled.

The army advanced on Bowling Green while the detachment I was with was on a scout down Green River; and on coming in, Captain Robie and myself galloped our horses all the way from Mumfordsville to Bowling Green, a distance of thirty-four miles. About a mile from Mumfordsville we found, by the side of the railroad, the corpse of a boy belong to General Sill's old regiment; he had died at a hospital nearby, and the steward had sent three other sick men to carry the body to Mumfordsville, and they had sunk exhausted by the road.

A train which had been out in that direction refused to take the body on for the men, and while I was looking at the corpse the same engine came back, and when it stopped I called the conductor, but he refused with an oath to take the body on the train, saying he had enough live men on. This enraged me considerably, and I drew a pistol on him, which had a very decided effect indeed, and he helped to put the corpse on the train. He, however, threatened to report me for stopping him, but at that moment Captain Robie came up, and the fellow found it convenient to have nothing more to say. I suppose he delivered the corpse in Mumfordsville, but he was mean enough to throw it off the train. The boy was a fine looking youth—sixteen years of age, and the sight of it and of the exhausted, sorrow-stricken soldiers, would have melted any but a heart of stone.

We arrived at Bowling Green just as Captain Loomis, of the Coldwater Battery, from Michigan, was shelling the Johnnies out of the place. At the instant I rode up to the river bank, I espied General Mitchell with his hat off, calling for volunteers—I did not know for what—but I volunteered, when I discovered that it was to carry a rope over Big Barren River, in order to enable him to swing a pontoon over the stream. Sergeant Frank Robie, another soldier and myself, mounted a little raft made of plank, on which we put a coil of rope, and then we pushed out, paying out the coil as we went. The raft was a small, frail structure, and the current setting against the rope made it swing up and down, so that we were frequently in the water up to our knees, and as the river ran very swiftly, the reader may very well imagine that we had a dangerous ride of it, to say nothing about the bullets of the rebels, from the opposite shore—about twenty of which were fired at us while we were engaged in the work, though luckily none of them took effect; but our infantry firing soon made the reprobates "light out" from their position.

Captain Loomis knocked the stack off the locomotive just as the train loaded with rebel soldiers was about to start out, and they barely had time to save themselves as we entered the town.

We finally got a rope over, through the protection afforded us by our infantry, and by the assistance of Lieutenant Shoemaker, of the Fourth Cavalry, Captain Yates, of the engineers, began throwing in his pontoons. The bridge would soon have been completed; but, at this point, General Mitchell rode up, and told us we could all go to bed now, as some of the men had found a ferry boat two miles below, which was capable of conveying two hundred men, and that that would be sufficient to accomplish his purpose.

Part of the 19th Illinois and 18th Ohio Infantry were double-quicked down the river, at once, to the boat, and crossed over, and then double-quicked up again, on the opposite side of the stream to the town, in time to drive out the rear guard of the rebels—some five hundred in number, who were busily engaged in destroying the place.

On the first night after our arrival at Bowling Green, an attempt was made to fire the stables where our horses were, with a view to the destruction of the animals; but Providence favoured us, and the wind suddenly changed, and the flames did not communicate to the buildings. Had they done so, our stock would have certainly perished in the flames, as we could not have released the horses in time. Seven large brick buildings were destroyed, and some frames were burned, between the stables and the public square. These were the first ones fired, and the incendiaries believed the flames would reach the stables, and destroy both horses and equipments; but their purposes were foiled, by the shifting of the wind.

On the following morning, detachments of our cavalry scoured the country in every direction, capturing a great many rebels, who were destroying property and pillaging houses, passing themselves off as federal soldiers. It was a common game and one easily played, amid the panic and excitement that followed the fall of Bowling Green; the people having been made to believe there was no crime too vile for the "Northern vandals." But the cavalry soon came over, and the citizens could readily discover the difference, and they began, at once, to inform us where these rebel depredators were to be found.

Seven hundred rebels were reported in the vicinity of Russellville, while yet others were prowling around in the county, and Lieutenant Harris with a small detachment was sent out to destroy the railroad, of which party I was one. We went to South Union, in Logan county, where I was sent out with seven men a short distance below, to stand picket. While on duty, a very remarkable looking man rode up to me and said:

"I am told you have come here to protect citizens in their lives and property."

"Yes," I replied, "that is our purpose."

"Well," he continued, "my name is Ray; I am a physician, and I own an interest in a large steam mill, five miles further down in the country, and it is to be burned tonight by the Texas Rangers; twenty-five of whom were detailed to burn it, and several others in the county. Can you do anything to save it?"

"Yes, sir," was my response, "get my men some supper, while I go back and see my commanding officer."

I went to see the lieutenant, back at the town, while Dr. Ray was preparing supper for the squad. The lieutenant at once gave me permission to go to the mill, if I desired to do so; and, after reaching the picket post, the doctor came with the provisions, and I told him I was ready. We started immediately for the town of Auburn, where the mill was located; when the doctor looked anxiously around, and asked:

"Where are your men?"

I told him I did not need any soldiers, but would call on the citizens for help, and inquired how many could be relied on in an emergency, and he said about twenty; and I told him that was enough provided I could get them out. When we reached the mill, we succeeded in raising but half a dozen men, including the miller and his employees. I then told the doctor that he must go into the mill and pile all the empty barrels up as high as he could reach, so that when one pile is pushed over, the whole lot would tumble down with it, and make a great racket. "Then," I said, "I will fire off my gun, and then you knock the empty barrels about, and shout: 'Turn out the guard;' and 'Fall in, men,' and we will make as much noise as if there was an hundred of us," after which I went into the coopershop to instruct the men. There were several good places for protection in the shop, from which they were to fire on any advancing party, after I had discharged the signal gun; and to all my arrangements the party agreed. The miller then went to his house and brought down hot biscuits, fresh butter, sweet milk and eggs, for a lunch, which we greedily consumed; after which two of the party went out to patrol the vicinity. We kept turn now guarding till about eleven o'clock at night, when one of the men came running in, almost breathless with excitement, saying, that they were coming from down the road.

I stationed the men to my notion, and began to walk a beat before the mill, taking good care to make sufficient noise with my sabre, resolved to attract attention. Very soon a small party of horsemen came at a gallop toward us; and when they were within gunshot, I shouted "halt," and immediately fired on them. The effect was magical. The rebels wheeled in confusion, running for their lives; while my men fired upon them as fast as they could, and the old doctor thundered the barrels about, and yelled like a madman.

The enemy were ignominiously defeated—put to flight. The doctor jumped and capered with joy, to see the effect of our strategy; it even seemed to make him young again. As soon as the excitement was over, we reloaded our pieces, piled up our barrels, and waited for a second attack, as we felt certain they would not give it up that way; but notwithstanding our expectations they did, and we were not disturbed by that party.

However, just after midnight another party advanced upon us, and we again stood on the defensive; but no sooner did I challenge the advancing men, than I recognized the voice of Major Dreisbach, of the 4th Ohio Cavalry, and among the men was Captain Robie, of Company A; and we were not obliged to renew either our firing or our strategy.

From this place I was sent to Russellville, to ascertain the strength of the force there, and such other particulars as would be of advantage to the service. I rode rapidly, in order to get in the town at night, and out again before daylight, so that I might obtain and communicate the desired information, before he came near enough to engage the enemy. They were represented at seven hundred strong; while the major's command only numbered one hundred men. I succeeded in getting into the town, and rousing some of the inhabitants, represented myself as a confederate quartermaster, and asked them to tell me where the Texas Rangers were, and inquired about Col. Wharton and other rebel officers, with the air of an old acquaintance. They informed me that the regiment had left town about an hour before; but if I would hurry on, I would overtake them at Whippoorwill Station; and that they intended to burn the bridge at that place, and would be delayed a short time.

I next inquired about the government property there; and one man went to show me the different stores of flour and other provisions, of which there was an immense quantity in town; after which I went to Grey's Tavern and ordered breakfast for a hundred Texan Rangers, telling him to have it ready for us just at daylight, which he promised to do, and I rode off to our command.

All this was done so quickly and coolly, that the citizens were not alarmed, and we even captured some of Wharton's men who were sleeping in town, at various houses; while the amount of stores which fell into our hands, was immense.

The landlord had taken me at my word, and we had a splendid breakfast, which had been prepared for the Rangers, who, alas, for my veracity, turned out to be real blue-coated Yankees. However, we devoured our meal with as much relish, and as great an amount of enjoyment, as if we had come from the banks of the Rio Grande, and ridden all the way to Russellville in a day. To tell the truth, we were fearfully hungry, and did as hungry men do.

Circumstances were such that the troops were soon recalled from the town, and they evacuated it, while I was down on the Tennessee line, whither I had been sent on another scout, by the major. When I returned, I found myself alone, and twenty-seven miles from our lines. On passing through, I discovered that the people had commenced to carry off the public stores; and I at once ordered them to stop, telling them if they did not, I would bring a company of men and lay the town in ashes; and my threat had the desired effect. At the depot I found another gang rolling out the flour, and hauling it off in wagons, and I gave them the same warning, but they did not yield so readily. They asked me if I possessed the authority to make the order, and if I was a commissioned officer, etc. This fretted me a little, and drawing my pistol, I rode in among them, and made them roll every barrel back into the depot again; and then shutting and barring the doors, I told them I would kill the next man I found near the place.

While I was down at Allensville, I met a two-horse carriage, in which were four old men and one young man, who seemed to be about twenty-five years of age. Entering into a conversation with them, I soon discovered that the old men were Union men, and that they had got stuck on some confederate money, and that they were going to Nashville to dispose of it for Kentucky State notes; but the young man, as if trying to draw my sentiments from me, expressed himself in the bitterest terms as a rebel. While the conversation was going on, one of the old gentlemen produced a flask of whisky, and passed it first to the other three, and then to me; asking at the same time, if I ever drank. I told them that I seldom drank anything stronger than brandy, and "laid hold." Raising the flask, I said, gentlemen, let us drink to the Constitution and the Union; when the old men shouted "hurrah for the Constitution and the Union," The young man, however, put his head out and fairly yelled: "No, sir, I'm a rebel; I won't drink any such sentiment; I will die first." My first impulse was to thrust my pistol in his face and blow his brains out; but he was unarmed and I would not shoot a defenceless man.

I was alone, and could not be bothered with prisoners; but I was fully determined to punish him in some way. Without answering his vehement expostulation, I turned up the flask and drank very leisurely, without the least show of anger, and then riding close to the carriage, I took the flask in my left hand, and passed it to the young villain, and drawing my pistol with my right, I deliberately levelled it on his breast, and said calmly: "Now, sir, you will drink or die;" and I meant it, for that was the only chance I intended to give him for his life. He seized the flask with trembling hand, his face pale with fright, and, in spite of his recent boasting refusal, he drank until I got afraid I would make him kill himself with whisky, and told him he could stop; that I did not want him to drown himself with Bourbon. Then giving him a few words of counsel, I allowed them all to proceed on their journey, and I turned my attention to the depot, which was surrounded by a villainous looking crowd of disappointed rebels, who had probably met to counsel over the evacuation of Kentucky and their own fate.

There were seven hundred barrels of corn at Auburn, three hundred barrels at Russellville, seven hundred at McCloud's switch, one hundred barrels at Whippoorwill, and as much more at Allensville; and at all of these places there were considerable quantities of wheat, and at Russellville there were stores of mess beef, pork, flour, and arms. I felt that all these things should not be left without a guard, and I well knew we had no men to spare, so I put each depot, and all the stores in the vicinity, in charge of the nearest wealthy citizen, telling him I would hold him responsible for the safety of the buildings and their contents; and that if a dollar's worth was lost or destroyed, he would be compelled to make compensation.

After this, I returned to Bowling Green, and reported my proceedings to Colonel Stanley, who was post commandant there. He approved my proceedings, and directed me to hold the things, till he could send down a guard, which I did, riding from one end to the other of my beat every day—a distance of thirty-two miles.

As soon as our forces had repaired the railroad, they began to remove all the stores to Bowling Green, and I was relieved from guard duty, and returned to South Union, on my way to Bowling Green. Here I was taken sick, with something bordering on pneumonia, and I was compelled to stop at the house of the agent of the Shakers, a venerable man, named Shannon. The women of the society took me into the house, and prepared a bed for me, and nursed me with the greatest care, until I was well enough to travel again. I was walking about in three or four days, and at that time a justice of the peace, named Carson, from Butler County, came to see me, telling me of two men, named Robinson and Keaton, terrors to his neighbourhood, who were constantly committing depredations. They claimed to be Union soldiers; but my informant stated that they robbed all they came to, regardless of their political sentiments.

All I could do in this matter, was to arrest the men, and take them to Bowling Green; and it was sixteen miles from where I was, to the place where the depredations were committed. I started, however, for the scene of the troubles, and on my way I met a man named Mobly, and another named Gines, who were known guerrillas, and who had done much mischief in the country. I told them I was informed that they were good, law abiding citizens, and I wished them to join me, and help me arrest a couple of men, who were "raising Cain" down below.

At first they objected, and did not at all like to go. One made an excuse that his wife was sick, and had no wood chopped; and he must hurry home and cut some; while the other (I believe it was Mobly), said that he was necessarily compelled to go to mill, otherwise his family "had obleeged to suffer."

"Where do you live?" I asked; and they pointed in the direction, which, as I suspected, was exactly contrary to the one they were riding. My suspicions were well-founded; they were just then going somewhere to plot, or execute mischief; they were mounted on extraordinarily fine horses, and appeared like very resolute men. I remarked that from the direction they were travelling, I did not think they were going to attend to domestic affairs; and added: "I am a United States officer, and you cannot refuse to assist me." Seeing that no excuse would avail, they went along; but I made it a point to put them in the road in front of me, so I could watch them. When I named the men I intended to arrest, they were greatly relieved; they were rejoiced at getting rid of two such men, as the ones referred to, who were their bitter enemies.

They even threw off all appearance of reluctance, and went with me willingly. Passing through the little town, I had another man pointed out to me as one who had been in the Woodbury fight only a short time before, and had come recently from the rebel army; and hailing him, without arousing his suspicion that I knew anything of his antecedents, I told him the same that I had told the others. He tried to beg off, pleading a sick wife; but I informed him I could not possibly excuse him; for if I excused him I must do the same for the others, as they had made a similar request. I stated that he had been recommended to me as a very proper man for the work; that he was anxious to restore law and order, and I could, under no circumstances, dispense with his services. He then invited me to dine with him, while his boy caught his horse, which I readily consented to do.

We then mounted and rode in the direction of Kitchen's still-house, where the parties were supposed to be. There had just been a religious meeting in the neighbourhood of the still-house, and a large number of men—good Union men, too—had gathered around to drink whisky, and talk politics; and among the number were Keaton and Robinson. I gave my rifle to Porter while I arrested Robinson, leaving Porter to guard the prisoner while I took Keaton into cusToddy. I then gave their arms to my citizen guards, and we mounted them on their horses, and made for Bowling Green, followed by threats and execrations of Union men, who did not know their real character. The last thing I heard was the voice of the old man Kitchen, who shouted that he had forty men and thirty muskets, and he would have the men away from me before we got five miles, adding: "The secesh are having a good time, Todday, arresting Union men with federal soldiers;" but he did not know the joke I had in store for the secesh. The next day I reached Bowling Green, after travelling nearly all night, with my prisoners, who were turned over to Col. Stanley, at the same time preferring charges against each.

I only claimed to have captured five prisoners; but Col. Stanley (of the 18th Ohio) tells the story differently. I had barely got my prisoners delivered to the Colonel, when the old man Kitchen, who really was a good Unionist, got to Bowling Green with about forty men, and demanded to know why Keaton and Robinson had been arrested. The Colonel answered him politely, and was about to dismiss him and his squad, when a well-known Union man identified three bushwhackers in the party, and the Colonel, who had an aversion for that class of men, ordered them all to be arrested and sent to jail. I do not know whatever became of the party, but Col. Stanley always told the story that I had brought him eight prisoners single-handed.

While at Shaker Town I wrote out the following advertisement for T. J. Shannon and other loyal citizens:

6 1-4 Cents Reward!

Ran away from the town of Bowling Green, in Warren County, Kentucky, one George W. Johnson, who claimed to be Provisional Governor of Kentucky. No inquiry would have been made concerning his whereabouts, but for the fact that he had notified the people of Kentucky that they must pay their taxes to him, for the benefit of the so-styled Confederate States of America; and whereas, the people of Kentucky, and Logan county in particular, are law-abiding citizens, and desire earnestly to pay their taxes promptly, and the said George W. Johnson and his ten legal advisers having absconded, and the sheriff appointed by said "legal advisers" being afraid to act, the citizens of Logan county will pay the above reward for his apprehension; but no thanks for his return. The person claiming the reward is to change a $20 Confederate States note at its face.

Many Citizens.

Feb. 22, 1862.

The advertisement was duly posted in three conspicuous places, but the money was never claimed. Johnson was afterward arrested, as I learn, but the captor never asked the reward. Death overtook him at Shiloh.

At the same place, I captured a rebel soldier, named Blewitt, and took him before Esquire Holland, where he took the oath of allegiance. We had no form of that oath before us, but the 'squire fixed up one strong enough, and he was about to administer it when a venerable old Shaker said:

"Friend James, thee had better swear him not to break open any more beehives;" and he insisted on a clause to that effect being inserted. The oath, however, was strong enough, when we were through with it.

I now started out in search of my regiment, which, by this time, had nearly reached Nashville. Going by way of Russellville, I got a comrade, who had been wounded when we charged the town. He was an Italian, named Garanchini. I had left him in care of parties at Russellville, and now that he was able to travel, I took him with me, proceeding by way of Springfield. We had no trouble in getting through the country, although we were the first Federals who had appeared in that section of the State.

We found the regiment at Camp Jackson, seven miles south of Nashville, which point we made a base for a great number of scouting adventures, in every section of the country, as we lay there for a considerable length of time.

I was very proud to learn that the 4th Ohio Cavalry had captured the city of Nashville, and that members of that regiment should be the first Federal soldiers to tread the streets of this stronghold of secession. Had "King" Harris known, at the time I applied to him for a pass, in company with my father, that I would become a member of the regiment which demanded and received the surrender of his capital, it is altogether probable that the petty monarch would have held me to a more strict accountability. As there was a misunderstanding soon after as to what troops captured the city, and not wishing to see my comrades robbed of their hard-earned glory, I beg leave to present the following, which is to the point, and, I think, will exhibit the affair in its proper light to every impartial reader:

Copy of H. C. Rodgers' Letter to J. Kennett.

Colonel Jno. Kennett:

Dear Sir,—According to my recollection, the Second Division commanded by Brig. Gen. Mitchell, advanced upon Nashville from Bowling Green, in the latter part of the month of February, 1862. On this march, the advance was led by the 4th O.V.

C., Col. John Kennett commanding. On, or about the 25th, the regiment marched to, and occupied, Edgefield Junction, some eight or ten miles from Nashville. From this place, Col. Kennett immediately ordered forward a detachment of the 4th O.V. C., under my command, with instructions to occupy the village of Edgefield, opposite the city of Nashville, to take possession of all steamboats, or other native craft lying there, and to hold the position.

These orders were fully executed—the detachment finding no enemy in Edgefield—a few straggling cavalry in Nashville—my command occupied Edgefield, two days before the command of Gen. Nelson arrived; during which time the Mayor of Nashville twice came over to Edgefield, for the purpose of surrendering the city: on his second visit, the city was surrendered. The mayor, Cheatham, tendering, and Col. Kennett receiving, the surrender. This took place at the residence of Mr. Fuller, in Edgefield. Mr. Fuller, myself and some others, whom I do not remember, were present. This occurrence took place the day before Gen. Nelson's command arrived.

The battery of Capt. Loomis, at the time of this surrender, occupied a position commanding, and within pistol shot of, the heart of the city. The 4th O.V. C. could have occupied the city of Nashville at any time after the occupation of Edgefield, had their instructions permitted it; in fact, a small squad did cross over to the city and back again, on the ferry-boat we had captured.

Mayor Cheatham was anxious to surrender the city, through fear we might shell it, and, in surrendering, he agreed to protect the public property until it was delivered to the United States' officers.

Capt. Loomis' battery was under the direction, at this time, of Col. Kennett.

Generals Buell and Mitchell both, certainly, must have known of the surrender of Nashville before the arrival of Gen. Nelson.

I, myself, brought to them the news of Nelson's arrival, two days after Edgefield was occupied by us.

            Yours, truly,
                (Signed.)   H. C. Rodgers,
Major 4th O.V. C.

Chapter 16

After John Morgan

The celebrated John H. Morgan was then in our front, doing his best to achieve notoriety, which he afterward succeeded in doing. To keep him in his place caused us much inconvenience; indeed, he was troublesome, and Gen. Mitchell resolved to drive him out of the country, if he could not catch or kill him. But before being successful, it became necessary to know exactly where to find him, and just how many men he had. The general told me what he wanted, and asked me if I would go down the country and hunt him up, and I replied that I would. He then gave orders that I should be fitted out to my own notion, and Captain Prentice, the assistant adjutant general, furnished me with a citizen's dress, and the General gave me his own saddle pony to ride, as it was the only unbranded horse in the camp.

Thus equipped, I put out from our lines in the night, and took the road to Murfreesboro. I had a lonely ride till morning, when I stopped at a house on Stewart's Creek, to get breakfast; and there I fell in with a man who stated that he was going to Murfreesboro, and proposed to ride with me; and, of course, I was glad of his company. From the familiar way he spoke of Hardee, and other southern officers, I felt satisfied he was a rebel scout, and had just been to Nashville. He was a large, well-built man, with homely features, but expressive of a good deal of cunning. He was very bitter against the Yankees, in his conversation, and could tell me more meanness they had done, than I ever before thought they could devise. All this I stored away, as "stock in trade," to be reproduced to the Johnnies themselves, when occasion should require me to abuse my friends.

We crossed Stewart's and Overall's Creeks, when we met with the first rebel pickets, standing in a field some distance away. As we approached they stepped up to know our business, where we were from, where we were going, etc. My companion was in a hurry to proceed, but I desired to converse with the pickets to get whatever information I could from them. They were as loquacious as I was, and had much to say about a fight they had been in a few days before, with the 4th Ohio Cavalry, magnifying their own exploits hugely. They represented the 4th Ohio as little better than arrant cowards, which worried me a good deal, but I must keep up my disguise. Little did they imagine that they were then speaking with a member of that very regiment; and less did they suspect that my fingers were aching to shoot them. If the General had not given me such very strict orders, I believe I should have stopped right there and given them a fight.

But a severer trial than that, even, was in store. One of the reprobates walked up to me, and with a flourish and an oath, handed me a pistol, saying it had been taken from the 4th Ohio Cavalry the day before, and that Captain Morgan had come in, at the same time, with eight buckled around him. I examined the weapon, and although it looked very familiar, I handed it back, and told him I had never seen one like it before.

Next my curiosity was excited by their guns; I represented that I had never seen any like them, and innocently wondered if the Yankees had any of the same pattern.

"No," said the man, "these are English guns;" and there, sure enough, on the lock was the crown and the words "Tower, London," stamped on the metal. There were but three men at the post, and when the fellow gave me his pistol, their guns were in a corner of the fence and they at some distance from them, so that I could have shot all three before they could have helped themselves.

No passes were required from men going south, but no one could travel north, without a pass from Hardee. On arriving at Murfreesboro, I found it was guarded by Morgan's battalion of cavalry, and three companies of Texas Rangers. Now, I had not the least idea of staying at the place, but had intended to ride through; and was proceeding along steadily, but carelessly, on the lower side of the public square, when I was hailed by a former acquaintance on the sidewalk. He was an old friend, and had served with me in Johnston's regiment, in Texas. I had intended to pass under the name of George Adams, but up to this time had never been questioned as to who I was; and it was very fortunate, as otherwise I should have been detected on the spot.

While talking with this man, a crowd soon assembled around me, to inquire the news from Kentucky, and wanting to know how I had possibly managed to get through the Yankee lines, and a hundred other such questions. I told them I had crossed the Tennessee sixteen miles below Nashville, at the mouth of Pond Creek, and hence did not come through the lines at all, but flanked them, coming down Richland Creek, and crossing the Charlotte Pike at Davidson's. I had been at home on a visit, I said, and was going back to Texas. When asked where I lived, I told them in Bourbon County, Kentucky; and when further questioned as to my motive for returning to Texas, I told them I had been making that State my home for years; and there was my Texan friend by whom to prove it.

As soon as I could do so, I turned to the ranger and asked him so many questions, that he had no time to interrogate me. While I was standing in the crowd, asking and answering questions by turn, a very fine looking man dressed in a plain black suit of clothes, walked leisurely up, and stood listening to the conversation. He at length addressed me in a mild but deep and manly voice, and inquired if I was from near Lexington. I told him that I was, and he asked the news from that locality, and I was giving him the "local items" in detail, when an officer stepped up to him and addressing him as Captain Morgan, called him away on business.

Well, for a little while the top of my head got cold, and the blood all rushed to my heart; but I do not think my emotions were betrayed in my face, for, in an instant, the danger of my position occurred to me in full force, and I resumed my devil-may-care manner, but surveyed him closely as he walked off. He was a man about five feet ten or eleven inches in height, fair complexion, rather red cheeks, round, manly features, with a light blue or gray eye, fiery red goatee of full dimensions, and a little coarse, light-brown hair, slightly inclined to red, which was closely cut. His appearance was genteel, and his manners very prepossessing.

He appeared to be a general favourite, as all eyes appeared to follow him, as he walked along with his fellow officers; and, perhaps, this was the reason that my very close investigation of him passed unnoticed by the men around me. I could not help feeling a little proud that I would now be able to report to Gen. Mitchell that I had seen the very man he had sent me out to find.

After Morgan had left, my Texas friend remarked that there were a great many Lexington boys in Morgan's battalion. I then asked him if there were any in town.

"Well, no," he said; then turning to a man at his side he asked:

"Is Jim B—— in town?"

"No," was the reply, to my great relief; "he is out on picket; we are looking for him in every minute."

This Jim. B—— was born at Leesburg, the place of my nativity, and could have identified me as an Ohio man. Without, however, appearing to be disconcerted, I expressed my regret that I was not able to wait and see him. Then turning the conversation, by asking if there were any Bourbon "boys" in the command, I pretty soon found it convenient to excuse myself without cultivating any further acquaintance. My companion was now ready to go, and coming up, mounted his horse and we rode for Shelbyville.

About five miles from town, I became sick—very sick; growing worse so rapidly that I was compelled to stop at a house. I was well aware that my companion was extremely anxious to reach Shelbyville that night; and, as for myself, I didn't want to get there at all. Stating my demoralized physical condition to him, I told him I was sorry we must part, but I must stop; so pulling up to a house by the roadside, I bade him "goodbye."

The "man of the house," whose name was Bidford, invited me in, and put up my horse. I had now cleared myself of my companion, and, therefore, recovered very rapidly. It was about five o'clock in the evening when I stopped, and shortly after, supper was ready, and I did it ample justice; and then, as soon as it was dark, I retired to bed. A great number of rebels were travelling along the road, and several of them stopped at Bidford's house for water and to have their horses fed. During the night I was there, an officer, with considerable of an escort, came in, and as there was but a thin partition separating the rooms occupied by us, I could hear every word he said. His name was Wood, and he was lieutenant colonel of the 1st Louisiana Cavalry, and was on his way to Murfreesboro with orders for Captain Morgan, and to Nashville with dispatches to Gen. Buell. He talked a great deal, and seemed to be on very intimate terms with my landlord.

Next morning I left early, taking the road to Shelbyville till I got out of sight of the house, when I took the first road that turned off, and started on my return to our own camp. At one point on the Las Casas road, I saw a detachment of Morgan's men coming down the road toward me. To be caught trying to go north would cause my arrest, if no other reason existed for it; so I turned into a lane, and quickened my gait. They pursued, and it was a tight race for about a mile, when I dodged them in a dense cedar brake; but I was driven a long way from my course. After wandering about for a good while, I rode up to a house, and was asking the woman about the way to Las Casas, when I heard a horse coming at a swift trot behind me, and turning in my saddle, lo! there was one of Morgan's men coming toward me, entirely without suspicion.

Turning to him, I remarked that I was glad to see him; that I wanted directions how to go to Brown's mill. I knew the way beyond that well enough, and had no necessity for inquiry farther. When he asked me where I was going, after exacting secrecy from him, which he readily promised, I told him that I was a Texas Ranger; that I had put on a citizen's suit to favour my plan; that I wanted to get into the country, as near to the Yankee lines as possible, in order to ascertain what had become of a very dear friend of mine, who had been missing since the day of our last fight with the 4th Ohio Cavalry.

"I want to find out," said I, "what has become of him, so that I can send word to his people, and advise them of his fate."

"Who is your friend?" he inquired.

"Well," I said, "his name is Corniel Warfield; he is an old friend of mine, and I will risk my life to find out what has become of him."

"Corniel Warfield," he repeated slowly, and with surprise; he belongs to my company. "Certainly I will do all I can to assist you, sir; he is a special friend of mine; I will go with you a mile or so, and put you in the right road to the mill; but you must not let the Yankees catch you."

"No, indeed," I said, "I will be sharp enough for that."

The fellow actually went a mile and a half with me, and put me on the road I sought, when he parted with me, wishing me every success. Thanking him, I "shook my pony up" with the spurs, and was soon out of sight, on the direct route to Nashville.

I had nursed this same Warfield, in our regimental hospital, the night after the fight; and knew very well where he was at the time.

I had only one more ugly place to pass, and that was La Vergne. I had heard a Ranger say, in Murfreesburro, that a party of them would be in La Vergne, that night, so that I knew I must be on my guard, when I approached the town. I rode at the side of the turnpike, on soft ground, and as it was after night, I passed unnoticed, until my horse's feet struck the plank which formed the crossing at the railroad, when almost instantly I heard the sound of some horses running down from a grove some distance to the left of the road. I "shook" pony again with the spurs, and away we went. Looking back, now, I saw the rebels wheel into the road after me. I waited to see no more, but struck out for our picket post, as hard as my horse could gallop. The Johnnies did not follow me more than two miles before they began to be afraid of running on our pickets; and I, too, had my fears; there was danger that our own men would fire on me unless I checked up in time; but luckily, I was recognized when I came in sight, and the boys of course did not shoot.

CHAPTER 17

Reconnoitring Middle Tennessee

I was soon at the general's quarters, and waked him out of a sound nap—the only time I ever found him asleep, though I have visited his quarters at all hours of the day and night. He was pleased with what I had done, and sent me away for a little rest and sleep, previous to starting out again.

In a few hours we started out with a detachment of cavalry and some infantry, among which was the 10th Ohio, mounted in wagons; and I have no doubt but we should have caught John right there, and thus addled the embryo general in the shell, but, as luck would have it, we met Colonel Wood, with the dispatches from Hardee to Buell, with Morgan, and about thirty picked men, as an escort. We halted, and then returned and delivered the dispatches to General Mitchell, who was not at all gratified at our meeting, as the Johnnies would know at once that we were meditating an attack on them.

While Colonel Wood and the general were talking, one of Morgan's men broke from the rear and started back to Murfreesburro, at his best speed; but anticipating something of that kind, Colonel Kennett had quietly sent a few men down the road, in the rear of the rebels, one of whom caught the Johnnie and brought him back to our camp. Morgan and Wood were astounded at the man's conduct; and General Mitchell was in a rage at the man's treachery, and held the officers responsible for it. He now had an excellent opportunity to keep the whole party as prisoners of war, and he submitted the subject to General Buell, who overruled him, and Morgan was allowed to return to his command, and he "skedaddled" without delay, and subsequently caused us much anxiety of mind, and many hard marches.

Soon after this, Captain Robie was sent with Company A, of the 4th Ohio Cavalry, to McMinnville, on a scout, and I was one of the party. The remainder of the regiment went to Tullahoma, and other parts, and we were to concentrate at that place. At McMinnville, we heard of some commands of rebels in our immediate vicinity, any one of which was superior to us in number. I had not started from camp with the captain, but coming in with a small body of scouts, who had been detailed by Colonel Kennett, to serve with me, I was told to push on and overtake him as speedily as possible. He had passed through McMinnville several hours before I got there; and while I was ascertaining which road he had taken, I was warned of the near approach of a party of rebels, by several persons—some of doubtful loyalty. I replied that we were fighting men and that we would be glad to meet Captain Bledsoe and Captain McHenry, and their commands, and give them battle. "We shall be camped on this road a short distance out," said I, "and you will confer a favour on us, to send these men word to that effect."

This they promised to do, telling me that Bledsoe had three hundred men, McHenry two hundred, and another man, whom they named, one hundred; and that the farthest command away was but five miles. Charging them again to be sure and send the rebels out, we took the road to Manchester, and, after dark, overtook the company in camp, when I told the captain about the rebels and the challenge I had sent them, and he approved it, and immediately put his camp in order for defence.

I was sent a quarter of a mile to the rear, with my party, to barricade the road, and hold it till the enemy made a demonstration. During the latter part of the night they approached us cautiously from the rear, but did not attack us, nor show themselves in any formidable numbers, but moved around and got on the Manchester road ahead of us, and charged down on the camp. But the captain had so disposed his men that they gave the assailants two sweeping volleys in their flanks as they approached; and perfectly astounded, they broke and fled, pell-mell, back in the way they came. One of their men, a lieutenant, tumbled headlong into our camp. We afterward ascertained that the rebel loss was eight killed and thirteen wounded; but this only came to our knowledge some time afterward. Captain Robie only reported one of them being left dead on the field, and his own loss nothing. We were unmolested after that, and reached Tullahoma in time to join the regiment.

The colonel had been at Manchester, and destroyed the powder mill there, and had driven a number of little squads of the enemy out of the country; and having consolidated his command, we moved in the direction of Murfreesboro, where our army then was, going by the way of Shelbyville.

Murfreesboro was taken by a detachment of the 4th Ohio Cavalry under Lieut.

While the 3rd division lay at Murfreesboro, Gen. Mitchell sent me out on a long scout to inspect all the roads leading to Shelbyville, and all the bridges over the river within five miles of the town, either above or below it. The reader will at once understand that this was a very long and dangerous task, as the roads were all picketed by the Texas Rangers and Morgan's battalion, and small squads of them were scouring the country, day and night, in every direction. To the right of the turnpike a couple of miles is a small town, called Middleton, the same place where Gen. D. S. Stanley gave the rebel cavalry such a trouncing. Near this little town I met a squad of rebel cavalry under the command of a lieutenant. I had just turned into the road, and did not see them until retreat was out of the question; for I was within half-pistol shot of them. For a moment I felt very bad, but the next instant resolved to "*face*" on them, and "*bluff*" through. Throwing up my cap, I gave a loud hurrah, as if I was immensely pleased over something that had just transpired. My first exclamation was, "Well, boys, I am glad to see you; how do you all get along, and what is the news from the army?"

"We are all well, I believe," said the lieutenant, eyeing me closely; "what command do you belong to, sir?"

"O, I belong to the 1st Louisiana Cavalry," said I; "my name is Bonham, and I am captain of Company I of that regiment."

"Ah! ha!" he said, dubiously scrutinizing my splendid uniform, which really had belonged to Captain Bonham, and who had died while a prisoner in our hands; "then, captain, allow me to ask what you are doing so close to the Yankee pickets, and *alone*?"

"O," I exclaimed, "I have had such a remarkable adventure, and if you are not in a hurry, I will give you the particulars."

"Certainly, sir, we should be pleased to hear it," said the Lieutenant, still surveying me intently; "but first tell me how far it is to the Yankee pickets, if you know, for so small a party of us may be in danger here."

"O, no," said I, "not in the least; for I have just come out through them, and the picket line is away beyond (north) of Old Fosterville, as much as three miles."

"Good on your head," said the lieutenant; "but, captain, what in the world were you doing in the Yankee lines?"

"Why, you see," I went on, "I was out here in this neighbourhood some time ago, with part of my regiment, on a scout. We went into camp at night, not far from New Fosterville, in a secluded place in the big cedar brake, north of town; after seeing the command all properly disposed for the night, I with two other officers, in company with Lieutenant Col. Wood of our regiment, who is, as perhaps you are aware, one of our most reliable scouts, went out on a reconnoisance toward the Yankee pickets. Wood, you know, is a perfect dare-devil, and what do you think he proposes to do? Why, sir, to go to a house in plain view of the Yankee pickets, and call for a supper for the whole party. Tickled at this novel proposition, in the excitement of the moment, we forgot the dictates of prudence, and consented to go. We had been there for perhaps an hour or more, and the lady of the house had laid a bountiful supper on the table, and we were just in the act of sitting down to eat it, when a little darkey came rushing into the room, in a terrible fright, saying, 'Oh masters, oh Miss Louise, de Yankee sogers hab dun cum, dey out dar in de road now, an dey all got hosses. Oh run gemmen, or dey done cotch you in a minute.'

"Wood and my companions rushed out and broke over a fence in the back yard, and into the cedar brake, and made good their escape, followed, of course, by a rapid fire from the Yankees. I knew very well that I could never be so fortunate on my wounded leg, for, you see, gentlemen, I was wounded in a skirmish in Kentucky last winter, and my right leg is very weak, (at the same time raising my foot from the stirrup, I showed an ugly scar on my shin, caused by being kicked by a horse years before), and realizing my inability to keep up with my more fortunate companions, I deemed it best to surrender without resistance, for I was afraid the infuriated wretches might kill me after I gave in, if not before.

"On passing my sword over to the officer in charge, who was a first lieutenant, judge my surprise to recognize in him an old acquaintance and friend who used to clerk in the same store where I was employed in New Orleans. His name was Dobbs, (he was first lieutenant of my own company); and he was glad to see me, and said that he was extremely sorry that I was a prisoner, but promised to use his influence to make my imprisonment as light as possible on me. He saw that the men treated me with respect, and as soon as he got to camp he went in person to intercede for me with Gen. Mitchell, who kindly paroled me and gave me the liberty of the cavalry camp; Lieut. Dobbs promising to become responsible for my safe keeping. The lieutenant did everything in his power to make me comfortable, and took me in his own mess, to eat at his table free of expense.

"Of course I appreciated the kindness of so generous a foe, but still was anxious to recover my liberty. Seeing that it was manifestly to my advantage to cultivate amicable relations with my captors, I sought by every means in my power to ingratiate myself into their favour; and so completely did I win their confidence that this morning the lieutenant proposed that I should accompany him on a short ride beyond the pickets. Of course I gladly accepted the kind invitation, and, the lieutenant borrowing a horse for me from one of his men, we mounted, when he said that he was going out to a farm house to procure butter, eggs and milk for his table.

"After we had got nearly a mile from the pickets the lieutenant dismounted, to arrange his clothing and adjust a 'Yankee button,' (made by poking a stick through the cloth) to his suspenders. We were standing beside a tree when the lieutenant took off his belt, and laid his pistols on the ground beside him; then turning his back to me, began working at his button. There was a chance that promised success. Springing forward I seized the belt, and drawing a pistol from it sprang upon the lieutenant's horse, and galloped away, leaving him overwhelmed with astonishment at his own foolish carelessness. Perhaps it was wrong in me thus to betray the confidence of so generous a man, but lieutenant, no man knows how sweet it is to be free, until he has once been a prisoner."

During the delivery of this story, the whole command had given me the utmost attention; and when I had concluded their admiration was almost unbounded. The lieutenant cordially extended his hand and said:

"Captain, allow me to congratulate you on your very fortunate escape," while his men expressed their feelings in sundry remarks, which, although meaningless to a citizen, are very expressive to a soldier.

"Bully for him," said one.

"Ah, he's a Tartar," said another.

"He's too old for the Yanks," remarked a third.

Seeing that now I had completely disarmed them of suspicion, I urged my anxiety to rejoin my regiment, and of hearing from home, and politely wished them a good day and a successful trip, and galloped away, followed by their congratulations.

As soon as I was well out of their sight, toward Shelbyville, I turned off on a by-road, and took my way to the "Widow's bridge." About two miles from this bridge, I stopped to get my supper, at a house occupied by a widow named Cheatham, who was a relative of General Cheatham, and of Cheatham, the mayor of Nashville. She received me with generous hospitality, and soon provided a bountiful supper for me. Giving my horse time to rest after eating, for I had to ride all night, I sat and talked to the lady after supper for some time. She had much to say about General Breckenridge, who had been camped very near her house, a few days before, and who had paid her a visit. She was very much flattered at this, and told me that part of the general's command were camped near, and that there was a picket post at the far end of the bridge. When night set in, I called for my horse, and told the lady that I believed I would ride.

It was in the latter part of March, and when I went out to my horse, the wind was blowing almost a gale, and snow was drifting in the air profusely. The widow went out through the storm to see me mounted at the gate. She expressed the liveliest sympathy for me in having to ride through that dark, cold, stormy night; and seeing that I had no gloves to draw on, she sent a negro into the house for a pair of yarn gloves, with instructions where to find them, and to hurry back, for she was already getting cold. Presently the negro returned with the articles, and as I was drawing them on, I began to grumble at the cold. "Wait a minute," she said, and away she went to the house, and soon came running back with a very fine white wool blanket, which she folded like a shawl and threw around me, pinning it under my chin with her own hands. Bidding this hospitable lady good bye, I mounted and was soon prowling around the picket post at the bridge.

I discovered that the structure was in good repair, and that it could be crossed with safety; then turning up the river, I inspected, in turn, two others across the stream. While prowling about the second one, which was only a mile from town, I unexpectedly run into a company of rebels, who were returning to their camp. I was just riding out from the bridge, when the sound of horse's feet approaching attracted my attention. How to escape meeting them I could not tell; so posting myself by the side of the fence, under the shadow of a large tree, when they had approached within a short distance, I sung out "Halt," in a loud and resolute tone, and in the next breath demanded, "Who comes there?"

"Friends," was the prompt reply.

"Dismount one and advance with the countersign."

"We haven't got the countersign," said the commander.

"What do you belong to," I asked.

"Morgan's battalion," he replied.

"Then break from the right," said I, "and pass us by file until we see what you look like; and if you prove to be confederates, you may pass in without delay."

Breaking by file, as ordered, they marched by me so close that I could have touched them with a ten foot pole. Keeping myself under the shadow of the tree, I pretended to inspect them as they rode by. When a few files had passed, I sung out, "All right, captain, you can reform your men."

"Form fours; forward, march," he shouted, and I soon heard his men clattering over the bridge and cursing it as an old "basket" that was unsafe to cross, and must soon fall down. They had not gone more than a few steps before the officer ordered his men to dismount and lead over by file, swearing that he believed the bridge would break if they did not do so. Of course this was information to me. I well knew that I must now ride for my life, for the trick would be discovered as soon as they reached the picket on the other side of the bridge. Turning up the road and keeping on soft ground, I followed until I came to a "timber" road, running through a cedar brake, where I turned off, and was soon safe from pursuit in the labyrinth of ways that ran in all directions through the woods.

Keeping up the country, I passed above the town about five miles, and hiding my horse in another brake not far from a house, (for I heard a chicken crow,) I followed the direction of the sound, and finding the house, roused a darkey, and got some corn bread and bacon from him, and directions where to find corn for my horse. I returned to where my animal was hitched, fed him, and laid down to sleep. I stayed in that brake until the next night, and then commencing at the upper bridge, I hunted down the river toward Shelbyville again, and found two more bridges, besides the one at the town, in good repair.

Riding cautiously as near the town as I could prudently, I took a good survey of it, but did not add much to my store of knowledge. Meeting an old darkey coming along the road, I stopped him, and in a low tone asked several questions as to what troops occupied the place, and if the bridge at town was in good repair. He informed me that the place was occupied by Morgan's Battalion of Cavalry and part of Wharton's Rangers; that some of them were quartered in the town, but the larger part were camped on the south side of the river, and were picketing the bridge, which was in good condition.

I had now accomplished all that I had been sent to do. I had learned all about every bridge, and had explored every approach to Shelbyville from the north side of the river. Feeling glad that my dangerous duty was over, with a feeling of relief I turned my horse's head once more toward Murfreesboro', where in imagination I could see "old Starry," poring over his maps by candle light, perhaps impatiently awaiting my arrival; but I was, as railroad men say, "on time," so I did not give myself any uneasiness on that score. I had not ridden more than three hundred yards when I saw a couple of men step into the road only a few yards ahead of me, and then facing me they commanded me to "halt." Knowing that death was my portion if captured in that disguise, I instantly spurred my animal forward at a charge, straight upon them.

When within about two jumps of them, I fired on the right hand man, when he gave an exclamation of pain and let his gun fall, and the next jump my horse struck him full in the breast with his knees and knocked him high in the air, and as he fell to the ground cleared his body with a bound. The left hand man fired as I passed, and so close were we to each other that the powder from his gun stung my face like fine shot. Seeing more men in the cedars on the right, I threw myself down, Comanche fashion, with my head by my horse's breast, but not a second too soon, for they sent a dozen balls whistling after me. Driving the spurs into my horse, I urged him to his utmost for about three miles, when I then checked up, to see if I was pursued; but I heard no more of the rebels that night, and pursued my way unmolested to camp, where I arrived just as the general was eating his breakfast.

I do not know who it was that was firing on me, unless I had blundered inside of the rebel pickets in the dark. The general was very glad that I escaped so well, and praised me to all the officers for venturing so far. But I soon had additional cause to feel proud, for my party of scouts were the first Yankees into Shelbyville, where we captured a bank and put it under charge of a guard until relieved by the authorities. This was the only institution in Tennessee which could redeem its notes; and I afterward learned that it did redeem its entire circulation in United States currency.

The rebels soon got over their scare and began to trouble us again. I scouted the country a good while as Captain Bonham, of the 1st

Louisiana Cavalry, but I accomplished nothing more worthy of narration, except that I had a few single-handed combats with members of Morgan's command.

Chapter 18

Trip to Decatur

On the 8th of April I was sent by General Mitchell down to Decatur, to get information as to the state of the country, and to destroy the railroad bridge at that point, if possible. I set out for Shelbyville, mounted on old Punch, my pet horse, properly armed and fully equipped with turpentine and matches, to do the required work. "Old Starry," (our pet name for General Mitchell), "blowed me up" that morning for being slow, which was the only time he was ever out of humour with me. He had given me a fine horse the day before, and I told him I was trying him to see if he was suitable for the trip; and that he was not to be trusted, and I would, consequently, have to ride old Punch.

This horse, for his services, deserves especial mention, and I will, therefore, describe him. He was a Spanish brown, fifteen hands high, with black legs, mane and tail. He was no fancy horse, but heavy and substantial, with a good honest trot, a fast walk and never failing wind. I had drawn him at Camp Gurley, and trained him to suit my purpose.

Near to the town of Fayetteville, in Lincoln County, Kentucky, night overtook me, and I left the road a short distance and slept in the woods. This was on Saturday night, and on Sunday morning I rode into town. The citizens were astonished to see a single man dressed in full Yankee costume—blue jacket, blue blouse and blue pants—and armed with the well known Yankee accoutrements, venture among them. They gathered about me in a great crowd, and seemed to regard it as the freak of a madman; but on approaching me at the hotel, they found me entirely rational, cool, and of decent deportment, and they at once changed their minds, and took me for one of their own men in disguise.

Seeing that it was my best plan to encourage this belief, I ordered my breakfast, went to the stable to see my horse fed, and then returned to my room at the hotel. There were about three hundred men gathered on the sidewalk to ascertain what the strange arrival meant, and to hear the news; and they were watching me with eager interest. I felt that I was playing a delicate game, with my neck in a halter. If they had only known my true character, they would but too gladly have hanged me to the nearest tree. They asked me my name, which I told them; next my regiment, and with a swaggering air, I said:

"The 4th Ohio Cavalry."

"What is your colonel's name?" said one.

"Colonel John Kennett," I answered, slowly, and with a dubious look.

"What is your captain's name?" inquired another.

"Captain O. P. Robie," I told him.

"Where is your command?" asked one who appeared to be a man of consequence.

"At Shelbyville."

"Well," he continued, "if your command is there, what are you doing here by yourself?"

"Why, sir," I responded, "if you want to know, I came to demand the surrender of this town."

"Well, well," said the man; "that is too good. One man to take a town like this," and they enjoyed the joke hugely.

They now began to look exceedingly wise; and I heard the whisper pass from mouth to mouth, that I was one of Morgan's men. This declaration I heard again and again, as I passed through the crowd. Soon after, a gentleman stepped up to me and requested to examine my gun, which I handed to him after removing the cap; but I at the same time drew out my pistol, cocked it, and held it in my hand till my piece was returned to me. After a brief survey of the gun, it was delivered over to me with trembling hand, when I restored the cap and put up my pistol.

At this moment I was called to breakfast, and walked into the dining room and sat down to the table, keeping an eye on everything at once. I seated myself beside a man of good appearance, who had on a handsome uniform and the three stars of a rebel colonel. Slinging my carbine across my knees, with the hammer up, ready for instant use, I loosed my pistols, in the scabbard on one side, and a vicious bowie knife on the other, after which I began to appease my appetite on the good things before me, watching the colonel closely. He looked at me three different times, and then rising abruptly from the table, darted out into the crowd, and I saw no more of him. A few minutes after, I heard the people on the sidewalk raise a loud laugh at the expense of some one.

After eating a meal—the first since I had left camp—I went out into the crowd again, and called for the mayor, saying I wanted him to surrender the town. Again the bystanders raised a laugh, and called for someone to go for the mayor, as he was not present. They then began to joke me about our gun-boats, saying the Yankees would never fight unless backed by them. I told them that General Mitchell had dry land gun-boats, with steel soles and spring runners, and that he had used them with great effect at Bowling Green. One of the men said:

"If you're a Yankee, show us a Yankee trick, and we will believe you."

"Gentlemen," said I, "I will do my best to show you one, before I leave this neck of timber."

"Where are you going?" said one.

"Down the country," I replied.

"Look here, now," one of the fellows pursued, "you may as well own up and tell us where the captain is."

"What captain?" I asked.

"Why, Captain Morgan, to be sure."

"Gentlemen," said I, slowly, "you have waked up the wrong passenger. I belong to the 4th Ohio Cavalry;" and again the laugh rung out at my preposterous assertion.

In obedience to directions, my horse was brought out, and it was a favourable time to leave, as they were all in a good humour, and I consequently mounted and took the road to Huntsville at a gallop. Just as I passed the crowd one fellow sung out:

"Hold on there, you haven't shown us that Yankee trick yet."

"There's plenty of time," said I, turning in my saddle to watch their movements, "before I leave this section of the country."

About five miles from Fayetteville, is a very noted highland called Well's Hill, and on the top of it there is a fork in the road, the left going directly south to Huntsville, and the right to Athens and Decatur. On reaching this road I was in the act of turning into it, when I looked across on still another road, called the Meredian road, and discovered a train of wagons slowly coming up the hill. I watched it, till I saw there was no guard near, and then riding around till I met the first wagon, I caused it to be drawn close along against the fence, and there stopped; then the next two to be drawn close along side, thus making an effectual barricade against any force which was approaching from that direction. Next I seized the wagon master, who was some distance in the rear of the train, and shoved him and the drivers up into the fence corner, making one of them turn the mules loose from the wagons. The loads were covered with corn blades, and other forage, so one could not see them, but the drivers told me that the wagons were loaded with bacon.

After arranging things to my satisfaction, I produced a bunch of matches, and fired the fodder, on the top of each of the wagons, which were of the old fashioned curved bodies, Connestoga pattern, each of which had on it four thousand pounds of bacon.

The guns of the party all happened to be in the wagons, and none of them had any side arms, except the wagon master, who had something under his coat, that looked like a pistol; and as he wore a belt, it is very probable he had one; and some of the citizens, I know had, for I saw three or four of them; but I was ready to shoot before they could recover from their surprise, so that it would have been foolhardy for them to resist, as I would certainly have killed the first man who made a motion to draw a weapon. I made no attempt to take their side arms, as I did not want to lose my advantage over them for an instant. There were three good guns burned up in the wagons, one a double barrelled shot gun, and two old muskets.

When the flames shot up, several citizens came to the scene of action, but I thrust them into the fence corner, along with the wagon master and teamsters. As soon as the wagons were so far destroyed, that they began to fall down, and I saw that it would be impossible to save anything of the wreck, I made the drivers mount the mules, and the wagon master his horse, and taking them on the road to Fayetteville, I told them that I was going to count one hundred; and that if, by that time, they were not out of sight, I would shoot the last one of them within range. I then began to count; "one" "two" "three," etc., very deliberately, while they put spurs to their steeds, and in a brief time they were beyond my ken, over the hills, toward Fayetteville, to give the inhabitants an account of my Yankee trick.

Wheeling my horse, I put out once more for Decatur, but at the same time inquiring the way to Athens, as if I intended to go there. As I passed the burning wagons again, I told the citizens standing around, that if they did not leave instanter, I would shoot the last one of them, and they scattered like blackbirds.

About ten miles farther down the road, I heard the deep, sonorous tones of a preacher, belabouring a sinful congregation. He was evidently a devout believer in a terrible and endless punishment for the wicked, for he was holding out to his audience the fearful picture of a lost sinner in hell, making a comparison between his condition, and that of Dives, who, he asserted, was once in a similar state of sinfulness, while on earth, and who eventually brought up in hell, and from whence he expressed a strong desire to visit Abraham in his new abode; adding that the wishes of the unfortunate Dives could not be complied with for some geographical cause—something in the topography of the country—a gulf in the way, I believe.

Over this subject he grew eloquent, and had probably got about to his "thirdly," and the congregation were almost breathless with attention, when it occurred to me that there might be soldiers in the church, and I had better look after them; otherwise they might give me some trouble. Riding up to the door, I made my horse enter about half way, so that I could see every man in the house. As his feet struck the floor of the church, with a loud banging sound, the people were astonished to see a soldier under arms, riding boldly in among them. Turning to the preacher, I inquired if there were any southern soldiers in the house. The clergyman was standing with his hand raised, as he was about to enforce some point he had made, being the very picture of earnest honesty, looking as if he believed every word that he had said.

When he saw me, his hand dropped, and he seemed as badly frightened, as if the identical devil he had so vividly described had appeared before him. He was almost overpowered with fright, and supporting himself by the rough pulpit, he glanced at the back door, and then faltered out: "Not now, I believe, sir." I saw that there had been rebel soldiers there, and that they had escaped in the direction of his glance; I instantly pulled my horse back, and spurred to the corner of the log church, just in time to see four men disappear in the brush across a field which lay back of the building. They were too far off for me to shoot at, and not desiring to disturb the worship further than the strictest military necessity demanded, I rode on, after desiring the clergyman to pray for the President of the United States. The rebel papers had an account of the affair, but they lied when they stated that I tried to make the preacher take a drink of whisky; for I hadn't a drop to bless myself with.

Pretty soon I met two soldiers riding leisurely along to church. I halted them, demanded their names, regiments, and companies, and informed them that they were prisoners of war; that I was a federal soldier, but that there was no way for me to dispose of them so far from our lines except one; I was sorry it was so—but I must shoot them. They begged that I would spare their lives, and pledged their honour that they would go with me in good faith, if I would not kill them. I pretended to be in a deep study for a few moments, and then told them if they would take the oath of allegiance to the United States, I would let them go; and to this they agreed eagerly.

Holding up my right hand, and removing my cap, they imitated my example, uncovered their heads, raised their hands, and with a solemn look, that would well become a court-room, waited for me to administer "the oath." I had joked them far enough, however, and not wishing to be guilty of blasphemy by administering an obligation I had no authority to require of them, I told them that I would rely upon their honour, but they must do nothing toward pursuing me, or giving information concerning my whereabouts; and I then told them to "go in peace."

The next man I met was an old citizen, riding a very spirited horse, and dressed in a suit of butternut-coloured homespun. Tall, thin featured, and gaunt, he was the very picture of a secesh planter. I stopped him, and inquired the way to Camargo; he pointed to the road he had just left, and told me to follow that. I now told him I was a confederate officer, and that I had orders from Gen. Beauregard to gather up all the stragglers I could find, and bring them forthwith to Corinth; that we were expecting a great battle there with our "detestable foe," the Yankees, and that it was absolutely necessary for everyone to be at his post.

"You will," said I, "do me a favour and your country good service by giving me the names of all soldiers who are at home without leave in your neighbourhood."

"Certainly, sir," he replied; "I will do so with pleasure; and if I had time," he added, "I would go with you, and help to find them."

I then drew out a note-book, and wrote down each name he gave me, with the company and regiment of each man, together with his residence; and then asked him to refer me to some responsible citizens, who would give assistance if necessary. He gave me the names of half a dozen, who, he said, would not only assist me, but would give the names of other delinquents.

He now prepared to ask me a few questions, and prefaced them with the statement that he was the "Chief Justice of Lincoln County," and that he was on his way to Fayetteville to open court on Monday morning.

"Are there many cases to be disposed of?" I asked.

"Yes, a good many," he said.

"What is their nature generally?" was my next inquiry.

"Why, they are mostly political," said he.

I was at no loss to know what the phrase meant; the accused were Union men, who, true to their principles, had refused to yield to the demands of the secessionists, but chose persecution rather than dishonour. I then concluded to have a little fun out of the old fellow, and render the persecuted loyalists what assistance I could. But as I did not desire to kill him in cold blood, I concluded to frighten him a little by way of punishment. Pointing to the dense column of smoke that was rising from the burning bacon, I said roughly:

"Look there, old man."

"Why, what in the name of God, does that mean?" inquired he, raising his eyes in utter astonishment.

"Why, sir," I responded, "it means that I am a United States soldier, and I have just burned a rebel train up there, and am now about to dispose of the Chief Justice of Lincoln County"—at the same moment raising the hammer of my gun, and drawing a bead on him.

"Great God! don't kill me, sir," he piteously pleaded; "don't kill me."

"Look here, old man," said I savagely, "if I let you live, do you think you will trouble Union men in this county again?"

"O, no, no, I will not."

"Won't bring 'em to trial?" I asked.

"No, indeed, I will not," he solemnly asserted; "I have been compelled to enforce the law," he then began in extenuation, when I interrupted him with,

"Don't talk to me about enforcing the laws, you old reprobate, or I will kill you in your tracks. Now, see here," I continued, "I will give you a chance for your life. This is a level road, and a straight one; now, I will count one hundred and fifty, and if you are not out of sight in that time, I shall kill you, just as sure as God made little apples."

I gave the word, and began to count, and he darted off, like an arrow, and was soon lost to my view in a cloud of dust.

Again taking the Athens road, I pushed on rapidly for some time till I passed several houses, and then, reaching a shallow creek, leading into the woods, I turned down it, so that the place where I left the road could not be found. I travelled up byways till near sunset, when I met with an old man, who had just crossed the Athens road, and he told me that he had seen twelve of Young's Tennessee Cavalry and fifteen mounted citizens after a man, "who had been raising a disturbance up the country." He said that I answered the description exactly, and that he believed I was the man.

"You had better hide somewhere, till after dark," he advised me; "for they are alarming the whole country wherever they go."

I saw that he was a Union man, so I told him that if I kept on riding they could better see and hear me, and perhaps it would give them a chance to bushwhack me. I then told him I wanted to find a sequestered spot, where I could leave my horse, and have him taken care of till I could get him again; and he told me of a very good Union man, who lived down in the woods, away from any public road, and advised me to leave my horse there; and he gave me such directions as would enable me to find the place, which I reached in safety.

Leaving my horse, I took to the woods on foot, making direct for Decatur, taking the sun for my guide. The second night overtook me in the woods very near Madison depot, on the railroad between Huntsville and Decatur. I had tried to travel in the night, but was overtaken by a terrible storm, and the darkness was so great that I could not find my way. Being very tired, I slept soundly, with no other bed than the ground, and no cover but my rubber Talma.

I awoke next morning just as it was beginning to get gray in the east, and found I had lain down in a low piece of ground, and the water had run under and around me, until it was about four inches deep. I was cold and wet, and hungry as a wolf. I made the railroad my guide after that, and passed through Madison just as the citizens were beginning to stir about, and I saw four or five rebel soldiers starting at that early hour toward a saloon for their morning drinks. I soon discovered that the railroad was the safest route I could travel, as there were no houses near it, and I followed it till I reached a point near Mooresville, where I stopped at the house of a Union man for breakfast, or rather dinner, for it was about ten o'clock. He took me for a rebel in disguise, sent there to try him and ascertain his sentiments.

He gave his name as Porter Bibb, and I gave mine as Gabe Fitzhugh. I was trying to sound him and he was trying to sound me. We spent about two hours in lying to each other, to discover each the other's opinions, but had mutually failed, and when we had commenced lamenting the death of A. Sydney Johnson in the battle of Shiloh, we were interrupted by the entrance of a Quartermaster's sergeant, who I ascertained to belong to Young's 2nd Tennessee Cavalry, and that they were guarding the identical bridge I was sent to inspect. I got into a conversation with them, and gave the 8th Texas—Wharton's Rangers—as my regiment. They were without suspicion, and I do not think they had ever seen a Yankee before.

My first business was to get their confidence—the next, to draw them into a conversation respecting the bridge. This was done without exciting the least suspicion as to who I was. They told me all about the bridge and its defences, and how they were built of cotton bales; and the sergeant gave me a description of how they tried its qualities as a defensive work.

"We took a six pound gun," said he, "and planted it three hundred yards from the fort, loaded with a heavy charge of powder and a solid shot, and then aiming at the fort about breast high to a man, we fired. The ball went through the first wall and turned downward, and struck the ground, glanced upward, struck and went through the top bale, knocking it to pieces, turned downward again and hit the water about the middle of the river, glanced up and struck a house on the opposite side of the river, then went through the walls and fell in the yard near the house."

"Why did not the officers make the fort stronger?" I inquired.

"Well," he said, "I asked that question myself, but the colonel said it wasn't intended to stand a siege, nor to turn artillery, but merely as a protection against Yankee cavalry; that the 4th Ohio was everywhere, and pitching into everything, and no one knew what day they might come to this section of the country. But let 'em come; we are fixed for 'em now."

He was so explicit in his description that he actually mapped out the fortifications on the floor of Bibb's shop.

While we were talking a rebel captain came in, who, I suppose, was a relative of Bibb. He was very inquisitive, and wanted to know all about me, adding that he hoped I would take no offense at his questions, as these "were very suspicious times."

"Not at all, sir," was my answer, "an honest man is never afraid of being watched?"

"Is not that a Yankee uniform you are wearing?" he asked.

"Yes."

"Why do you wear it?" was the next inquiry.

"Because," said I, "it is unsafe to wear any other where I have been."

"Where was that?" he wanted to know.

"Near Shelbyville."

"How came you to be there? Why are you not with your command?" was his next query.

"I was," said I calmly, "left behind at a house, on the retreat from Nashville, too sick to travel."

"Whose house were you left at?" he persisted in asking.

"I was left with a man named Butler."

"Where is your horse?" he wanted to know.

"I let a comrade have it," I told him, "because I was afraid I would never be able to ride again."

"Where are you going now?" he asked.

"To my regiment."

"What is your regiment?"

"Wharton's Rangers."

"What is your captain's name?" he would like to know.

"Captain Cook," I told him.

"What part of Texas were you from?" he asked.

"From Waco, on the Brazos River," was my reply.

"Ah! I have been there; were you acquainted with Dr. Tindsley?" he inquired.

"Yes, sir," I said; "he is president of the vigilance committee of McClennan County."

He then went on to ask a great many more questions about the county and the people, and finally became fully satisfied that I was all right, and a good soldier. He then took his leave, and in a few minutes the corporal and sergeant got through their business and departed. Bibb then told me that dinner had been waiting for some time, and that he thought the men would never get away.

"But," said he, "I never would have asked them to eat with me, if they had staid till tomorrow morning."

I swallowed a hearty meal, the reader may be sure, as I had not eaten since I left Fayetteville on Sunday morning, and this was Monday noon; and, after dinner, I started out for Decatur, still following the railroad. When I passed houses, it would be so far off that I was not noticed; and when a train passed, I would be standing behind something, so that those on board could not see me until they had passed, when it would be too late to either stop, or shoot, or do anything else. When I arrived at the first railroad bridge in the swamp, not far from the Y in the road, I came to the camp of the 2nd Tennessee. I walked in, unconcernedly, and called for Colonel Young, but was informed that he was over the river, at Decatur.

"Do you wish to see *him*, sir?" asked the Major.

"Yes, sir," I replied, "but I will call again; what time do you expect him back?"

"About ten o'clock, this evening," answered the Major.

"Then I will call tomorrow morning," I said, and turned to go away.

At this point the major began to evince anxiety as to who and what I was, and I answered that I was on my way to rejoin my regiment, at Corinth. This satisfied him, and he went into his tent; but an idle soldier bawled out:

"Say, thar; what are you doin' in a Yankee uniform?"

"Why, I always like to wear the best I can get," said I, and moved on.

No one pretended to stop me, although several asked me questions. Just as I was leaving camp, someone hailed me, and wanted to know where I was going. I told him to a house that I pointed out in the distance, and that I intended to stay there all night.

"You had better stay all night with us," he said; "we will treat you to the best we've got."

"No, I thank you," I said; "I have been sick for some time, and prefer sleeping in a house when it is convenient."

"Don't blame you, sir," he responded; "I would do it myself, if I could."

When I got to the house, I told the lady I was sick, and would like to lay down awhile; and she invited me to rest on a bed which was standing near the fire, and I had a short nap, when I was aroused by the entrance of two men. Without moving, I surveyed them unobserved, for they had not seen me yet; and then I affected to be sound asleep, being well-concealed by a blanket. They inquired for me, and said they desired to speak with me. The woman pointed me out, and said I was a soldier, that had just stopped there, and inquired if I was the man they wanted.

They said they supposed I was, and inquired of the woman who I represented myself to be; and she told them substantially my story, which was the same as that I had told before. One of them wanted to wake me up immediately, but the other said that I should be allowed to sleep a little, while they warmed themselves. The first man, however, could not brook delay, and he walked up and shook me roughly, saying:

"Come, soldier, get up; we want to talk to you."

I got awake, finally, and without offering to get up, asked them what they wanted, in a tone expressive of no pleasure at their intrusion. They then began to question me as to who I was, where I was going, what my regiment was, and so on: all of which I answered promptly and carefully. Pausing a little, one winked at the other, who nodded in return; then addressing me, he said:

"Well, my friend, we want you to go to camp with us."

"I have been to your camp," said I, "and came from it, over here to stay all night."

"Well," said the spokesman, "we want you to go back with us."

"I don't propose to go back there tonight," I responded.

"Well," he continued, "I think you will *have to go*."

They had not yet drawn their pistols, and, without giving them time to do so, I seized my own, under the blanket, and jumped to the floor, ready to fire.

"Now," said I, "get out of this house, and do it quickly, or I will shoot you."

They began at once to stammer apologies for their conduct, but I shut them up:

"I treated you like gentleman," said I indignantly, "and you have insulted me by your outrageous pertinacity, and I want you to get out of my sight. I don't allow any man to intrude on me, while I am attending to my own business."

They saw that they could not draw their weapons without exposing themselves to a shot, so they walked out of the house. Knowing very well that they would go to camp and get more men, and then return, I began to study how I should proceed. One thing was certain; I could not get to the bridge immediately, for it was too strongly guarded; so, sitting down to the table, as supper was announced, I made the people believe I was not in the least disconcerted at what had passed; but, all the time, I was studying how to beat the rebels next. I carefully calculated the time it would require for them to ride to camp and get a squad of men and ride back; and after eating I stood in the door a moment, and then said to the woman that I guessed I would go over to camp and see those fellows; that I didn't know what was the matter with them; and that they must have thought that I was a suspicious character; and the woman thought my plan a good one, and I started out, going across a very large wheat field, and then all around it, trying to find my way through the swamp, to the river, calculating to steal a boat and float down under the bridge.

I failed in this, however, and knowing that I had no time to lose, I started back up the country to find our army. I took a course by the stars, and travelled till late in the night, when I heard the deep-mouthed baying of a hound behind me. I stopped to listen a few minutes, and heard it repeated several times, and then came a chorus, loud and strong, of several dogs. Listening attentively, I knew by the sound, that they were following my track. I was near a dense body of timber, and darted into it, at the top of my speed, and did not run far, till I found, to my great joy, I was plunged into a stream of water waist deep.

I now felt confident of breaking the trail; so, wading across the stream, I raised on the other bank, into a dark, shallow swamp of considerable extent. Holding on my course by the stars, I wandered for nearly an hour, when it became so dark and cloudy that I could not see. I, however, kept on, till so thoroughly exhausted that rest was a necessity; but still the swamp seemed interminable, and the water was about waist deep. I was almost ready to fall from fatigue, when I discovered a white spot on the surface of the water. It is an old adage, that a *"drowning man will catch at a straw,"* and it was true in my case. I pushed on, and found it was a pile of new rails, rising above the water about five inches, and I clambered upon it, and stretched myself out to rest, and was soon in a deep sleep. I could still hear the dogs occasionally, as I mounted the rail-pile, and was astonished at it, for I thought I must have travelled ten or twelve miles.

Next morning, I awoke chilled almost to death. I could scarcely straighten myself up, I was so benumbed with cold. I got down into the water, which, by contrast, actually appeared warm; and I waded through it for almost half an hour, when I reached dry land, in the rear of a plantation; and, looking across a field, I could see the negroes just turning out to work. I immediately slipped across to their quarters, and approaching a gray-haired veteran, I told him I was a Yankee soldier, and needed his assistance, and he replied that anything he could do, would be done quickly and cheerfully. I told him I was hungry, and he went in and brought out an ash-cake, and a very large, thick slice of ham, and gave it to me, saying, he was glad to be able to do something for "his people," adding:

"Massa, I allus calls you 'our people,'—God's people—'coz I knows you wants to make de poor brack people free, and don't want to keep dem down, crushed down like dumb beasts, and make slaves of dem as long as dey live. God will take care ob his soldiers, dat he will; and dem what gits killed in battle, he takes right home to glory. Tank de Lord, for his mercy; de day ob 'liberance is at han', wen do poor brack man kin hol' up his hed, an' say I'ze a man, and not a beast. Tank de Lord, tank de Lord, for bringin' de brave norden solders to fight our battles, and make us free, like oder people, and de Lord bress you, my son, an' I hope you git back to your own people, an' not a har of your head be touched."

Had I listened a moment longer I must have shed tears, so feelingly earnest, and with such deep sincerity were the old man's words uttered. As I was in haste, I broke off here, and taking a young negro with me, to show me the way through the next swamp, I jumped over the fence, and was soon out of sight in the thicket.

When I parted with the old man, he asked my name and regiment; and the last words I heard him utter, as I pushed out on my journey, were:

"Ole Jacob will pray to de Lord for you dis night; may de Lord always keep you in his han'."

My guide seemed to be perfectly at home in the swamp, and piloted the way for three miles over a string of logs, which seemed to be arranged by accident, and not design, so as to form a complete chain across it, so that we were landed on the opposite side without wading a step. I now made my way across that immense body of timbered land which lies between Athens and Fayetteville, to a mill, on the road to Huntsville, and seventeen miles north of that town, and found that our army had encamped there on the previous night.

Every horse in the vicinity had been picked up by our men, or I would have now confiscated one to overtake the command. I, however, was compelled to go on foot, till I reached Meridianville, where, as good luck would have it, I met a negro in a buggy, who was driving a very fine horse, and I at once concluded to ride, and make up for lost time. I accordingly concealed myself until he got close to me, when I stopped him and jumped into the buggy, and, turning it around, I was off—not only with the horse, but with the negro, baggage, and buggy, all of which were impressed into the service of the United States.

Putting the horse out to the top of his speed, I drove into Huntsville just as the men were raising the headquarter tents. I reported the condition of the country, down below, on both sides of the river, as far as Tuscumbia, and that it was clear of rebels with the exception of the 2nd Tennessee and 1st Louisiana—both cavalry regiments; but it was impossible for me to get to the bridge, and learned that the rebels had it already tarred, and that pitch-pine was piled in it, ready to be fired at a moment's notice.

CHAPTER 19

Carrying an Important Dispatch to General Buell

When Huntsville was captured, a great amount of rolling stock fell into our hands; indeed so sudden was the blow struck, that a train already fired up, was unable to escape. Upon this latter, Colonel Turchin's command mounted and started for Decatur, at once; and in two hours the town was in the Colonel's possession, and the flag of the Republic waving over it—my friends of the 2nd Tennessee Cavalry having a hard time to save themselves; and some of them, who were out in pursuit of me, on coming back, being unaware of the change, rode directly into our camp, and were captured.

The occupation of Huntsville took place on the 11th day of April, 1862; and the amount of public stores which fell into our hands was immense. We likewise took about five hundred prisoners; and in the telegraph office was found a dispatch from General Beauregard, giving the strength of his force at Corinth; together with his position; the disposition of the command; the amount of supplies on hand; the number of reinforcements required; and by what time they must be on the ground, or he would be compelled to evacuate the place; and adding that if that place fell into the hands of the enemy, the cause of the South was lost. This dispatch was given to me in a few hours after I got to Huntsville, and I was ordered to take my own way to get the document to General Buell, at Corinth, but to get it there without delay.

I saw the importance of the dispatch at once, and I mounted my wild horse—the one the general gave me—and, as he handed me the document, he told me that he had sent two other men with copies, and expressed the fear that they would not get through, as they were inexperienced in the country. "Now," said he, "I depend on your getting through with it."

I turned my horse down toward the Fayetteville road, and put him out at a rapid gait. He was a large, thorough bred animal, six years old, and perfectly wild, not even being "bridle wise;" and, when once I got him started on a straight road, I "let him out" to his best, till I got him pretty tired, when I checked him up to a more moderate speed.

He made the trip to Fayetteville in three hours, a distance of thirty-six miles. When I reached the town, I stopped with my old friend, the tavern keeper, and got another good breakfast, for I had been riding in the latter part of the night. Colonel Pope, of the 15th Kentucky Infantry, was in command of the town, and I went to him and asked him for a fresh horse. He immediately summoned some of the leading citizens to his headquarters, and told them they must furnish me with the best animal in the town, and bring him to me forthwith; and they were not long in obeying, but brought a magnificent horse—the property of a doctor who lived near. The owner expressed some dissatisfaction at parting with it, but a Yankee guard is inexorable and it had to come; and Colonel Pope was a man who allowed no trifling.

Mounting the doctor's horse, I went by way of Fishing Creek ford, to Columbia, the county seat of Maury County, Tennessee, which place was commanded by General Negley; and to him I delivered the dispatch, with the request of General Mitchell that it might be sent immediately by telegraph to General Buell, at Pittsburg Landing. General Negley was in bed when I arrived at his quarters, but he rose and called on his adjutant general, Captain Hill, to take it to the telegraph office; while he directed me to the best hotel in the place, offering to pay my bill.

About four miles from Columbia, I had fallen from my horse from fatigue alone, and I presume I lay for at least an hour, entirely unconscious; but on recovering, I found my horse tied to a bush nearby; and in the vicinity was a woman's track in the dust, showing that someone approached me, while in a state of insensibility and had gone away immediately, supposing I was merely sleeping; and it was probable that she tied my animal. It was a lucky circumstance that none of the many squads of guerrillas infesting that region, discovered me, in that unguarded condition, or perhaps I would never have reached my destination.

I cannot say exactly what caused me to fall; I remember distinctly that I was wide awake and whistling at the time; when suddenly it seemed as if a great weight was lowered down upon my right shoulder, and I felt myself sinking; then suddenly the weight seemed to shift to my left shoulder, and I remember no more.

On my way back to Huntsville, and about eight miles from Columbia, a negro waved his hat at me, and I stopped. He was more than a quarter of a mile from the road, but when he saw me halt, he came up at a run. He then asked me, almost breathless with excitement, if I was the man that had gone up the road two days before, and I told him that I did pass there about that time, "the day before yesterday."

"Well, den," said he, "you bin de bery man dat I want to see. Massa, I'ze gwine to tell you sumthin' now, but you mus' promise neber to git me into no trouble."

I told him to speak out; that I was a Yankee soldier and his friend, who would never betray him, and he then proceeded with his information, which was to the effect that his master and eight other men were waylaying me in a small mill, intending to kill me, as I went down the country. He said that the plan was laid in his master's house, and that he was the owner of the mill; and that the other men were to come there, as if on business, but bring arms with them, concealed. There was a bridge above the mill, within short gunshot, and a ford below it, even a less distance away. They were to stand in the mill and fire on me; and if I went by the bridge, my body was to be sunk in the pond, and if I crossed at the ford, my remains would be swept away by the current; while my horse was to be given to one of the party, who was going to the rebel army.

When I received this notice, I thanked my informant, and then rode down to the mill at a charge; and instead of going to the bridge or the ford, dashed right up to the door of the building. The miller saw me coming, and ran in; but I called him out, and, keeping him between the mill and myself, took him to account about the proposed murder. At first he attempted to deny all knowledge of the offense; but I told him it was useless; that one of the best proofs in the world was his running from me, when I had not yet turned toward him. I told him that I did not want to kill as old a man as he was, but if he did not tell me all about it, I would go back to Columbia, and get a party of cavalry and come out and burn his mill, his house and barn, and carry off every dollar's worth of property he had, that we could haul away. He hesitated a little, and then asked if I intended to hurt him if he did tell.

"No," said I, "but I must know where your men are, for I have come for a fight."

"They are not here at all, sir," said he; "they have gone; they only staid one night and day, and then gave up your coming back this way;" and he said this in such a way as to convince me that he wanted it to go a long way in extenuation of the act.

"Well, old man," I replied, "I will advise you a little. Never, as long as you live, offer again to molest a Yankee soldier. Nothing but your gray hairs now saves you from a bloody death. Let this be a warning to you, and I will spare you; but you must give me the names of those other men. I will bring them to an account."

As he gave the names, I wrote them down on a slip of paper, and then giving the hardened old sinner a parting admonition, I crossed the ford, and resumed my journey.

Not far from Meridian, a little while before night, I overtook Sergeant—now Captain—White, of the 4th Ohio. I was very much fatigued and sick, and we stopped to stay all night near where we came together. Our host was named D———n, who is a prosperous citizen, and to him I mentioned the fact that I was not well. He stated that he was scarce of bedroom, but that I could sleep in the store-room with his clerk; while he put the sergeant to sleep with a safe guard named Greathouse.

Late in the night I heard a noise outside, on the ground. It appeared like someone walking softly on a loose board; and listening, I heard it repeated; and at the same moment, the figure of a man's head was visible before the window, and presently another was seen; after which they suddenly disappeared. Soon afterward, however, they returned, one at a time, and I cautiously whispered to my companion, who, to my astonishment, was wide awake and watching the window. I told him to slip out cautiously into the other room, which he did; but as he went he stumbled against a chair, and the figures disappeared instantly.

For a long time I saw no more, and was on the point of calling the young man back, when they slowly approached from opposite sides of the window. Soon the one on the left moved noiselessly over to the right, and another appeared in his place; and all stood gazing intently into the darkened room. I could see them distinctly, but they could not well see me. At length the last man who came up, raised a large, heavy gun, in such a position that it crossed the window diagonally; and while this was going on, I had quietly raised myself up in the bed, and as I was not undressed, I drew my pistol and cocked it noiselessly, by keeping my finger pressed on the trigger; and while the man with the gun was gazing intently into the room, I fired with a careful aim directly at his face.

There was a fall, a low moan, short, heavy breathing, hurried whisperings, and then a heavy shuffling sound, as of men running and supporting a considerable weight. My first impulse was to spring out, and by firing rapidly upon the retreating party, rouse my two comrades; but upon reflection, I concluded to hold my position, as they were probably watching the door to shoot me if I went out. I then waited till the moaning sound had died away, and then whispered to my comrade to return to bed. He did so, and we both enjoyed an unbroken rest till morning.

I never was able fully to explain this mysterious intrusion. The men may not have been enemies; I may have misjudged their character; but in all cases, when mistakes are made which result in shooting, *I want to be the party who makes the mistake.*

I arrived in Huntsville again without further adventure, but greatly fatigued. But there is an old adage that there is "no rest for the wicked," and I found it so in my case. I went at once to headquarters to report. Although it was night, I found the general, as usual, wide awake and busy. Turning to me quickly, he asked me if I was not "almost tired to death." I told him I was very tired, but was ready for any service; to go anywhere, or do anything he might desire, in the line of my duty.

CHAPTER 20

Reconnoitring Bridgeport

After I had made my report, the general turned to me and said: "How many rebels are there at Bridgeport?"

I told him I did not know, but would go and see for him.

"That is just what I want you to do," he remarked; "go and see. But do you want any money, or disguise?"

"No, sir, I will go in uniform."

"Then," he continued, "I want you to use all diligence, and report as soon as possible; you will find our troops at Bellefonte, and then you will have seventeen or eighteen miles to scout alone; do this for me now, and when you return, you shall have a long rest."

I mounted my wild horse again, and was off at once. I had time to get to Maysville, a town twelve miles out, before morning, and there I stopped for breakfast. While I was staying there I was overtaken by Lieutenant Criss, of the 4th Ohio Cavalry, with about thirty men, who were going to Bellefonte, which is about ninety miles from Huntsville. We had no adventure on the route; but when we reached the place, we were surprised to find that it had been evacuated by our troops. Lieutenant Criss said that he must go back, as he had already gone further than he was ordered; and he turned toward Huntsville immediately. I dismounted, and as my horse could be of no further service, I sent him back to camp by one of the men. I was now alone, and nearly one hundred miles from our lines, and the little party which came with me was rapidly disappearing from view.

When they were out of sight, I walked into a little grocery to see what was in it and to hear the news. The room was literally packed with men—some dressed as citizens, but by far the greater number sporting the tawdry trappings of the rebel soldier. I scanned the crowd closely for arms, but could detect none. What the men were there for

I could not tell, nor did I stay to inquire. My eye fell upon the landlord of the hotel, and I "saddled" him for a dinner, but he refused to get it, telling me it was after the usual time. I replied that I must have a meal, and that immediately; and he again began to make an excuse in return, and in an under tone muttered: "I don't keep tavern to feed Yankee soldiers at," when I drew my pistol and told him to get out of that grocery and order my dinner at once, or he would be a dead man; and I was about to suit the action to the word when he darted out.

I then began to question the crowd to know how so many men should collect together in so short a time after the Yankees had left, but no one answered me. I knew that they were furloughed rebels, and professional bushwhackers by their appearance, and that they had just come down from the mountains, when they saw our men leave, in order to see what it meant. What they had done with their arms, or why they were unarmed, was a mystery to me. Their frightened appearance showed that they had just huddled into the little grocery when they saw our squad approaching; and nothing prevented their capture, in a body, but the fact that Lieutenant Criss had failed to search the town before he turned back.

Pretty soon the tavern keeper appeared at the door and invited me to dinner, which I found to be a very good repast, though it was cold. Some people would scarcely have relished a meal given under such circumstances, by an unwilling host, and it prepared behind their backs; but I never feared "pizen," and ate with a relish. While I was eating, a train whistled in the distance, and in a minute it dashed into town.

The crowd rushed out, and off into the mountains, at the first sound of the whistle; and I was happy to be thus suddenly relieved of my ill-looking neighbours. The train was loaded with troops, under command of the lieut. colonel of the Thirty-third Ohio Infantry, and Major Driesbach, of the 4th Ohio cavalry.

The major did not like to see me start out on foot, so, yielding to his advice, I took a horse that he provided for me. I did this against my better judgment, for I very well knew that I could not ride two days without detection. The major then sent a detachment of men with me as far as Stevenson, under command of Capt. Crane, and on the route we were continually beset by high waters, which overflowed large sections of the country. It was dangerous to travel through the swamps, for it was impossible to know the moment we might be precipitated over a bank, into deep water, or the channel of a stream, so swift that it would carry us away in the current. However, after great labour, and several "duckings," we found ourselves in Stevenson, a little town in the Cumberland mountains, where the Memphis and Charleston railroad crosses the railway from Nashville to Chattanooga; and here we stopped at the "Alabama House," then a very good hotel.

There was no enemy nearer than Bridgeport, which was ten miles away; and as it was my business to reconnoitre that town, and ascertain the strength of the garrison defending it, Capt. Crane retired from Stevenson to a post three miles out, and encamped, to await my return. I was favoured by the darkness, and rode along the main road, while the rebels were extremely careless, not anticipating the presence of an enemy. As I approached the camp, I stopped a big booby of a boy, who had not sense enough to know one kind of soldier from another, and got him to tell me where the pickets stood, and all about the lay of the camp, which he could not help knowing, as he had just been there, and was on his way home; and he also gave me a very close estimate as to the force the rebels had in and around the place; and he further pointed out a railroad bridge across Widow's Creek, which the enemy were rebuilding, or rather had rebuilt, but on the first trial the structure and locomotive were precipitated into the stream together.

Bidding the boy goodbye, I followed a road he described, and after travelling about four miles, I rode into the rebel camp. Up one way, and down another, I went swiftly, through the dark, without being once halted or disturbed by a Johnny. If they noticed me at all, they probably supposed me to be an orderly.

Having thus a good opportunity to judge of the number of their forces around me, I arrived at the conclusion that, on the north side of the river, there were about five thousand men, thus confirming the statement of a negro, who had visited us, some time before, and who also estimated that there were about three thousand on the south side. I saw two pieces of artillery near the river bank, above the bridge, but these were all the cannon I saw. Bridgeport was, as I discovered, a "flourishing village," consisting of one house—a well built one story frame, with two rooms.

Having reconnoitred to my satisfaction, I returned to Capt. Crane's camp, reaching it a little before daylight, when I found him in the act of starting again for Bellefonte. I gave him my report to deliver to the general, telling him that I would remain in the mountains, till our troops came up to take the place.

Parting from him, I climbed up into the mountain, with my horse, taking a route which would lead me toward Bridgeport. When I got to Widow's Creek, again, I went down into the valley, passing the picket at the railroad bridge, and passing around by a ford, some distance below, and attempting to ride again into their camp, in broad daylight. I had proceeded about one hundred yards toward the camp, when I was halted by a picket, consisting of a sergeant, and eight men.

When I turned, they were standing at a "ready," and I saw that something must be done quickly, or it was all over with me; so, quietly wheeling my horse around, I made back toward them very quietly, and when within about thirty-five yards of the post, raised my gun quickly, levelled it at the sergeant's breast, and fired; then spurring my horse well back in the flank, I started him off with a spring. I saw the sergeant reel, but saw no more. At that instant they fired, but missed so badly that I did not even hear the whistling of the balls. Again they drew a bead on me, but I threw myself down on my horse's side, and went past them at a charge, and the missiles went far over my head, and I was safe. They had double barrelled shot guns, and had each barrel loaded with a ball, and three buck shot; this I learned afterward.

I had to run, through a straight lane, about eight hundred yards; and while going down it, several bullets were fired, some of which passed near me; so I concluded that there must have been more rebs about than the eight at the picket post, though I did not see them. When I got to the end of the lane, I wheeled into the mountains, and for the first time looked back. Here I saw a squad of cavalry, just entering the other end of the lane.

When I got about half way up the mountain I had to dismount, as my horse was now thoroughly exhausted. Stooping down to take a drink of water at a spring, I distinctly heard the rebs at the foot of the mountain, yelling to an old miller whom I had passed, asking him which trail that bareheaded man had taken. I at once hurried on up the mountain, and when on the top, struck out on a path which rather led me back toward Bridgeport—a piece of strategy intended to deceive my pursuers, who would naturally conclude that I was heading for Bellefonte—something I should have done, had my horse been equal to a straight race. As it was, however, I had to rely on woodcraft alone.

The main body of them missed me at the spring, but a few held on the right trail, and we had it up and down five high mountains, and across a many valleys, back and forth through the different little trails, until we were overtaken by night. I now began to think my escape

"Then spurring my horse well back in the flank, I started him off with a spring. I saw the Sergeant reel, but saw no more."

certain, but on coming down into the valley of Little Coon, I found every road picketed, and the citizens aroused; and I heard of several squads of cavalry scouring the country in search of me.

Some of the citizens were ready to befriend me, but others were shy; while one, and only one, shot at me, and he stood at least three hundred yards off, and as soon as he touched the trigger of his piece he wheeled and took to his heels, as if Old Nick was after him. After dark I thought I would have time to stop and get a bite to eat, as I was exceedingly wearied and nearly famished; and I accordingly stopped at the house of a man named Terry. He was moderately wealthy, but like a great many others in that section and at that time, was not bountifully supplied with provisions; but his daughter gave me some corn bread and milk, together with some fried bacon; and after eating what I wanted, I discovered that I was so exhausted from over exertion, that it was next to impossible for me to move. Rest was absolutely essential, and I threw myself down before the fire, putting my feet as near to it as I could bear, in order to take the soreness out of them.

I had been there, I presume, about half an hour when two men entered, whom I supposed, judging from their appearance, to be citizens; and our orders were to treat such with kindness, and not molest them unless they showed signs of hostility; and I accordingly used them politely when they entered. They told Terry that they were greatly wearied, and desired to stop for a while to rest; but they were scarcely seated, when a knock was heard at the door, and when it was opened a soldier, in full uniform, entered. In an instant I was on my feet, and clearing the space between us at a bound, levelled my pistol on him. We were but about two feet apart, and the muzzle of my weapon touched his breast, and I ordered him to put down his gun; and as he perceived no time was to be lost, he lowered his piece until it nearly touched the floor.

This was done in much less time than it takes to tell it; but at this stage of affairs the other two sprang at me with pistols in hand and jammed them violently against my head on each side, and ordered me to surrender, and at the same instant they seized hold of my pistol-hand, and jerked it back over my head. Thus relieved, the soldier raised his double-barrelled gun, and thrust it against my breast, and ordered me to surrender; and although further resistance was useless, I did not and could not speak. I was completely taken in, and it was all the result of my foolhardiness and carelessness. I could have done without anything to eat, and I might have abandoned my broken-down horse, which was, at best, but an incumbrance to me; and I might have concealed myself in the mountains till our army advanced on Bridgeport, which I very well knew would be in a few days; indeed, there were many things I could have done, and avoided my embarrassing situation; but it was then too late; I was a prisoner.

I was taken from the house into the yard, when, for the first time, I discovered that the place was surrounded. About two hundred yards from the house was the captain of the gang, and we marched out to him; he ordered me to be tied, and then I learned that my captors belonged to Stearns' battalion of Tennessee Cavalry.

The reader will be able to derive a faint idea of what I saw and suffered, from this time till I was exchanged, from the following report I made to Gen. Rosecrans, and which I extract from the *Annals of the Army of the Cumberland*, and which was written just after I had been exchanged and had reported to my regiment for duty:

Murfreesboro, March 22nd, 1863.

On the 24th of April, 1862, I was taken prisoner near the town of Bridgeport, Tennessee, by a battalion of rebel cavalry under command of a Colonel Stearns. I was alone on a scout at the time, and fell in with nine of the enemy's pickets. I got the first shot and killed the sergeant, (so I was told by Captain Poe, who had command of the pickets.) I was pursued by five companies of cavalry. After running several miles I was obliged to stop and dismount at a house to get something to eat, and while there was surrounded by one of the pursuing companies and captured. I was then tied on a horse and carried over a mountain to where the battalion was camped; arriving there about nine o'clock p. m.

When we got there I was immediately surrounded by about two hundred men, some crying "Hang him!" "Shoot him!" "Shoot the d—d Yankee!" and several of them levelled their guns on me; some of them being cocked. A Captain Haines told them I was his prisoner and under his protection, and he detailed twenty-four men to guard me, placing two men at each corner of my blanket. When we went to bed the Captain lay down on one side of me, and his first lieutenant on the other; and in this way I was preserved from assassination.

The next day I was taken to Bridgeport. I fared very well at that place, but the day following I was taken to Chattanooga

"When we got there I was immediately surrounded by about two hundred men, some crying 'Hang him!' 'Shoot him!' 'Shoot the d——d Yankee!' and several of them levelled their guns on me."

and confined in the jail, a two story building. The upper story, where I was confined, was about twelve feet square. Here were confined nineteen Tennesseans, a negro, and myself. In the dungeon, which was only ten feet square, were confined twenty-one men, belonging to the 2nd, the 21st, and 33rd Ohio Infantry, who were charged with being *spies*. They were under command of a Captain Andrews, who was then under sentence of death by a court martial recently held at Chattanooga.

They were waiting for the Secretary of War at Richmond to ratify the proceedings of the court martial previous to executing the captain, and they said if they were ratified, the rest would certainly be hung. I was afterward informed by the rebels that Andrews and eight of the men were hung at Atlanta, Georgia. I was told subsequently by a rebel citizen, that they hung Andrews and seventeen men. I once went into the dungeon where these men were, and found them handcuffed and chained in pairs by the neck with a heavy chain, which was locked around each man's neck with a padlock that would weigh two pounds. These padlocks were larger than a man's hand. We were fed twice a day on tolerably good bread, spoiled beef, and coffee made of cane seed. There was no sink in the jail, and our offal stood in a bucket in the room where we were confined, day and night, and was only emptied twice a day, and of course the stench was intolerable. We were denied the privilege of washing our clothes, or of having it done. The jail was literally swarming with vermin, nor was it ever cleaned out.

From Chattanooga I was taken to Knoxville, to another jail, and confined in an iron cage. Here I was told by a man named Fox, the jailor, that I was brought to Knoxville to be tried by a court martial as a spy, and that if I was tried I would no doubt be hung. This court martial adjourned without bringing me to a trial, as did the one at Chattanooga. From there I was sent to Mobile, where another court martial was in session. After keeping me about eight days at this place, I was next sent to Tuscaloosa, Alabama. From this city I was taken, in company with all the other prisoners at this post, to Montgomery, Alabama. The first day out I was taken sick with pneumonia and typhoid fever, but the rebel surgeons refused me any medicine, and even a bed, and I was left for twelve days lying upon the deck of the boat, with nothing to eat but corn bread and beef, which latter

"I ONCE WENT INTO THE DUNGEON WHERE THESE MEN WERE, AND FOUND THEM HANDCUFFED, AND CHAINED IN PAIRS BY THE NECK WITH A PADLOCK THAT WOULD WEIGH TWO POUNDS; THESE PADLOCKS WERE LARGER THAN A MAN'S HAND."

the rebels said had been packed five years.

At Tuscaloosa they shot a federal soldier for looking out of a window, and wounded another in the face for the same offense. At Montgomery they refused to let me go to a hospital, although in an utterly helpless condition. Here they shot a federal lieutenant under the following circumstances: he had been allowed to go out for milk, accompanied by a guard, and he was waiting for a woman to hand the milk out through a window, when the guard gave the order to '*come on.*' 'Wait a moment, till I get my milk,' said the lieutenant. The guard made no reply, but instantly shot him in the breast with a shot gun, killing him forthwith.

From Montgomery I was taken to Macon, Georgia, in company with twelve hundred others. Here we were allowed seven pounds of corn meal and two and a half pounds of bacon of bad quality, for seven days. We were allowed two surgeons and but very little medicine. Our men fared very badly here, being punished severely for the slightest offenses. One man, named Cora, was kept tied up for three days by the wrists to a tree, so that his toes just touched the ground, because he helped kill a yearling calf that got into the camp.

A Floridan and two Kentuckians, political prisoners, were confined in the jail at Macon on quarter rations for twenty-two days. The only offense they had committed was to attempt to escape from the prison lot. Our men were pegged down on the ground for any misdemeanour. This was done by stretching out the limbs and driving down a forked stick over them, and the operation was completed by driving one down over the neck. It would be impossible to tell all the hardships to which we were subjected, but I have endeavoured to portray a few of them. They may be summed up thus:

We were confined in bad quarters, and many were without any quarters. Our dead were left unburied for days together, and some entirely so—at least to our knowledge. We were denied medical attendance. Our chaplains were forbid preaching to us or praying with us, (by order of Major Rylander.) Our men and officers were shot without cause. An insane federal was shot at Macon, Georgia, for no offense. We were compelled to bury our dead in the river banks, where their bodies were liable to be washed out. We were beaten with clubs on board the steamer en route for Montgomery, Alabama. We were fed on foul and unwholesome diet, and frequently left without any rations for two or three days at a time. Our exchange was delayed as long as possible, and we were confined in camps surrounded by swamps, as the rebels said, that we all might die. I find it impossible to enumerate all the hardships put upon us, but have enumerated such as were the most intolerable.

James Pike,
Co. A, 4th O.V. C.

While we were proceeding along through the mountains, we came to a narrow shelf, with a deep abyss on our right, and a perpendicular rocky ascent on our left; and along this I passed watched by five guards—two before and three behind. At some parts it was so narrow that it was almost impassable for one to walk along; and at one place, we came to a rock which almost blocked up the way. There was not room for a man to walk squarely between the rock and the cliff, while on the outside, the trail ran so close to the great precipice, that it was extremely dangerous to attempt to follow it, even on foot.

When we reached this place I asked the guards to untie me, so that I could keep my feet from being hurt by the rock.

"No," said the sergeant, in a rough way; "ride on and hold your feet up."

"You forget, sergeant," said I, "that my feet are tied under the horse, and that I cannot raise them."

"Well, ride on," he replied in a tone of command, "or you may fare worse."

"Let me ride on the outside of the rock, then," I requested, "or my feet will be jammed against the rocks."

He now turned partly round in his saddle, and drawing his pistol, said: "Look'ee here now, sir, you ride right through thar whar I did, or I'll shoot you."

Seeing that expostulations were useless, I rode into the narrow channel, although I saw I should be hurt. Turning to one of the guard, I said:

"Guard, will you untie my feet till I get through this place?"

"No," he said, with a horrid oath, "we've got orders from Colonel Stearnes to keep you tied till we get you to Bridgeport; he says you are a mighty hard case, and he gave us orders to shoot you if you didn't go along willingly, so you had better ride in."

My right foot caught on the top of the rock in the trail, and my left against the side of the cliff; and for about three steps down the mountain the whole weight of the horse's foreparts rested on my ankles by the rope under his belly. The torture was excruciating, but acting on Indian principles, I uttered no complaint. The horse lunged forward three times on his hind feet, until he dragged my foot over the rock to the end of it, when I was released, and the horse's forefeet came down to the ground again. The rebels seemed to enjoy my sufferings, but otherwise they treated me well enough.

My imprisonment was not entirely without its sources of amusement. Everything was not tragedy, but I was delighted by occasional comedy. One circumstance, in particular, may be worthy of a rehearsal. When they were taking me from the Chattanooga jail to Knoxville, I was kept in the depot about an hour, awaiting the departure of the train; and as was natural, the citizens who were lounging around, had a great many questions to ask me, and my answers gave them evident satisfaction. Two young officers and a lawyer came up and engaged in a conversation with me, and attempted to turn my arguments by ridiculing my cause, being particularly severe on Yankee prowess. I at once waived all further conversation by remarking that I had taken them for gentlemen. They at once whirled away through the crowd, exceedingly indignant, and I thought no more of the matter, when in a short time in came Colonel Bibb, post commandant, or provost marshal—I believe the latter, and shouted:

"Where is that Yankee? Where is the sergeant of the guard?"

"Here I am," said the sergeant.

"Mr. sergeant," added the colonel, "if you allow the people to talk to that man any more, I will put you in irons, sir;" and then turning to me, with a fierce gesture, he fairly screamed; "and you, sir, Mr. Yankee, if I hear another word out of you, *I will put you in double irons.*"

"Crack away, sir," was my response, "there is nobody afraid but you."

He immediately whirled around, and left the depot, trembling with rage; and I expected every minute to see a guard come in with the irons; but the train was soon after ready and I was put on board.

When I was in Ledbetter's camp, they put me under a guard of eight men in Colonel Stearns' tent, as he was not in camp; and while there, the major of the battalion came to me and told me that General Ledbetter would have me released and commissioned, and put in command of a company of conscripted men if I would renounce my cause, and take the oath of allegiance to the Southern Confederacy; but I declined, telling him I would be a private in the Union army than a brigadier in theirs. He then left me and did not renew the proposition.

Next morning I was turned over to the provost marshal, and put in the guard tent, along with two other men who "wouldn't soldier." The Johnnies crowded around to see me, sometimes passing into the tent, past the guard, contrary to all order and discipline. The lieutenant of the guard, a fine portly fellow, finding that it would do no harm to let them in, came and sat down by me on my blanket, in the most social manner possible; and we passed some time in friendly conversation, when an Indian adjutant forced his way into the tent. He began to boast of the prowess of the southern troops and decry the pluck of the Yankees, affirming that the latter would not stand the bayonet.

"You are a liar, sir," I fairly shouted. He was on his feet in an instant, as well as myself; he reaching for a pistol, while I raised my fist to knock him down. At this juncture, however, the lieutenant of the guard stepped between us, and taking the adjutant by the collar with one hand, and the seat of the pants with the other, raised him on one knee, and tossed him headlong out of the tent; then turning to me, in a good natured manner, he resumed his seat and the conversation.

The men asked me in the presence of this lieutenant how to get to our lines, and I told them; and he then informed me that, if I were only outside of their pickets, under his charge, he could turn me loose, and go with me to our army, and deliver himself up. He then remarked in a whisper: "I'll bet there will not be less than fifty of our men leave this camp to-night, and go to your lines."

While I was in this camp, the major of Stearns' Battalion told me that ten of his command had been detailed and sent down to Steveson to arrest or shoot me, but that when they started toward me, they became frightened, and came back on the run. That same day I had shot a rebel near that place, but whether or not he was one of the ten I do not know. He was on the run and refused to stop, as I ordered him, and I shot him while running, and he sprang as high as a man's head in the air, and fell on his face, when I went back to them, and told some citizens where he could be found.

While at the Chattanooga depot, and after Col. Bibb had threatened the sergeant so severely, a stout, heavy man, of very pleasing appearance, came in. He was clad in a plain suit of blue homespun, without a single mark or strap to show military authority. He walked past the guard without a word, apparently in search of someone, and then suddenly turning toward me, said: "Oh! this is that Yankee, is it?" and walked directly to me and extended his hand in a most friendly manner.

The sergeant of the guard, without a word, ran at him, seized him by the arms, and clasping both of them down to his sides with the grip of a vice, he stooped under him, and threw him clear across the railroad track. He did not touch the ground, till he reached the opposite rail. The man then walked out of the depot as quietly as he entered it, but did not utter a syllable. After he had left, an officer on the platform said:

"Do you know who that man was?"

"No, I don't," was the surly answer.

"It was Major General Ledbetter," said the officer.

The sergeant dropped his head a moment, when he looked up in a resolute way, and said:

"Well, I don't care a cuss; I won't be punished for every man's misdoin's."

While on the route to Knoxville, my guard was under the charge of the very Indian who had been so unceremoniously thrown out of the guard tent for insulting me; and he now exhibited all that spirit of revenge inherent in his race. I was subjected to every annoyance that his malice or his caprice could invent, or he dare inflict. On my arrival at Knoxville, I was put in an iron cage in the county jail, and fed twice a day, on good bread and beef, and some seed coffee; and when taken out, I was placed in charge of the Eufaula Light Artillery from the State of Alabama, and taken to Mobile, and thence to Tuscaloosa by railroad, and from there to Montgomery by river.

While at Selma, I was once more solicited to take charge of a company of rebel cavalry; and was tendered the influence of Gen. McTyre; the offer of the general being made through his son, who was the lieutenant in charge of me.

It would scarcely interest the reader to give a more extended account of our sufferings; and I will only add, that they were of the most horrid character, and thousands upon thousands died beneath their crushing weight. At Macon, I escaped in company with Lieut. Ford, of the 8th Iowa Infantry, but was recaptured six days afterward, so weak and sick that I could scarcely stand alone. Ford was only out one day, when he was recaptured, having been run down by bloodhounds. When I was recaptured, I was saved from punishment by the adjutant

"The sergeant of the guard, without a word, ran at him, seized him by the arms, and clasping both of them down to his sides, stooped under him, and threw him clear across the railroad track."

of the battalion of guards; but the lieutenant was ironed, and kept in that condition, till sent off to be exchanged.

While in prison, we owed much to the care and kindness of Dr. Hezekiah Fisk, surgeon of the 8th Iowa Infantry, who was a prisoner with us.

We were sent off for exchange in October, 1862, going by way of Savannah, Augusta, Columbia, Raleigh, Petersburg and Richmond. On the trip we suffered fearfully; men were left dead at nearly every station on the entire route. I finally reached my destination safely, and, on the 18th of October, 1862, was exchanged. The officers on the flag-of-truce boat, and especially the surgeons, exerted themselves to their utmost, to save the men; but a large number had suffered so much that human skill was unavailing, and died before reaching Washington City. For my part, I was reduced to a mere skeleton, and was sent to the Cliffburn Hospital—an institution in the care of the Sisters of Charity, and received every attention that could be bestowed, until I became well once more.

CHAPTER 21

Arrival of Wounded from Fredericksburg

A short time after I was taken to Cliffburne hospital, the Battle of Fredericksburg was fought, and thousands of wounded were sent to Washington, to the different hospitals. Cliffburne received its full share, and the Sisters had all that they could attend to. They had but few sick men in their care, at that time, their patients being generally wounded men. There were men with legs off; men with arms off; men with, I might almost say, their heads off; at least, they were minus a large part of them. The wounds were made by every kind of missile known to the science of gunnery, as well as sabre cuts, and bayonet thrusts. There were patients who had suffered two and even three, amputations, and these wounded men represented almost every State in the Union; indeed, I might say, every nation of the earth.

There were Americans, Irishmen, Germans, Frenchmen, Spaniards, Italians, Austrians, and I believe Danes and Norwegians; but they were all groaning under grievous wounds—suffering in a common cause; all were Yankees now. There were men there, who had scarcely been in the country long enough to know how to ask for a drink of water in English; yet whose first act on landing in America, was to volunteer in the United States Army, to battle for the maintenance of the government that had always been an "asylum for the oppressed of all nations;" and whose first initiation into the American service, was to be hurried into a terrible battle, and stricken down in death or with painful wounds, to pine away months of patient suffering in hospitals.

But all that I saw here bore their sufferings with heroic fortitude. The wounded veterans would spend their time in telling stories of battles and adventures; in reading books and papers left for them by charitable or religious persons; in dressing their own wounds, if they were able; or in recounting the circumstances under which they received them. Letters from home formed their greatest solace. When one got a letter from home, he would appear like a new man—it would make him so cheerful. It was astonishing with what devotion the sisters would nurse, and watch over them.

Here, in this bunk, would be a patient, feeble little boy—a drummer, perhaps, who had left his mother and sisters to join the army, and by the stirring notes of his drum, to cheer the war-worn soldier, now stretched on a bed of suffering, with no mother near to nurse or care for him—perhaps, even she did not know where her darling was; but he was faring just as well as he would with her, for the Sisters of Charity were hovering over and nursing him, supplying every want, and soothing, as far as possible, every pain; there, in that bunk, is a brawny man, wounded by a shell; his injuries are terrible; perhaps he is fearfully wicked, and as he writhes in pain, upon his bunk, cursing his cruel fate, at every breath, a sister's hand smooths down his hardened pillow, and a sister's voice speaks words of comfort to his soul.

Perhaps she is repelled with fearful oaths—but only to return to him when he is calmer, with redoubled kindness. Here, in this ward, is a poor soldier dying. All their loving labours and pious prayers have been in vain; the hand of death is on their patient. Perhaps they have watched and cared for months over him, and have had great hopes of his recovery; but now, alas! they are called upon to perform the last kind offices for him, and consign him to the grave. It is a sad trial to them; and as they cluster around the dying man, they tell him of a better world, and their prayers ascend to the throne of grace, for the welfare of his soul.

For weeks, they watched my almost hopeless case; for some of the surgeons said I would die; but under their kind treatment, I rapidly recovered, and was soon able to travel and wanted to go to my regiment; but to pass through the "Government mill,"—would be quite enough to kill me in my weak condition, so I applied for a special order.

CHAPTER 22

At Home—French Leave

By the aid of Hon. C. A. White, General Wadsworth, and General Martindale, I obtained permission to leave Washington, and go to Camp Chase, near Columbus, where my company was on parole, for they had been captured on the day that I was exchanged—and while at Columbus I took "French furlough," and made a visit to my home, where I had a pleasant stay; but took care to report at Camp Chase on "pay day." I was still very weak, but improved rapidly, from the time I next "struck" hard tack.

The surgeon, in Washington, offered me a discharge, if I wanted it, telling me I would never be able to do any duty again. I refused him, telling him I would soon get well, and go to the field again; and I lived to verify my word, for I have done an immense amount of hard service since then. I went to the field again with my company, sometime in March, 1863. Our route lay by way of the Ohio and Cumberland Rivers; and as we landed and remained at the little town of Dover, for some time, I had an excellent opportunity to survey the old battlefield of Donaldson. The ground was rough and hilly, and exceedingly difficult to manoeuvre troops on; while the fort itself stood on a commanding eminence overlooking the river. The field was strewn with missiles of all kinds, while the dismounted guns, the scarred and fallen trees, and the furrowed earth, all told the terrific struggle that had taken place upon the hills.

Having no guide, I could learn nothing save what was then discernible—such as the respective lines of battle of the two armies. Here and there, along the interval between them, would be places where the timber was unusually cut up, and the ground terribly torn by artillery, while every visible object on the surface would be riddled with bullets—so many mementoes of violent charges under a murderous fire. When we consider the almost impregnable position of the enemy, fortified at nearly every assailable point with extreme care and skilful judgment, the nature of the ground our troops were compelled to charge over, the Battle of Fort Donnelson must appear to every reader of history, as one of the most gallant victories which our troops have won during the late long and bloody war.

In due course of time we arrived at Nashville, and, on landing, set out for Camp Stanley, near Murfreesboro; and there we found our regiment—the glorious old 4th—sadly thinned in numbers, but as full of fight, and as enthusiastic in the cause as ever. I missed many a familiar face, and many a voice that would have given me a friendly greeting, had it not been hushed in death. My comrades gathered around me, and welcomed me among them once more; and now, again, I really felt at home. No one knows the deep attachment existing among soldiers; they can scarcely realize it themselves, until surrounded by adversity; then it is that we *feel* how devotedly we love one another.

Company A had not been long in camp before it was put on picket; and on this duty we continued for fourteen days under command of Lieut. Charles D. Henry, being stationed on the East Liberty pike, about two miles from Murfreesboro. For several days nothing occurred to mar the even tenor of camp life, except that a squad of bushwhackers, five or six in number, fired a few random shots at us, which resulted in a quick chase and a final escape.

After this the lieutenant put me on patrol duty, outside the lines, to watch all suspicious points; and while on this duty I was one day joined by Lieut. Frank Robie, the captain's brother. We rode out together much beyond my ordinary trips, having crossed Cripple Creek, and gone about three miles beyond it, when we met an old black man riding along the road, apparently buried in deep thought. There appeared to be a feeling of calm felicity pervading his soul, for it shone out in his face. Such were his meditations that he did not notice us till we addressed him:

"Uncle," I asked, after saying howdee? "ain't you a preacher?"

He raised his eyes, and seeing only a strange officer and soldier at his side, opened them wide and replied:

"La, massa, how did you know dat?"

"We only guessed at it; but what is the news?"

"Well, marsters," he said, "if I ain't mistaken, you is some dem gemmen dey call Yankees, and if you is, I ain't afeard to talk to you; but, Lor', a body doesn't nebber know who dey is talkin' to now-days."

"You are right," we responded; "we are Yankees, and if you know anything about the rebs, we want you to post us."

"Well, marster, I is de widder Trimble's Willis, an' I *is* a preacher, a Methodist preacher, and last winter, on de fust day of December, our soldiers cotch me an' whipped me, kase dere was one of our boys on the plantation tole 'em dat de widder Trimble's Willis prayed for de Union."

Of course we sympathized with the old man in his persecution, but he was not the only one who was persecuted then for opinion sake. He then proceeded with "Marster, it jes seems to me that you Northern men knows ebery ting, an' you don't seem to be afeard of nuthin'; why our men would no more think ob ridin' so fur frum dere camps dan nuthin' in de world; but gemmen, you is in a great deal ob danger here. You is mity close to a big company of *our* men, an' you better be keerful, for dey mout do ye harm."

I asked the old man how far off they were and which way. He told me very explicitly that they were near a little town called Milton, close by. I told the lieutenant that I would go and see where they were. He went back to the picket post, while I thanked the old preacher and left him. For awhile I wandered around through the brakes and over the hills, passed through the town of Milton, but still saw nothing of the rebels. After hunting in vain for some signs of them, I looked all around for smoke, but none was to be seen in the timber, or any place where it was likely that any considerable number should hide. The old darkey had reported them at nine hundred, but added that it was only hearsay with him. I now turned off all the public routes and went to searching the byways, and taking one of these by-roads that led through the farms, I made for a little, low gap in the hills, which here rose almost to the grandeur of mountains.

As I approached the gap I discovered two men, one standing on the ground, the other seated on his horse. They seemed at a loss to account for me coming on perfectly unconcerned toward them. They suffered me to approach within about forty steps, when the one that was mounted wheeled his horse, and aimed to run off down the opposite side of the gap, but I halted him twice and then fired. The shot took effect between the shoulders, just to the left of the backbone. He yelled murder twice in a terrified voice, and then fell forward on his horse's withers, while the frightened animal rushed madly down the hill. My whole attention was instantly devoted to the other man, who was mounting and preparing to follow his comrade's example. I was afraid he would shoot me while I was reloading my gun, which was a Smith & Wesson carbine, but he was too badly scared; he never stopped, but went down the hill at a break neck pace. I ran to the top of the hill, and behold—just at the foot of it were about one hundred and fifty rebels, who had been, as I afterward learned, foraging.

They were somewhat scattered, for when I got my first view of them, they were running from every direction for their horses, which were standing in a bunch under a strong guard, right where two roads crossed. For this point my second man was running. Just as he got to it I fired, he being about one hundred and twenty-five yards off when I did so, and without looking to see what damage I had done, I turned in my saddle and called out, *"Forward the 4th!* forward the 4th Ohio!" then turning upon the enemy again, I drew my pistol and tried it three times, but every cap was wet. I then attempted to load my carbine a third time, but it got out of fix about the trigger works, and I could do nothing with it. All this time the rebels were mounting, and each fellow as he gained his saddle took the road for Auburn without stopping to look back.

A few stopped long enough to discharge their guns, so that there were perhaps fifteen shots fired at me, some of which cut very close, but did no damage. One fellow, braver than the rest, walked right out in the middle of the road and raised his gun to his face, took a long, careful aim, and pulled the trigger, but the gun missed fire; the cap bursted clear and loud, but I suppose the powder was damp. He broke for his horse then as fast as his legs would take him. I thought it was very questionable whether my friends would ever hear from me again when I saw him taking such deliberate aim at such close quarters, as we were so near together that I could have counted the buttons on his coat. I waited till they all got well started down the road, which was in a surprisingly short space of time, and wheeled my horse and took the road for Murfreesboro, and there is no mistake about it, I rode rapidly.

As I passed the next house, I saw a woman standing in the porch, watching my actions all the time; but she could not see the enemy from where she stood. I told her to tell the rebels, when they returned, that there was but one man in the attacking party, and that he said he had flogged one hundred and fifty of them, and could do it again.

This fight, if fight it might be called, took place at Hooper's Tanyard, two miles from Milton; and on my retreat, I passed through the latter place. Stopping a moment, I called a man to me, and gave him the same message I gave to the woman, and as I expected pursuit, I made for Murfreesboro, at once, which was fourteen miles distant. However, I saw no more of that party, though I did see another squad of twenty-six, that did appear as if they were after somebody. The fear of a pursuit by the first party, gave me a good speed; and the sight of a second, caused me to persevere, until I was once more safe within our lines.

I knew no more about the affair at that time, than what is contained in the particulars I have related; but a party of our cavalry soon afterward went out in that vicinity, to scout, and there learned that my first shot had killed a picket, and mortally wounded a horse; and that my second had wounded a man severely, and passed through the neck of one horse, and subsequently wounded a second one; and that the enemy had went to the town of Auburn, seven miles distant, without halting, or breaking their gait; and that they deserted a large forage train, which I could have destroyed, had I known where to look for it; but it was behind a projection of the hill. Lieut. Henry, of Co. A, was out on a scout, in the same direction, shortly afterward, and the same particulars were learned by him. He had a talk with the woman I saw, and she told him that she had communicated my message to the men, and that one of them exclaimed: "*Oh, he is a liar, there were but eighty-four of us.*"

It was big enough, the way he told it; but I must still adhere to my original statement, although I could only judge of the number by the ground they covered, after they got closed up.

My next adventure was in Breckenridge's lines, at Dry Hollow, not far from Bradyville. I got inside of his pickets, and was taken suddenly sick, and was prostrate a couple of days, before I could get out. I think, however, that hunger cured me, if anything did, for when nearly famished I was able to travel. I was only sent to see if he was still at his old place, in force, or if he had skedaddled, and was only making a show of holding the position. I succeeded in getting the desired information, and in the darkest part of the night, got out of his camp again, and made for Gen. Hazen's camp, near Readyville. On the way, I stopped at a house near the Readyville and Woodbury road, very much fatigued, and also exceedingly ill, and was waiting till the people got me some breakfast.

While laying before the fire, I heard a rapid firing on the Woodbury road, and on going to the door, I saw nine men of the Third Indiana cavalry, fighting with more than thirty rebels. They were only three hundred yards off, and I had no time to get closer, so I stepped behind a tree, and commenced firing, with a Spencer rifle.

The Johnnies held the Indianans very close for two or three minutes, and at one time I thought they would all be captured—there appearing no hope for them against such odds. I was still unobserved by either party, and I therefore was enabled to use my rifle expeditiously, and accurately. The Johnnies did not discover where the cross fire came from, but when they found bullets coming so rapidly, from another quarter, they wheeled round, and fled in a hurry, several of them being badly hurt, as I discovered from the way they rode. When the rebels left, the Indiana boys put out for camp, taking with them several articles I could see them pick up, although I could not ascertain what they were, from where I was located.

The fight being over, I swallowed my breakfast in a hurry, and took to the woods, fearing unpleasant consequences, and was soon in Gen. Hazen's camp.

Chapter 23

Scout to Woodbury

When I got back to Murfreesboro it was necessary to know how many rebels were at Woodbury, and I went from General Rosecrans, under the direction of Captain Swaine, chief of scouts. I left our lines at Readyville, and went a mile or more, when I got an old woman to hide me in her house in a back room, where I slept till the moon went down; and then taking up a branch of Stone River, I slipped into the rebel lines without raising the slightest alarm. It was only about seven miles by the high road, but it was more than ten by way of the creek to my point of destination. I kept constantly in the creek bottom, until I was nearly opposite Woodbury, when I struck off to the hills which surround the town, and from which a full view could be had.

I got to a good position on a hill, but could not see all that was going on. I waited till day light, in the hope that I could then see plainer; but I was disappointed in that, and at once resolved to change my quarters to another hill. To do this, I had to go down into a valley and walk across it, and then ascend the other elevation, in plain view of the reserve picket. I had a small glass, and was so near them that I could see the lint on their coats very distinctly, and I discovered they were eyeing me closely. I walked quickly out into the road, took a position, and began to walk a beat, as though I was standing sentinel. Presently a spruce looking old farmer came walking along, and supposing himself inside the pickets, he moved carelessly, and did not stop till the second "Halt," and an unmistakable motion of my gun claimed his attention. He seemed very much surprised to see a guard there, saying: "Nobody stopped me here yesterday."

"Well," said I, "I belong to a regiment which just came in last night, and the officer of the guard put me on this beat and told me to stop all persons going into the town unless they had proper papers." He at once showed me a pass from John Morgan's provost marshal, and I told him he was all right, and could go on. He was highly tickled at the eulogies I bestowed upon him, and before I let him go I managed to draw from him all that he had seen in Morgan's camp on the day before.

When he left, I told him it was probable that I might be relieved before he came back, but that he would find our camp just over the hill there, and pointed in an opposite direction from that I intended to go. I then resumed my walk upon the beat for a minute or two, when I affected to see something suspicious on the hill, which I started to go to, and raising my gun as though I intended to fire, I aimed at a fancied object; then lowering my piece, I pushed rapidly up, while the pickets watched me intently.

When on the top of the hill, I stopped again, and looked intently in the direction of the picket, and then passed around the summit with my carbine raised, as though I expected to see the object every instant; till, in a few minutes I turned the point of the hill, so they could see me no more, when I ran along the side for about half a mile; then climbing nearly to the top, I doubled my track and ran back, till nearly opposite the picket again; then getting down on my hands and knees, I crawled up the hill cautiously, and concealed myself in a hollow log which lay on the top.

I was now enabled to see the rebels in part of their encampment, and everything that passed, either on the Readyville road, or in Woodbury. It was very early in the morning of a tolerably cold day when I got in the log, and by night I was nearly frozen. During the day, I heard something running on the dry leaves outside, and I immediately prepared for a defence, thinking, perhaps, it might be a man who had seen me secrete myself. Suddenly, however, it sprung lightly upon the log and dropped itself through the opening right over my face; it was a coon, but it saw the place was occupied, and politely withdrew. Possibly I was intruding myself into its quarters, but as it did not wait to demand any apologies, I offered none. It was large and fat, and would have made a famous roast; but I had to lay still, for my neighbours on the hill were vigilant, and had they seen me for a second, they would have been after me with a sharp stick, which they would have applied without mercy.

That night I left my log, and took the back track for Readyville. I went across the country till I had passed the last of their picket fires, of which there appeared to be several lines, these being formed by Morgan's men, who was conscripting every man he could find. I passed very close to some of the posts—so near that I could hear the men talking in a low tone. At one place I chased two soldiers out of an old log house, who were inside talking to some females. As soon as I discovered they were in there, I secreted myself behind the chimney, and began "peeping" through the cracks. The fellows seemed to be on very friendly terms with the old man and his three daughters, the latter being very pretty, and at that time, putting on their sweetest smiles. I felt a little anxious to change places with the Johnnies about that time; or, if I had felt entirely assured that they would not have became "unlawful," I would have been content to talk to the odd girl; but that I knew was an impossibility, and I dismissed the idea.

On the table sat a wooden tray filled with cakes, a few of which I knew would do me an immense amount of good at that time, for I was hungry; and I determined, if possible, to have my fill. I, therefore, scrutinized the yard and out-buildings to satisfy myself there were no other men there, and glanced around to see if any picket fires were in that section; and finding all was right, I walked off a few steps, and fired off my gun. The Johnnies jumped out of the house, and as they did so, I screamed: "Run, boys, run; the Yankees are on us!" and away they went, as fast as their legs could carry them. I fired one shot at them as they appeared in the yard, when the women commenced shrieking fearfully, supposing themselves surrounded by those horrid Yankees—the terror of all the chivalry of the South, male and female. I was so near the rebel pickets that I dare not remain long for fear I would get myself into "business," so I put out for the low ground, and at three o'clock the next morning was once more in our lines, where I slept till daylight; after which I proceeded toward Murfreesboro.

When within about six miles of that town, I was walking along the high-road, inside our lines, when I saw a party of eight or ten men coming down from toward Murfreesboro. Thinking they were our own soldiers, I trudged along, confidently expecting a friendly chat when we met; but when they got nearer me, I discovered they were partly dressed in gray. I, however, still could not think they were other than Yankees—perhaps a detail of scouts on some breakneck expedition—and I was still expecting a friendly confab, when I noticed that they stealthily raised their guns. That was enough for me, for I knew that they could not mistake my character, as I was in full uniform, and under arms; and I sprang through the cedar brake as fresh as if I had just started out after a long rest; the sight of an enemy in one's rear generally has a magical effect on the gait even of a wearied man, and certainly it materially accelerated mine.

Running through the densest part of the brake, where they could not follow me on horseback, I felt confident of escape, as they could not see me before I saw them. I heard them crashing through the bushes only for a short time, when I stopped, after a mile heat in the cedars, exhausted. They were now no longer in hearing, and I, therefore, rested myself awhile, and then took a route through the brake, that I knew would bring me out at old Jack Dill's, within four miles of Murfreesboro. Jack was a fair specimen of a backwoods Tennessee Union man; large, sun-browned, and muscular—honest and patriotic. He invited me into the house with a hearty welcome, and told me of a brush he had had with the rebels the day before; and while the old man was recounting his adventures, his pretty daughter Jennie set me out a nice dinner, with fresh butter and new buttermilk, hot biscuits, and venison steak; and who could not enjoy a story under such circumstances?

The rebels had thought to surprise him in his house, and drag him off to the army; but old Jack was roused by the barking of a faithful dog, and took to the brake near his house; and in pursuing him, the rebels exposed themselves to his unerring rifle, and went back unsuccessful—minus one of their men.

On returning to the house they vowed vengeance to his daughter; she told them to go and make their threats to her father himself; but they didn't go. Old Jack was very proud of his gun—a long, full-stocked rifle. Patting it affectionately, he said:

"You see she is so old and is worn so thin, that when I push a bullet down her, she strains and swells out her sides, like a snake swallowin' a toad; but, by hokey, I can knock the spots out of a secesh yet."

From Dill's I took the main road to town, and in an hour I was at headquarters making my report.

CHAPTER 24

Gen. Stanley's Great Raid

The next duty I was on was when Gen. D. S. Stanley, chief of cavalry, made his dashing raid on the rebel camps near Middleton, Tennessee. It was a brilliant affair, and managed with consummate skill. Leaving Camp Stanley late in the evening, about the last of March, or first of April, 1863, he led a heavy column of cavalry down upon the camps in the vicinity of Middleton; the march being conducted in the night, the darkness and dust so impenetrable that a man could scarcely see his file-leader; indeed, the general had to station guides all along the route, at cross-roads, to prevent some of the columns from taking the wrong way. The Fourth Regular Cavalry had the lead, their advance-guard consisting of about twenty men, who behaved most gallantly, driving in the rebel pickets, and throwing the first camp into confusion, by an impetuous charge, entering it simultaneously with the flying pickets themselves.

The rebels being taken by surprise, leaped from their beds or blankets, without coats, pants or hats,—some, even, without drawers. Our men cut and hacked away as they advanced, until the rebels discovered that their assailants were but a handful of men, when they rallied, and drove the regulars out of camp, with a withering fire which caused our boys to suffer severely. But that was only for a moment; Gen. Stanley was almost immediately upon the enemy with his heavy column, and he swept everything before him, by one grand, irresistible, overwhelming charge. On and over the terror-stricken rebels, rode Stanley's daring men with their flashing blades; and the Spartan band of regulars, being thus relieved from bearing the whole burden of rebel fire, rallied again and dashed headlong into the thickest of the battle. On and on they sped, and so the first camp was carried, and the second brigade, under the gallant Col. Eli Long, rushed upon the foe, the ground fairly trembling beneath the mighty host of maddened horses, while the air was filled with the clash of steel, the rattle of sabres, the hurried fire of the enemy, the shouts of the victors, the hoarse commands of officers choked with dust, and the groans and shrieks of the wounded and the dying. Woe to the man, be he friend or foe, who fell on that field amid that impetuous charge. He sank only to be trodden under foot and crushed to death.

On rolled another wing of the command under Gen. John Turchin, sweeping over all opposition, till it was suddenly fired upon from a third camp. But, even here, there was scarcely a momentary check. The doughty general raised himself in his stirrups, and shouted:

"Now, boys, ve makes von more scharge"—

And before the sound of his voice had died away, the column was sweeping pell-mell through the camp, among the tents and shanties of the enemy. Frightened beyond measure, the rebels almost ceased to fight, but threw down their arms, and thought only of escape. Our men rushed madly on, after resistance had ceased, until recalled by the bugle sound; after which they returned in triumph to Murfreesboro, leading with them five hundred of the rebels as prisoners of war.

Every regiment—the 7th Pennsylvania, the 4th Regulars, the 4th Michigan, the 4th Ohio, and 3rd Indiana—all seemed to be in their element that morning; and each member of those regiments must ever regard as a proud day in their history, that one on which they charged and cleared the rebel camps at Middleton. It was a glorious victory to them, and a withering defeat to the enemy.

The scene after the fight surpasses all description. The ground was strewn with arms and accoutrements—guns, pistols, sabres, cartridge-boxes, belts, blankets, quilts, coverlets, torn tents, riddled with balls, cooking utensils, filled with food, mess pans, smoking hot, containing cow-peas and bacon; dead and dying men—some of them cleft, with the deadly sabre, from crown to neck—wounded unfortunates staggering about,—some supplicating for mercy, and others begging to be relieved of their tortures by death—some with bodies so hoof-beaten as almost to defy recognition—these were the sights which met our gaze on every side, and startled and sickened the hardiest soldier, as he gazed at the result of his morning's work.

Here and there one of our brave boys had succumbed to the enemy's fire—but they were fortunately few—and these engaged our earliest attention; and while we were attending to these, the rebel infantry, encamped two miles away, having been aroused by the fighting, came upon us at a double-quick; but our worthy general was not to be caught napping; and, having accomplished his object, he recalled his men, mounted them, and returned in triumph to Murfreesboro; but not until the enemy's quarters—winter quarters at that—were committed to the flames; and with them were burned thousands of small arms, while hundreds of horses were killed, and as many saddles destroyed. This raid resulted in almost the complete destruction of the famous 8th Confederate Cavalry, which bore the brunt of our heavy charge. Hundreds of the bodies of men belonging to that command lay scattered over the field; while many more graced our triumph by being led away as captives. Our loss was small in numbers, but no man who fell there, could have been well-spared, as each was a hero—almost a host. We carried off our dead and wounded; not a strap or buckle fell into the hands of the enemy, when they returned again to their old haunts. We shot every horse that fell into our hands—even some of our own that broke down on the march'

In this fight, I had little in the way of personal adventure, of an unusual character—perhaps not so much as occurred to hundreds of others on that day. One fellow fired a load of buck shot through the right knee of my pants, but in return, I worked a new button hole in his coat, with my rifle. Colonel Long sent me with an order to Major Dobb, who was in command of the 4th Ohio; and I "lit out," amid the dust, smoke, confusion and clatter, in search of the major, but succeeded in running up to the wrong crowd, and did not discover my mistake till within fifty yards of the rebels themselves. I had reached the end of a lane which ran around a ten acre field, and come out into another that ran from a house, through a cedar brake; and coming to this last lane, I turned down it to a party of soldiers I saw close by. Our men were all covered with dust, and almost as grey as the rebels; and when I saw them, I hailed, but they refused to answer me. I hailed them again, thinking still that they were our men, and this time rode out from behind the fence, in full view of their lines, so that they could see my accoutrements; and instantly a volley from the cedar brake greeted me; and after discharging their pieces, five of the men nearest, charged out after me.

I was riding a very pretty little mare that I had taken from them, when we charged the first camp—my own horse having fallen headlong in the fight, and as I had no time to ascertain the cause, I seized the one I was then on, and saddling her in haste, mounted her—and she ran past the end of the lane I had come down, and then up into the other, so that I was nearly hemmed in; but I wheeled instantly, and dashing back again, gained the end of the lane I wanted to follow, about thirty feet ahead of them. My mare was as fleet as a deer, and I left them so fast that they soon ceased to pursue; but halting, they kept up a steady fire across the field, while I ran around three sides of it, and until I was out of their sight behind the friendly cedars. I at last found the regiment in another part of the field, up to their eyes in a fight, and delivered Colonel Long's order to the major and then retired to the company ranks. It was my first attempt at playing *aide-de-camp*, and I readily reached the conclusion that as an occupation, it was not calculated to prolong the natural term of a man's life.

After my return to Murfreesburro, I went to Harpeth Shoals, on special service. Van Dorn was then foraging in that region; and the country was overrun with marauders. I went about leisurely, and called on all the famous guerrillas in that section, at their homes. They were chiefly De Morse's men, and I spent ten days rambling about with them, scouting the country daily, from Indian Creek to Harpeth Shoals, and back to some of the many little streams which flow past into the Tennessee. I was disguised as a Texas Ranger, and was violently secesh, of course; and in this character I was stopping at the house of a notorious guerrilla, named Tom Couch. I grew patriotic during our interview, and boasted of the prowess of the Rangers, and expressed my opinion of those who favoured the Yankee cause, in no very flattering terms; extolled the devotion of those who proved faithful to the South, and abused the black hearted Abolitionists of the North, till I got old Tom's "Southern heart" thoroughly "fired," and he could no longer retain himself, and he spoke unreservedly:

"The people of this section have always stood true to the South, sir; we can never be conquered; *never!* NEVER! NEVER! This is Dixie, and a Yankee has never *dared* to put his foot on these hills, although we are only sixteen miles from Nashville. If we should even catch one here we would hang him instantly. They dare not give us a chance, but keep far enough from us. They never can take this rough country; our hills are all free from them, thank God!"

Old Tom lived on Pond Creek, and there was a Tennessean, an officer in our army, with whom I was personally acquainted, whose family were next neighbours to him; and I told him that I was on secret service for Gen. Polk, and that I was authorized to give five hundred dollars for the capture of that officer—Dave Knight—and his delivery to me on the spot; and he was delighted to know that the general was after the Lincolnites with such earnestness, and promised me every assistance in his power. He told me that Gen. R. B. Mitchell had arrested a great many men and women, too, and confined them in the penitentiary at Nashville, to be sent South, or punished as was thought best; and Couch told me very confidentially that Dave Knight's wife was to be arrested and taken South, to be held for retaliation, along with many others. This was news to me, and I asked him if I could *afford any assistance*, and told him if I could, it should be cheerfully given. He then told me that the duty had been committed to De Morse's men, and that about three hundred of them had crossed Harpeth River, and encamped on Dog Creek. Telling him that I would go down to their camp, I jumped on my horse, and put out. I had been in that region the day before, but of that Couch knew nothing; and I was aware that there was a high, steep ridge, that I could travel a mile or so on, and see everything on Dog Creek. I reached the hill, and, sure enough, there were the camp fires of the Johnnies.

After dark I went up the country again, and warned Mrs. Knight of her danger, caught her a horse, and took her to Nashville for safety; and this I had barely time to do, as the rebels were ahead of us, picketing every avenue of escape for several miles around, in order to catch as many Union people as possible; but had not yet visited her house. She was a very brave woman, and buckled on her navy revolver without hesitation, and when within a few hundred yards of the rebel pickets she showed me a by-road, which she said she knew perfectly, and that it would take us through the hills to Nashville without going on the Charlotte Pike; and this path we followed, and reached our place of destination about twelve o'clock, in the midst of a terrible storm.

Returning to Murfreesboro, I found orders to report for duty in Ohio, and I left camp on the 3rd of June, 1863, and arrived in Columbus on the 10th of the same month.

CHAPTER 25

After John Morgan in Ohio

My mission to Ohio was a purely military one; but I had only one personal adventure, and that was in connection with the Morgan invasion. When the famous and fugacious John was making his raid, I happened to be at my home in Highland County; and as the rebels passed within fifteen miles or less of Hillsboro, of course, I sallied out to see what big things I could do. Everybody and his son were after him, and why shouldn't I go? Mrs. John A. Smith, a patriotic lady in Hillsboro, kindly furnished me a spirited little pony to ride, and in company with several of the young men of the town, I started for the scene of action, supposed to be near Sardinia. When we had passed Mowrytown some distance, we found where the rebels had thrown the fences down, as if to accommodate mounted skirmishers, though it might have been to favour their horse-thieves, but which of these things I do not pretend to say; but this put us on the alert for straggling parties of the enemy.

Sure enough, not far from Sardinia, after passing a large body of timber, I espied a number of men, about three hundred yards off; two of them standing in the road, talking to a man in his shirt sleeves, while several others were in the timber. It seemed as though all of them had horses, but some were dismounted. Well, it was a suspicious case. Eyeing them for some moments, I made up my mind that it was a rebel picket post, and so I raised my gun, and blazed away. How they jumped! but they started right toward me. At this time the citizens who accompanied me were a little way behind; so throwing up my hand as a signal for them to stop, I turned my horse, and started back on the jump, attempting to reload my gun at the same time. The motion with the gun gave the pony a scare, and with a couple of quick side-jumps to the right, the little rascal flounced me out of the terrapin-shell saddle, and the next thing I knew, he was making his best time back to Mowrytown. Jumping to my feet, badly "stove up" by the fall, I called out to my comrades: "Stop that horse! stop that horse!" but the more I hallooed, the faster they went, until in a short time they were lost in a cloud of dust.

Thinking the Johnnies were still coming, I bounced over a fence, and off through the woods, to a house, and borrowed a two year old colt to ride back Mowrytown; and at the next place I came to, I borrowed a saddle of a woman, telling about the scrape; and in due course of time I arrived at Mowrytown, where I found my pony, but my comrades, having succeeded in stopping their runaway horses, had again pushed on after Morgan. Hurrying after them, I overtook them at Sardinia, and learned that I had fired on—a lot of citizens; and that, too, within fifteen miles of home. We scoured around till long after night, when I and comrade named McKee, succeeded in overhauling them.

A couple of darkies, belonging to Morgan's command, with horses and equipments, had wandered into a settlement of blacks in that neighbourhood, and some of the citizens thought they had been sent as spies, and that some of Morgan's men intended to make a raid on the village and carry off some of our black folks into slavery. Not caring to have our black folks reduced to servitude, we started after the supposed spies, and after a sharp chase, caught one of them, and got both horses; and the other afterward came in and gave himself up. The horses belonged to Captain Thorpe, of Morgan's command; and one contraband was his servant.

We thought we ought to be allowed to keep the horses, which were fine Kentucky stock, and so stated our claims to Governor Todd; but that honest functionary failed to get the matter before his obtuse official optics in that light, and so we had to give them up. McKee couldn't see the profit of the chase; but I told him that must consist in glory; that the credit of fighting to save the Union, was pay enough for any man. He admitted that point, but said, dolefully, that it was *poor pay*. After all my running around, however, I did not get to see a Morgan man, except in the distance. It will hardly be necessary for me, after this story, to say that mine was not the party that captured John and his command; but we were willing souls, nevertheless.

CHAPTER 26

Off to the Hiawasse in Search of Steamboats

Having performed the duties assigned me in Ohio, to the satisfaction of my superiors, I was ordered back to my regiment, and on the 7th of August, 1863, I reached it, and reported for duty. I found the boys in high glee over the Tullahoma campaign, which had just been gloriously terminated; but at the same time all were busily engaged in making preparations for the advance on Chattanooga.

I was at once detailed as a scout, to act under Gen. Stanley, chief of cavalry; and under his directions I went up the mouth of the Hiawasse River, while the army lay at Winchester. The rebels had some steamboats, which Gen. Stanley was anxious to get possession of, before they had time to destroy them; and he knew they were laid up somewhere along the river, between Chattanooga and Knoxville.

Starting out afoot from Winchester, I took a road in the direction of Cowan's station, and followed it for several miles; and when I thought I was far enough up the country, I crossed over on Little Coon, and passed near where I had been taken prisoner the year before. On Little Coon I stopped one day to get dinner, and was not long in discovering that the people were "secesh," and thinking it might be of some advantage, I concluded to secede for a few minutes too. As soon as I had established the belief that I was a rebel, I inquired for old man Terry, and asking if he was still alive; and the woman of the house answered that he was well, adding that he was her brother-in-law.

"Let me see; didn't he catch a Yank at his house about a year ago?" I asked, carelessly.

"Why, no," she said, "he didn't catch him himself, but he sent word to Colonel Stearns' men, who were camped close by, and they went over to Terry's house and got him."

"Did you see him, yourself?" I asked.

"No, I didn't see him, for I was a milkin' when they rid by, but the gals all seed him; they said he was a savage lookin' feller."

"Pretty hard case," I remarked.

"Yes, the gals sed he had a real "hang-dog" face."

"How did he behave himself?" I asked, for I now remembered the place perfectly well; and also of having seen a couple of buxom girls standing in the door, who enjoyed my fallen condition hugely, and laughed at my being tied on the horse.

"Why, the gals said he was a sassin' of our men as far as they could hear him; and the gals said ef they had a been in our men's place, they wouldn't a took it, for he was as black as any nigger."

"Did the Yanks ever find out that Terry had him captured?"

"Oh, la, yes; and they sent a power of their men thar, and took off nigh about everything the old man had."

"What did our men do with the Yank?" I asked.

"Why, we did hear," said the garrulous old woman, "that our men took him off down to Chattanooga and hung him; and then we heard again he had got away from our folks; ever since Terry heard that, he's been mighty oneasy, for the Yankee soldiers that took his truck away, said our men couldn't keep him, and if ever he got back, he would be jest as sure to kill Terry as ever he set eyes on him again."

"Well, I reckon the old man would rather he hadn't have had anything to do with it, in that case," said I.

"Oh, la, yes; for the Yankees liked to have broke him up for it; they driv off every cow and every hoss creetur he had, besides he's afeared the feller will git back some time."

"How far does Terry live from here?" I asked.

"About two miles and a half," she replied, adding in the same breath; "La, it would be mighty bad ef he should happen to git killed off and leave all them pore little children without anybody to take keer of them."

"Do you remember that Yankee's name?" I inquired.

"Well now, soldier, I did hear it, but raily I have forgot it; gals—Virginny—does ary one of you gals remember what that Yankee's name was that got taken over at your uncle Terry's, last spring, a year?"

"Virginny" now appeared in the door of the sitting room, and no sooner did her eyes light on me, than she gave a sort of terrified start, and retreated to the innermost recesses of the kitchen.

"La, gal, why don't you tell a body!" said the old woman; "Virginny, do you hear?"

Thinking I would see a little fun with the old woman, I said, solemnly: "Madam, I am the man."

"La, bless my soul an' body," she said, and sinking into a chair, she burst into tears.

"Don't be alarmed, madam," I said, "I don't intend to hurt any of you; and you may tell Terry for me, that he need not be afraid that I will hurt him, although he caused me six long months of imprisonment, and I nearly lost my life by it. You can tell him that I will spare him for his children's sake, and not because I do not think he deserves punishment. Tell him to stay at home and take care of his children, and I will see that the Federal soldiers do not molest him."

The young ladies made their appearance at this time, to soothe their mother's agitated feelings, when I bowed to them, and with excessive politeness said:

"Ladies, I wish you a very good day."

Finding that there was a considerable force of rebel cavalry on Little Coon, I concluded to go back on top of Cumberland mountain, and travel along it until I got out of danger of falling in with them, and I accordingly changed my route.

Not a great distance from Cowan's station I was going down through a long, narrow, and very crooked pass in the mountains, when I heard ahead of me a great deal of chopping. None of our men were in the country, so I concluded, as there were too many axes going for the chopping to be citizens, that the enemy must be up to some "dirt." Clambering to the top of the mountain, I followed along it till I came to a projecting spur, which I followed out and presently stood on the edge of the bluff, almost over the cause of my alarm. At the foot of the mountain was a party of rebel cavalry—home guards, as I supposed—who had about fifty darkeys chopping down trees across the road, thus effectually blockading the gap at a place where it could not possibly have been seen until turning this short spur that projected into it. It didn't require much soldier sense to tell what that meant.

They were fixing a trap for our cavalry, or some other body of troops that they were perhaps expecting to pass that way. The thing had been well considered, and would have been a serious obstacle to anybody of troops, at that point, for a few sharpshooters deployed along the sides of the mountain could have then defended it against a large force. There were about twenty rebs guarding, and fifty darkeys at work. The Johnnies were scattered about among the choppers, urging them to their utmost exertions; while right at the end of the spur were their pickets—three in number—but I was now behind them. After surveying the condition of things, I saw that I was perfectly safe from them, for the sides of the mountain were very steep, and I could kill every white man there before they could climb up to me; and as for the blacks I did not fear them. They had not fallen many trees up to that time, so I thought I would file my objections to the whole proceedings, and selecting a good position behind a huge, craggy rock, I picked out the most prominent man, who was a portly fellow, in his shirt sleeves, riding about among the darkeys, whip in hand. He rode a fine, light gray horse, and was a splendid target.

He was about four hundred yards off and "downhill," and knowing that a "downhill" shot is apt to carry over, I pulled right on the horse's rump, as he was going straight from me. A puff of wind raised the smoke from my rifle, and I could see when the ball struck. It must have missed the man entirely, for the horse reared almost straight on his hind feet, and gave a terrific bound, which tumbled the rider out of his little old "terrapin shell" saddle upon the rocks so violently, that he must have been severely injured, for some of the negroes ran to him and helped him up, while several of the white men caught and brought back his horse, which was bleeding profusely from a point in the middle of the right hip. While this was going on, everything was in the highest state of excitement. The soldiers ran together, looking in every direction, in the wildest alarm, and every darkey ceased chopping instanter. One fellow, who was much closer to me than the others, bawled out at the top of his voice:

"Who fired that shot?" But he received no answer save the echo of his own voice; but determined to know, he raised himself in his stirrups, and bawled louder than ever:

"I say, who fired that shot?" but he still received no answer.

By this time my gun was loaded, and I took good aim at him, and fired, just as the word "shot," "shot," "shot," was echoing among the hills; and without waiting to see the effect of it, I sprang upon the rock, in plain view of them, and began to order an imaginary comrade to "run back and tell the regiment to 'hurry up,'" and then turning, with my gun loaded, I sent another shot whizzing among them, at the same time ordering some skirmishers to come down from the opposite ridge, and close in with the rebels, accompanying my speech with a violent gesture, as though pointing right at my supposed friends. I then fired a third shot and raised a loud "hurrah boys, and we'll surround 'em," when the Johnnies fled in the wildest confusion, hardly taking time to help their comrade to mount his wounded horse, which was almost unmanageable.

As the cavalry was speeding down the pass, and the darkeys were shuffling after them, I ran back up the mountain, and descending it, climbed the opposite side and kept on my journey, following the top of the ridge the rest of that day, and also on the following night and the next day until about nine o'clock in the morning, when I was suddenly startled by the sound of horses' feet coming behind me. I stepped behind a tree and listened, and discovered there were several of them.

A spur put out ahead of me from the main mountain, and I thought if I would run out on this, they could not see me, and would ride past. The timber was very open, and I was disappointed; for, in coming around a bend in the road, they observed me just as I arrived on the brink of the mountain, which was very steep. There was about a dozen of them, well-mounted; and they came upon me as fast as they could run through the timber; but they necessarily had to run up to the place where I turned off to gain the top of the spur, to follow me, and this gave me time, and I improved it by scrambling down the steep sides of the mountain, very fast; but I presently came to the top of a cliff, about three hundred feet high. This looked like a bad chance for escape, but, turning along it to the right a few hundred yards, I again found a place where I could descend some distance; but was then once more stopped by another cliff which projected out like a shelf.

Below the right-hand end of this cliff, a huge hickory tree was growing, and its shaggy top just reared itself above the shelf on which I stood, the trunk being about eight feet from the edge of the cliff. There was no time to lose, for already I could hear my pursuers clattering over the rocks above me, and once I heard a sabre jingle; therefore, running to this tree, I looked over the giddy height, then slung my rifle across my back, and leaped out headforemost with all my strength. I grasped the body of the tree with my arms and succeeded in holding, although the weight of my heavy accoutrements almost jerked me loose again. Sliding rapidly down the tree, I lit on another bench in the mountain, from which I made my way down into the bottom of a deep ravine.

When I got down to the foot of the tree, my clothes were badly torn, and great slivers of hickory-bark were sticking through them

"There was no time to lose, for already I could hear my pursuers clattering over the rocks above me, and once I heard a sabre jingle; therefore, running to this tree, I looked over the giddy height, then slung my rifle across my back, and leaped out headforemost with all my strength."

in every direction. My hands, arms, and breast were bleeding profusely from several wounds, cut by the rough bark. When I struck the tree the breath was nearly knocked out of me, and it required all my strength to hold on. I was now safe, and never saw nor heard of my pursuers again. I followed this, to the bottom of the mountain, and just as I got to the mouth of the ravine, I saw a man raise his head up from behind a log, so that I could just see the rim of his hat.

Supposing, of course, that no one but a bushwhacker would be caught in such a suspicious place, I pulled down on him with my Spencer-rifle and took a careful aim right on the centre of his hat. I was not more than fifty yards from him, and was just closing my finger on the trigger, when I saw a woman's bonnet raise up beside the hat, when I noiselessly lowered my gun, and stepped behind a tree and waited to see what this could mean. Presently, a fine, athletic man raised up, as straight as an Indian; though he seemed to be labouring under the most intense excitement. His hands were clenched, and his eyes were fiercely glaring with passion.

The next moment, a woman stood up beside him, and set a little bucket on the log, at the same time weeping bitterly; and as she strove to restrain her tears with her little white hands, her bonnet fell back upon her shoulders, and exposed a beautiful face of dazzling fairness, and features of perfect regularity. The man raised his right arm in an excited manner, and, instinctively, I clutched my trusty rifle, and the thought flashed through my mind, "if you strike that woman you are a dead man;" but, before I had time to give it utterance, the woman, throwing her arms around his neck, fell sobbing upon his breast, locked in his loving embrace. Great God! how deeply my soul was agitated as I remembered how nearly I had come to rashly firing, when the man first raised his head from behind the log! What an escape from shedding innocent blood, and bringing a blighting, overwhelming sorrow upon that beautiful woman, who was now clinging so affectionately to him! While I was thanking God that I had not fired, the woman's voice broke upon the still mountain solitude, and she save utterance to her frantic grief:

"Oh, Henry, my love, you must not, shall not go. They shall not take you from me, and drag you away to fight a people who have never harmed us; perhaps to be killed, or thrown into a cruel prison! No, no, you shall not go; I will feed you here in these mountains as long as I live, before they shall take you from me," and she nestled closer to his manly bosom.

Raising his hand again, as before, he replied: "Suzie, Suzie, I will not leave you; no, I will not leave you; but I will hover around our home, and watch over you and Willie as long as I can; but if the worst comes, and I must fight, so help me God! I will fight for the Union of the States as long as God lets me live." His voice, although choked with emotion, was deep and manly, and sounded through the solemn stillness of the forest until the awakening echoes of the great mountain caught up and repeated the "patriot's vow."

His loud, excited tones seemed to rouse a little child, that had been sleeping behind the log; for pretty soon I heard "mamma," in childish accents, and then a little, bright-eyed, chubby-faced boy, about three years old, ran out from the log, and caught his father with infantile affection; and winding his little arms around his parent's knees, he looked wonderingly up at his mother, and said, in a pleading voice: "O, papa, don't go!" The man laid one hand fondly on the child's head, and the woman raised herself from his breast, and taking the child up, said to it: "Willie, kiss papa."

As the child stretched out its arms, and put up its little mouth, I stepped from behind my tree, and advanced toward the group. At first they were startled at my footsteps; but when they saw it was a Yankee soldier, they were reassured, and gave me a cordial greeting. The man then told his wife it was time for her to go home; and bidding her to "take the soldier to the house, and give him his dinner," he turned up in the mountain gorge, while the woman led the way out into the valley to her dwelling—a neat little log house; and in a few minutes she laid before me an elegant supper; and although it was the last of August, the heat was scarcely felt in this cool retreat.

I have forgotten this man's name; but, if I remember rightly, he was a son-in-law of old man Russell, who lived in the head of Dorin's Cove, where I staid that night. He had been compelled to hide out in the Cumberland mountains for several months, to keep from being dragged away to the rebel army; and his wife told me how she had to take his provisions to him, and that even her steps were watched. That she often carried his food to the mountains in the back of her bonnet, and laid it in some place where he could find it; but that sometimes he would be two or three days without food.

I was once almost tempted to ask the old man Russell if he didn't want another son-in-law, for he had a second good looking daughter, whose admiration for Yankee soldiers was only exceeded by her devotion to the cause of the Union. She complained bitterly that their part

"His voice, although choked with emotion, was deep and manly and sounded through the solemn stillness of the forest, until the awakening echoes of the great mountain caught them up and repeated the Patriot's vow."

of the confederacy was not able to afford her a pair of shoes, although she had offered fabulous prices in gold for them, and I, therefore, promised to bring her a pair the next time I came that way; but this is not the only promise of this sort that I have left unfulfilled in that country. Of course, at the time they would be made, I would mean it; but I seldom saw the parties a second time.

After passing a pleasant night at Russell's, I made my way to Bridgeport just as Gen. Lytle arrived there. He had some important service to do in scouting through the mountains after some bushwhackers, who were harbouring in the country from Little Coon up to Widow's Creek. Having been in that region before, I knew just where their hiding-places were, and, of course, we soon routed them, and I pursued my tedious journey in quest of steamboats. While scouting for Lytle, I was introduced to Gen. Sheridan, who was then a division commander; and he then told me that the service was for him, and that he would see me handsomely rewarded; but the general, I suppose, has never had a chance to fulfil his promise, for I have not seen him since.

However, it makes no difference, for soldiering, like virtue, must be its own reward. The rebels having taken all the water craft to their side of the Tennessee, General Lytle made a detail of men to dig out a canoe in which I could cross the river. It was made in the night, and early next morning I put it to a good use, running over to the island opposite Bridgeport, and catching a Johnny for the general.

The reprobate, not knowing that the Yankees had a boat of their own, had paddled defiantly down the river before Lytle's headquarters, when the general said: "Pike, go and fetch that man to me; can't you catch him in your boat?"

"You just watch the race if you don't believe it," said I, and away I went, and soon had the Johnny standing in the presence of the general; and like all the rest of the secesh clan that ever I caught, he exhibited the most abject humility.

CHAPTER 27

After Steamboats Again

Leaving Bridgeport, I once more was off on my steamboat exploits, and as I was crossing over Walden's Ridge, about fifteen miles below Chattanooga, at the top of the "cut off" I heard a very long, and loud scream, or more like an exultant yell. Thinking of nothing but bushwhackers in that locality, I "treed" instanter, and stood with my gun at a "ready" to fire on any suspicious object. Soon the sound of a horse's feet, coming almost toward me at a run, roused me to renewed vigilance, that I might get the first shot; for I made sure it was some rebel cavalryman. I was not kept long in suspense, however, for in a few seconds a magnificent horse bounded into view, mounted by a beautiful young woman, who was riding "man fashion," or, as the little boys say, "astraddle," utterly unconscious of observation.

Her long, brown hair was streaming in the wind, as she was without bonnet or shawl; her short sleeves and low necked dress, left a beautiful neck, plump arms, and a voluptuous bosom, partially, but not immodestly exposed, while the skirts of her dress being drawn up by her peculiar position on the horse, exposed limbs perfect in development, and of dazzling whiteness. She was singing, in a clear musical voice, snatches of some song which she occasionally stopped, to give a shrill whoop at a half wild cow she was driving before her, at a fearful rate through the thick timber. She rode her horse with a fearless grace, and a firm hand, guiding the spirited beast by a rope halter turned into a loop around his nose. She soon vanished from my view, to the left, following a well beaten trail which I was confident must lead to a house. So quick did she come and go, and so beautiful did she appear, galloping away through the green woods with such a happy gracefulness, and fearless air, that I could almost imagine that I had seen a real nymph of the mountain.

227

"She was singing, in a clear, musical voice, snatches of some song, which she occasionally stopped, to give a shrill whoop at a half-wild cow she was driving before her, at a fearful rate, through the thick timber."

Following the trail she took, in about a mile and a half I came to a house. A panting horse, of magnificent proportions, had just been turned loose in the yard to graze, and I instantly recognized it as the one I had seen careering so proudly through the woods with the fair rider. I at once went to the house, and at the door was welcomed by a pleasant looking matron, who invited me in, and treated me with much civility, as soon as I told her that I was a Yankee soldier and wanted lodgings. Soon after, the fair equestrienne came in with a bucket of milk on her head, "nigger" fashion. There was no poetry in that, it is true; but she was really very pretty, and as she placed her bucket of milk on the table, the elder woman addressed her:

"Eliza, here is one of *our* soldiers come to see us at last."

Then turning to me, she said:

"Stranger, what is your name?"

I told her my name and regiment, and asked what her husband's name was, and judge of my astonishment when she answered "Bob White"—he whose patriotic efforts in behalf of the Union, were a theme of admiration far and wide, in that section of Tennessee. He was what the rebels called a Yankee bushwhacker, and was a great terror to small bands of rebel cavalry who had to pass any where through the Sequatchie Valley. He had about thirty men under his command, and sometimes could raise as many as sixty, on special occasions.

While my hostess was preparing supper for me, she and her sister were full of curiosity to hear from the north, and especially what our expectations were in regard to the rebellion, and our hopes of maintaining the Federal Union. I gave them the best satisfaction I could, consistent with duty; and they were much pleased to hear that our numbers were so great, and our army so well appointed, and expressed the most encouraging hopes of our final success.

Supper dispatched, I went to bed, as I was very tired. I had just got well off on a scout to the land of dreams, when I was aroused by the sound of horse's feet. The reader will understand that on these trips I never undressed, and sometimes slept with all my accoutrements on. The two women had put me to sleep in a room separated from theirs by an entry; and at the sound of horses, I sprang out of bed and bounded noiselessly to the door and tried to open it quietly; but lo! it refused to open; and on stooping down and peering through the crack between the door and the wall of the cabin, I found it was fastened by a strong chain, which was passed through a hole in the door, and around the facing between the logs, and was locked on the outside with a strong padlock. There was no time to lose, so turning to the window—a single sash, held in by two nails,—I broke the latter off, and laying the sash on the bed, I jumped out on the ground and ran behind the house as the men hailed the inmates at the front door; and peering around the corner, I discovered a large squad of rebel cavalry; Mrs. White answered them at the door.

"Was there a man passed here about dark, afoot and dressed in Yankee uniform?" they inquired.

"Why, yes, there was," said Mrs. White; "he stopped at my house, and got his supper, about dark, and as soon as he was done his supper, he left to go the 'cut off' way to Chattanooga."

"Who did he say he was?" was next asked.

"Why, he told us that he was a Georgian, and that he was going home."

"You say he went the 'cut off?'" said the officer, interrogatively.

"Well, now, I don't know for certain that he did go that way, but he told us that he was going by the '*suck*,' and, of course, he would be obliged to go the 'cut off' from here."

With a polite "Thank you, madam," the officer rode away, followed by his men, some twenty in number. Waiting to see the last of them disappear over the brow of the mountain, I crept back through the window and replaced the sash again, and was soon sound asleep. Nothing more occurred to rouse me till midnight, except that one of the women opened the door cautiously, and looked in, I suppose to see if I had been disturbed. I feigned to be asleep, and she closed the door and locked it again. Near midnight, I was again awakened by the sound of approaching horses; and as they halted at the door, I again removed the sash, and jumped out of the window. This party hallooed and Mrs. White asked: "Who's there?" and one of the men answered: "Mack."

I peeped around the log house again, and discovered eight resolute men, all well mounted, and armed to the teeth.

"Is that you, McArthur," said the woman.

"Yes, come out a minute," he said.

She hastily dressed herself, and throwing a shawl around her shoulders, went fearlessly out to see them. Their conversation was carried on in a low tone—so low that I could only catch a few words now and then.

"We heard of him down at the foot of the mountain," they said presently, in a louder tone, as if to end an argument; "Well, tell him to come out here, we want to see him."

"Oh, boys, let him sleep," pleaded the woman, "for I know he's tired; besides, I am certain he is a Yankee, for he was talking to me and Eliza, until he got so sleepy he couldn't hold his head up."

"Oh, there are a heap of men claims to be Yankees now," said Mack; "tell him to come out."

I now walked out to them, for I was certain they were some of Bob White's men. They were very frank, telling me their suspicions; but I had no trouble in satisfying them that I was all right, and a friend; and then, after inquiring of the woman whose company of rebels it was that had passed, the whole party rode on in the same course they had gone.

This party had a good looking young woman with them, who was piloting them over in the valley, to catch a notorious guerrilla, by the name of Pickett; and the men vowed they would hang him if they caught him. When they had gone away, I asked Mrs. White what made her lock me up in the room:

"Why, you know," she said, "in these troublesome times a body never knows who they can trust; and you know we had no men folks about the house, for Bob is gone over the river, on a scout for Gen. Rosecrans."

I now got along without further disturbance till next morning, when, after a good breakfast I resumed my journey, feeling very grateful to my generous hostess, who refused pay almost indignantly.

At the mouth of Soddy Creek is a place called Penny's Ford. The rebels were picketing on the south bank, and on the north lived a very old woman, named Martin, in a house entirely alone. Some of our prisoners, who had escaped from the south side of the river, crossed over at Penny's Ford, and the old lady had fed and secreted them, till they got strong enough to travel. Of this the Johnnies had heard, and to show their *chivalry*, I suppose; would amuse themselves by shooting at her. It was at long range—about nine hundred yards—and to have hit her, would have been mere accident. Every time she showed herself, they would vault a ball over, more, probably, to see the old woman run, than with any other object in view. She stood out nobly, for several days; but, finally, one time, while sitting in the door of the cabin, knitting, a ball struck the door facing, about four inches from her head, and this so frightened her, that she closed her house, and went to live with the old man Penny, where I heard her relate her story.

I went down the river bank, and halloed across the stream, to the

Johnnies, who immediately answered; and one of them, bolder than the rest, ran down to the edge of the water and asked what I would have. Without answering his question, I fired a shot at him, from my rifle, putting my sight up to eight hundred yards. It seemed a long time going, but presently the rebel stooped to dodge the whistling bullet, and I saw that I had over shot; so I aimed again, and discharged my piece, holding this time full on his head. He was standing erect when I did so, holding to a willow bush, with his left hand, and his gun in his right; and after a long time the ball reached its destination, and I had the satisfaction to see the Johnny tumble headlong on the sand, his gun flying several steps from him. I then had it hot and heavy for a while. His company, concealed by the woods on their side, made the balls rattle on the bank where I was, cutting the trees up cruelly, but doing no further harm, for I was hidden in a deep ravine where I was perfectly safe; and from which I could fire on them leisurely, whenever I got a good "sight."

After having my own fun with them for an hour, I took the road to Colonel Cliffs', on Sail Creek. He was a colonel in our army, and I was told, at one time was on General Burnside's staff. He was at that time away from home, on duty; but I was hospitably welcomed by his family. I stopped here for two or three different nights, on the last being hunted out by fifteen or twenty rebels; I fortunately, however, received notice of their coming before they got in sight of the house, and moved my quarters promptly.

While in that part of East Tennessee, I was fortunate enough to hear a real, heartfelt sermon, preached in favour of the Union; and the services were closed with an ardent prayer for the President of the United States, his advisers and counsellors; for Congress and the success and welfare of our armies in the field. There was no milk and water, nor soft solder about it; but it was a real old fashioned, upright, square-toed Union sermon. The preacher was an old, white-haired man, and his crowded congregation were, for most part, of venerable age. The meeting took place after night, and as there was danger of it being disturbed or broken up by straggling rebels, I was invited to be present. Every man was armed; and this meeting took place in a country where some men say there were no Union men!

From this neighbourhood I went to Chattanooga, which was now being invested by the army of the Cumberland. On the north side of the river was Colonel Wilder's famous brigade, and I reported to the colonel, and was sent by him with a dispatch to Bridgeport, where

General Rosecrans was supposed to be. I had walked since morning from above the mouth of Soddy Creek, a distance of thirty-three miles; and the same evening I started from the camp before Chattanooga, to Bridgeport, a distance of fifty-four miles, over a rough mountain road. At Bridgeport I found the general, and reported to him, and learned that the cavalry were a long way in the advance of the infantry, and that it would be impossible for me to overtake them; so, after receiving orders to "knock around loose," I put out over Raccoon mountains.

These mountains are the lower or southern range of the Allagheny mountains, and are high, steep and rugged, while lower down the country, they are called the Sand mountains. It is a ridge of a very irregular shape, and extends from a point where the Tennessee forces its way between it and Walden's Ridge, on the north side, to Blountville, Alabama. Its many recesses and deep forests have always made it a constant place of resort for bushwhackers. In it is the celebrated Nickajack cave, one of the largest in the United States. Over this mountain a part of the army had already toiled, and the road was strewn with wrecks of wagons, splintered wheels, broken harness, crippled horses left to die, and poor broken down men who were unable to keep up in the impetuous march that would allow of no delay. On they were toiling over the mountain toward Trenton, in the hope of overtaking their commands at that place; but I fear it was a vain hope for some of them, for they seemed very much exhausted.

Trenton is a small town in Georgia, and is the county seat of Dade County. It is situated in a fine valley between Raccoon mountain on the west, and Lookout mountain on the east; and the valley is watered by Lookout River, and several creeks. Here General Reynolds was encamped, and I slept there till morning, and then pushed on for the advance. I passed Sheridan's division, and the next was General Negley's command. Learning from General Lytle, of Sheridan's division, that General Negley was to lead the advance, I concluded to report to him for duty, and found his division encamped on Lookout River, in the valley between Lookout and Raccoon mountains, at the foot of Johnson's Crook, a narrow and meandering defile that led up the precipitous sides of Lookout mountain to Stevens' Gap.

It was a terrible undertaking to put an army up into that gap, as a handful of men might defend it against a host. It was held by Wharton, with a division of cavalry, mostly Texans; and Negley was to scale the mountain with his division and take possession of it. General Stanley was hovering on the enemy's communications far down in Georgia, in the neighbourhood of Alpine, Broomtown, and other points, almost, and at one particular time, quite in rear of Lafayette; and at the same time, Gen. McCook, with his corps, was toiling over Lookout at Niels' gap, between the cavalry and Thomas' corps and Stevens' gap, his being the right of our infantry. Reynolds crossed over with his division, if I remember rightly, at Doherty's gap, while Crittenden's corps moved up the railroad around the north end of the mountain, and General Wagner continued to threaten Chattanooga in front with Wilder's and Minty's brigades of cavalry. Chattanooga lays in the wide end of a Y, formed by Lookout on the west, and Pigeon mountains on the east; the north end of Lookout rising about one mile and a half from the west side of the town.

Pigeon mountain is a spur of Lookout, which projects itself over to the Tennessee, about four miles east of Chattanooga. For about one half its length, it retains the name of Pigeon mountain; while the north end of it is called Missionary Ridge. In the Pigeon mountains are three gaps, besides the one right at its junction with Lookout, the most southern of which is Bluebird Gap, the middle being called Dug Gap, while the most northern is known McCowan's Gap; and the intermediate valley between these two mountains is named Ma-clamore's Cove. It is, at Dug Gap, about nine miles wide, running to a point at the south end, while at the north end, at Chattanooga, it is about five and a half or six miles in width. The railroads running from Chattanooga to Knoxville and to Atlanta, pass through Mission Ridge at the north end; after which one keeps on up the Tennessee to Knoxville, while the other turns down on the east side of the ridge to Lafayette, the first point to which the enemy was compelled to retreat, and which is situated about six miles east of Dug Gap, bearing a little south.

The reader will bear in mind that I knew nothing of the plan of the campaign, beyond what was developed on the field, and what was patent to all. I had passed in two days from our left, near Cottonport, Tenn., where I saw a part of Minty's brigade, of the 2nd Division of cavalry, down to Chattanooga, where was Colonel Wilder's famous brigade, with General Wagner, and some force of infantry and artillery, busily engaged in shelling the place; thence to Bridgeport, where the commanding general was with a few troops, just preparing to go to Trenton, then already in the hands of Reynolds' division; I also passed the 33rd Ohio on the opposite side of the river, and saw Crittenden's troops ferrying the stream about the mouth of Battle Creek; and from the top of Raccoon beheld the most of our centre and right encamped opposite the respective gaps, where they were to scale Lookout Mountain, and from whence they were to be hurled like an avalanche down, down from the giddy heights of that cloud-capped range in resistless columns into the valley, where they were to deploy in line, and sweep across upon the unprotected flank of the enemy, who were then in full retreat.

The plan was certainly projected by a master mind, and had it been properly executed, would have proven the death blow of Bragg's army. After having gained his object, it *seemed* to be the intention of the general to draw his men in quietly, and without bloodshed, into the fortifications around Chattanooga; and had the entire command been properly handled, nothing could have transpired to thwart the design.

General Negley began his ascent of the mountain early in the morning of the 9th of September, I believe, and by noon had his whole command camped on top of the mountain, and here he sent me out to reconnoitre. It was a pretty long and dangerous tramp, but I made it safely, and discovered that Wharton's command was on the opposite side of the gap. The advance of the division was soon followed by the balance of Thomas' corps, and at the same time Gen. McCook was scaling the heights at Neil's Gap, twelve miles below, and Crittenden's was moving round and over the north end of the mountain, while Gen. Stanley was threatening La Fayette from Broom Town Valley, almost in rear of the rebel army. On the 10th the army was fairly bivouacked in the clouds, on the top of Lookout, which is very broad; in some places being four miles wide. Heavy clouds are constantly hanging over and lapping down upon the summit, and if it be a damp day, the top and sides are completely enveloped in the lower clouds. It is not, however, a high mountain, being only fourteen hundred and sixty feet perpendicular, I believe, above the level of the Tennessee river.

I believe we rested a day on top, and scouted out the summit, while in the afternoon Col. Stoughton with his regiment went down the gap to drive back the enemy, in order that our engineers could repair the road. I was sent out again toward night, and passing through Stoughton's command and the rebel skirmish line at a dead run under fire of both sides, I gained unharmed the top of a very high spur of Lookout. I was aided in this by the dust raised by the rebel cavalry, while the fire was going on, and by the darkness after the fight was over. I clambered over cliffs during the night, to gain the top, over which, next morning, I could not look without getting on my hands and knees. It was risky work, but it was in a good cause, and was of advantage to the service, which was enough.

At the first crowing of the chickens I was on my feet, waiting for light enough to see the valley below. The view extended all over Maclamore's Cove, and is one of the finest landscapes I ever beheld. Far to the left—perhaps sixteen or eighteen miles—could be seen the heights around Chattanooga, while directly in front was the range called Pigeon mountain, together with McCowan's Gap, Dug Gap, and Bluebird Gap—all clearly revealed by the light in the east. I had a splendid signal glass with which I could see very minute objects in Dug Gap, and I discovered that it was well defended by rifle pits and artillery—two batteries being distinctly visible; while in rear of the gap rose a hill that thoroughly overlooked it, and on the crown of this hill was an extensive earthwork, running its whole length, and I counted within it sixteen guns. On the side of this hill I could see a great many brush shanties, with light, fleecy smoke rising above them, thus clearly indicating that they were occupied.

From the top of the mountain I descended by a very precipitous and rocky ravine, the bed of which in the wet season was a roaring torrent, but now shrunk to a little babbling brook, that found its source on the top of the mountain at some boggy springs I had passed. At the foot of the mountain I discovered a house nearly at the mouth of the gorge. I made for it, at first, with the intention of quizzing the people, to see what they knew about the enemy's movements; but when within a few hundred yards of the place, I discovered a man sitting in the hall or porch, which lay between the wings. He was leaning back, with his right leg thrown over his left knee, while opposite him, and leaning against the other wall, sat a beautiful young lady. I knew he was a Texan by his free and easy lounging style.

Running noiselessly in the bed of the ravine, under the cover of its bank, I stepped up out of it behind a huge tree, about sixty yards from the house. Now, if I shot the fellow there, the woman would take conniptions, so I thought I would scare him out, and then shoot him. I stepped back into the ravine, and hid myself, and then fired a shot in the air, and it had the desired effect. He rose, and walking out to where his horse was tied, picked up his bridle, and began to put it on. I got up behind my tree again, and shouted: "Don't you put that bridle on that horse!" He paid no attention, but as he approached the animal's head I recognized him. His name was Bowers, and he had served with me in Texas. Leisurely he adjusted his bridle, even taking time to buckle the throat-latch. Again I shouted to him to "put down that bridle," but he paid no attention to me whatever.

As he stepped to the side of his horse, I ordered him not to mount; but slowly, and without the least excitement, he swung himself into the saddle. I wanted to save him, and so I cried "Halt!" loud enough to be heard half a mile; but he turned quietly from me, as if to show his contempt for danger, and I was compelled to fire on him, or allow him to escape to the enemy, and report. Taking a good rest, against a tree, I fired full on his back; and we were in such close proximity, that I could see the hole made by the bullet. His horse sprang off into the woods, but he clung to the saddle, although in the agonies of death.

Hearing others on the opposite side of the house, I at once began to play officer, and deploy skirmishers at "double quick;" and so completely successful was the ruse, that the rebels did not await the development of my plans, but skedaddled as rapidly as possible in the direction of Dug Gap, taking with them the wounded man, whom they left at the next house, where he died.

I missed getting his horse, which was a very fine one; as the intelligent animal, with his dying rider, ran steadily along with the horses rode by the others for over a mile, and until they reached the house indicated, where the wounded man was left to die. I was at the house an hour afterward, but found that the horse and equipments had been taken off, and that an ambulance had also been sent for the body, and that it, too, had been conveyed to the rebel camp.

After this, I hurried over to the road by which our army was to descend the rugged mountain, and found Col. Stoughton's regiment in the valley, where they had skirmished the night before, and then prepared my report for the general, in writing, and forwarded it to him from the skirmish lines.

CHAPTER 28

Battles of Dug Gap and Chickamauga

We had not been skirmishing more than an hour, before the army began to pour down the steep, rocky, dusty road. On they came, winding to and fro, down the serpentine road, now enveloped in clouds of fog, then emerging from the mist, their bright arms and brass trappings glittering in the sun; now submerged beneath a dense cloud of dust, they would again remain hidden for a time, till it was lifted off by a passing breeze, and again the mighty army, as if by magic, would stand out in full view before the beholder, martialing for the fray below.

The rebels beheld them in terror, and they fled in confusion in the direction of Dug Gap, leaving only a small cavalry force to skirmish with our advance. Gen. Negley then pushed a regiment or two out on the road, as far as Davis' cross roads, to feel the enemy, and ascertain his position. The reconnoissance was gallantly conducted—the rebels disputing every foot of the ground; and as soon as the reconnoitring party began to fall back, they hung upon its rear, until we gained our old position, at the foot of Lookout Mountain.

Early in the morning the general advanced with his whole division upon Dug Gap, when the enemy's cavalry again disputed our progress, and the same ground was once more fought over, till we reached Davis' cross roads, at which place our army rested for an hour. The men being refreshed, pushed on again for the gap, where the rebels were found in overwhelming force. An engagement at once ensued, which lasted for several hours; but as the enemy was soon strongly re-enforced, Gen. Negley ordered a retreat, and his men were drawn off, slowly and quietly, one brigade at a time. Slowly the artillery was taken off the field, occasionally halting to throw a few shells into the advancing enemy, till finally we regained our old camp.

Our loss in this skirmish was about forty killed, wounded and missing; but we lost nothing else; so leisurely were our forces withdrawn, that the teamsters stopped to reload a wagon which was upset. The 19th Illinois, and 18th Ohio Infantry, did noble work in this encounter, fighting at short range, and repelling two or three handsome charges. They killed thirty odd men, at a single volley, near the gap, all of whom were left on the ground by the enemy.

As we were proceeding toward the gap, I was frequently far in advance of the column, looking out for ambuscades, and performing the other delicate duties which devolve upon a scout; and while reconnoitring, I discovered a stone wall to the left of the road, which looked like a splendid place of concealment, and I accordingly jumped behind a tree and scrutinized it carefully, to discover signs of the enemy, but for some time I was unsuccessful in my efforts. Presently, however, I saw a man partly concealed by a clump of willow bushes, at a little distance from the wall; and observing him closely, I saw that he was motioning with his hand, as if to keep men down.

In a little while I discovered another, and then another, until I saw four men crowded under the bushes, when I opened on them with a few shots from my Spencer rifle, and as they were but about two hundred yards off, I soon made it too hot for them, and they hustled down to the wall, when I lit out to report the ambuscade to General Negley. He immediately ran down a section of artillery into a position that commanded the wall, and then led a charge in person over the intervening hill, and down upon the rebels, who delivered a hasty volley before our men raised the hill, and then fled in confusion, leaving several of their dead on the field. I chased one horse, with his rider, over a bluff bank, about twenty feet high, into a creek; the rider sticking to his animal all the time, till he struck the water.

The horse mired in the quicksand, and the man was compelled to leap from his back, and leaving him, gain the opposite bank, where he leaped a fence and disappeared in a corn field, while I was loading my gun. I then took the fellow's horse and saddle, and broke his gun and threw it over the fence after him, though I am not aware that he even stopped to think about it, much less to gather up the pieces.

Our artillery was managed with great precision, and the enemy must have lost heavily. We occupied the ground next day, and we had a considerable number of their dead to bury—the bodies having been abandoned on the field.

"I opened on them with a few shots from my Spencer rifle, and, as they were but about two hundred yards off, I soon made it too hot for them, and they hustled down to the wall, when I 'lit out,' to report the ambuscade to General Negley."

A rather amusing incident occurred just before the engagement. I was on a scout up to the very foot of the gap. The rebels, for a long time, refused to show themselves, seemingly to draw us up into the gap, while they held another force that I had reported, ready to pounce upon our flank, when their masked batteries in front were to riddle our column with shells. Near the gap lived a venerable widow, who had two beautiful daughters, all Union, or at least so they told me, when they thought me a *rebel*. Her house stood within easy shooting distance of the rebel sharp-shooters, and inside their picket line, although they had no post on the road. I went into the house, and told the old lady that I was very tired, and wanted to rest awhile, and she told me to lay down on a bed, but I preferred the floor. I was only doing this in order to see what I could find out; and I had been there but a little while before her little son ran up to the door and said:

"Mother, mother, here comes an officer."

I rolled over carelessly and asked where he was, and he told me in a whisper that he was out at the end of the house. I was after him in a moment, and I jumped over the fence between him and his men, and walked stealthily along behind him, until raising a little hill, he spied our pickets, about half a mile off. He quickly concealed himself in a fence corner, till he had taken a good look, then turning to go back to his own lines, he met me, with my rifle raised and my finger on the trigger.

"Just take the road before me, sir," was all I said.

He raised his hat very politely, bowed low, and remarked:

"Why, really, sir, I am very much surprised to see you here."

Finding himself a prisoner, he took it with the best possible grace. I allowed him to keep his sword until he reached the post, and let him walk by me. He was such a perfect gentleman that I hated to turn him over to the hard fate of a prisoner; but my good manners never saved *me* when I was in *their* hands, and so I consoled myself with the thought that he might have had better luck. After I reached camp with him, I ascertained that he was a second lieutenant on Colonel Corbyn's staff.

From some unaccountable cause, the army was detained in the vicinity of Stevens' Gap for five days; and during this interval, the enemy was reinforced by Longstreet's corps, and other troops from Virginia.

During the morning of Saturday, the 19th of September, little was done except closing up the trains, and getting them over the mountains, before it was discovered that Bragg was attempting to flank us on the left, when instantly our army was put in motion toward Chattanooga, to prevent him from accomplishing his object. Our march was soon discovered by the rebels; and now began the greatest foot race the eye of man ever beheld. My duty often caused me to ascend high points of the ridges and hills, to see how the enemy were progressing; and wherever they moved, the tell-tale dust would disclose their operations. Each army was intent on gaining their fortified ground near Chattanooga; and we had an even start, and if anything, the shortest road—our army marching down on the west, and that of the rebels on the east side of the Chickamauga River.

Great heavy clouds of dust hovered in the air, revealing the course of each army, through its entire length; as well as disclosing the movements of the smallest bodies of troops.

About ten o'clock in the morning, Bragg discovered it would be impossible to flank our army, and prevent us from gaining the desired point, and immediately began to close with us. His artillery thundering on our flank, gave notice of his intentions; and General Rosecrans accepted the challenge, and soon our batteries were answering shot for shot, and shell for shell.

This artillery duelling was very destructive for some time, particularly on our right, where the guns thundered with uninterrupted fury. Guns were dismounted, caissons blown up, wheels splintered into fragments, horses torn almost limb from limb, while the mangled gunners lay scattered in all directions and wounded in every manner. Still the work of death went on. When the heavy shot failed to strike among the gunners, it was only to pass among the boughs over their heads, and by splintering them, carry additional destructive elements into the ranks of the supporting infantry. The shells, shrieking through the air, burst among the men, and horses, sweeping down whole squads of the one, or teams of the other; and when a caisson was struck, the effect was terrific. The vehicles would be shattered to fragments, while the powder of the shells would ignite, and throw them in every direction, bursting as they went, and sweeping scores of heroes to untimely graves.

While this was transpiring on our right, the heavens appeared rent by a sudden crash, and the earth trembled beneath a steady, rolling sound. The battle had began on the left, and the musketry had opened in dreadful earnest. Peal, on peal, the sound was borne to us, on the right, by the wind, almost drowning the heavy roar of artillery near us, which of itself was well nigh deafening.

Rapidly General Rosecrans shifted his troops from right to left, to meet each new assault of the enemy. Each time, as the roll of musketry raised above the sound of the cannon, it told us that the battle continued to surge to the left, and that the lines of our army were being stretched to the greatest possible length. Stout hearts began to feel a misgiving, and brave men watched the enemy with wary eye.

McCook's corps, on the right, held its ground. Battery after battery of rebel guns had been silenced, but they had not yet given back, keeping continually closed in upon our men; and in the evening they charged upon Van Cleve's division, pouring in three terrible volleys; but they met with a fearfully bloody repulse, and were compelled to fall back to their old position, after which they soon began to retire from the field they had occupied.

Concentration on our left was the next movement in order; for on that wing the battle was yet raging with unabated fury. Our lines were faced to the East, with the right to the South, and left to the North; and in rear of this were our teams, and non-combatants; and these were hurried off in hot haste, toward Chattanooga.

Sunday morning, the 20th, revealed to us the enemy in a new and stronger position, and much nearer to Chattanooga; and at daylight, the contest burst forth again with redoubled fury, on our devoted left—General Thomas this time taking the offensive. For hours the contest continued, without decided advantage to either side, when suddenly the enemy concentrated in tremendous force, on McCook's corps, rushing impetuously forward and driving it flying from the field. God grant that I may never again behold such a scene as I there witnessed. The assaulting column charged to within sixty or eighty paces of our lines, under a fire so murderous that they halted, and wavered, at least five minutes, when, reinforced by another line, the foremost men were literally driven upon us.

At this critical juncture, our ammunition failed, and the enemy was upon us, pouring in withering volleys upon our almost defenceless ranks, so that no troops in the world could have withstood the assault. Panic stricken, the corps rushed to the rear; but they were true men, and heroic leaders were there to rally them, and thrice they formed, and turned upon the advancing foe, who forbore to pursue so determined an enemy. Most heroically did the fugitives cluster around their battle flags, with tear-streaming eyes, fondly caressing the banner they were now helpless to defend.

Here and there a gallant colour sergeant would halt and raise aloft the ensign of liberty, shouting out to the men not to abandon their colours—not to give up the flag—to remember Stone River, and not to yield, for our troops would yet be victorious, as they had been on many a hotly-contested field. Here and there an officer pleaded frantically with the flying men; now using words of hope and encouragement, or orders and menaces, as either were demanded by different characters; calling upon them to remember their country and her honour, to reflect that they were Americans, and must fight to save their banners.

They could not resist the appeal, and three times they rallied and waited determinedly for the enemy; each time in better order and determination, standing ever in well-formed ranks, until ordered to take up a new position. Nobly did those colour sergeants discharge their duty that day, not one of whom yielded his banner, till he had first fallen beneath it. Captain Johnson, now colonel of the 13th Indiana Cavalry, contributed much toward rallying the men; as did also Captain Rockhold, of the 15th Pennsylvania Cavalry, and many other officers both of the staff and line, whose names I do not now remember. The last man I recollect seeing on the field—and I was one of the last to leave it—was Major-General McCook, riding even into the thickest of the enemy's fire; and it indeed appears miraculous that he escaped with his life.

While this was transpiring on the right, the thunder of battle still reached us from the left. What befell the fugitives now, I know not; for, thinking they were taking a wrong road, I left them, and going immediately to the left, reported to Gen. Thomas for duty. He held his ground firmly until toward night, when, during a lull in the battle, he began to retreat. His corps was in the best of spirits, and full of confidence in the general.

Deliberately every man supplied himself with a rail—whole brigades facing to a fence for this purpose—each fellow shouldering the biggest one he could lay hands on; and then the brigade would reform and resume its march, the men laughing and joking each other over their heavy work as gayly as if they had not seen thousands of their comrades fall that day. The enemy pursued, but the corps with its portable breastworks was invincible. Halting in a noted gap in Mission Ridge, the troops put their rails to use by raising, in a few moments, an effective barricade. The general made his headquarters just in the rear of the gap, and under short artillery range of the enemy; and he maintained his position, in spite of the rebel shells, which were whistling over his head for hours together; and here he was reinforced by two or three brigades of Granger's reserves, and renewed the contest.

On the 21st our line reached around the crest of Mission Ridge, something like a half-moon, with the bow toward the enemy. The battle, however, was not severe on that day, as the rebels appeared disconcerted. They made several feints upon our lines, but our general was always ready for them, and checked them at every point. At times their artillery would send shell after shell shrieking over our heads, as if determined to frighten us from our position; but they fired badly, as if they had lost their best gunners in the late terrible contest. At times they would pour volley after volley of musketry upon us, but did but little damage, as the balls either struck our barricade, or flew harmlessly over us, and clattered among the trees.

Their next ruse was to try to turn our right with their cavalry, and it was said that Forrest led the charge in person. Scaling the end of the ridge, where our right was posted, they charged furiously upon the 21st Ohio Infantry, and were handsomely repulsed, without loss to our side; while eight of the enemy fell dead within a few feet of our lines. The 21st followed them with an uninterrupted fire from their revolving rifles, until the rebels were driven from the hill. This was about the closing demonstration; and that night the army quietly retreated to Chattanooga, leaving their camp fires burning brightly, to deceive the rebels.

General Thomas did not leave the field until all had gone from the scene of the late conflict, but the rear guard; and about midnight, part of General Stanley's force appeared upon the ground, to cover the retreat. While the battle had been raging, they had been hotly engaged with the enemy's cavalry under Forrest, and had also been beset with infantry. Their duty had been of a most dangerous nature, and was performed in a gallant manner. Our cavalry lost many daring men during the battle, chiefly, however, in killed and wounded, though they lost a few in prisoners.

Noiselessly the army marched to Chattanooga that night. Not a sound was to be heard save the rumbling of the trains or the occasional word of command. When the troops reached the town the whole aspect was changed. Uncertainty was now certainty. We had gained the point for which the campaign was planned and for which we had struggled so hard. Determination could be read in every face. Filing along the breastworks the rebels had constructed, men and officers took off their coats and engaged in strengthening their position.

I now saw General Rosecrans for the first time since I left Bridgeport. He looked wearied and care-worn, but hopeful and determined. I spoke to him and wanted to burn the jail where I had been confined with Andrews' men, but he refused permission, telling me it would raise too much smoke over the town and impede the aim of the artillery. His countenance did not change till he rode along by some familiar regiments and saw their thinned ranks and worn looks, when he appeared ready to burst into tears; at that moment the men raised a hearty cheer for "Rosecrans," when he rallied from his momentary weakness, and galloped to the outworks in front of the town. I heard many a man and officer swear that the town should never be surrendered—and it never was; while the rebel columns were soon hurled, flying back for Mission Ridge, a position they deemed impregnable.

Chapter 29

Personal Adventures During the Battle

I had some personal adventures during the battle, two or three of which may be worth the reader's perusal. The lamented General Lytle, who was killed in the second day's fight at Chickamauga, held the right of McCook's corps most of the day; and when he saw the evening closing in on him he sent me down to the left, telling me to post on a mile or so and see how everything stood, saying that the service was of the utmost importance. This was on the 19th.

Away I went, first down in front of the rebel lines, and in full view of them, till I saw they were preparing to advance, when, dashing across the open place, I came over to our own front. I turned down it to a long break in the line; I then followed the general direction of our front for half a mile, when I reached one of our own batteries which I found to be literally dismantled. The caissons were blown into fragments, the guns dismounted, and the gunners were scattered, dead and wounded, thick around it. Poor fellows! they had been stricken down at their posts, torn and mangled, by shell and grape.

I had no time to stop, as much depended on my diligence; perhaps I held the lives of many men in my hands. I rode on, some three-quarters of a mile further, still seeing no troops, when I turned back. I passed the dismantled battery again, and stopped a moment to see if I could identify it, when one of the wounded men feebly called out:

"Soldier, cover me up; cover me up; I am cold; oh! so cold."

The supplicatory tones were hard to resist, but I saw the enemy advancing, and hastened back to the general. As I reached our line again, I hailed a body of troops with:

"What brigade is this?"

"One of the wounded men feebly called out: 'Soldier, cover me up, cover me up; I am cold—O, so cold!'"

"Third brigade of Van Cleve's division," was the hurried response.

I had barely passed it when a double crash of musketry told me that they had closed in upon the advancing enemy. I now put my mare out to her best speed, to pass the next brigade; and in answer to my hail, they shouted: "second brigade of Van Cleve's division;" and I had hardly passed when a heavy volley of the enemy's musketry whistled over the heads of our men, and was immediately answered by the brigade.

The firing behind me was now both rapid and destructive. As I passed on, hailing the next command, I found it was the first brigade of Van Cleve's division, and as I had just reached the end of its line, it, too, joined in the furious contest, with a deafening crash of musketry. The firing, now, for a short time, was intense, and the work of death terrific; but the enemy gave way, and retired to their old position.

I reported to General Lytle the condition of things on his left, and as the enemy remained quiet for a little time, Van Cleve now closed up the gaps in the line. Before this change of position, however, I was again sent over toward the enemy, to see what they were doing; and I reached the creek in the thicket, and crept on my hands and knees until I got close enough to hear them talk.

"There, that's right," said one fellow.

"Hand me that glass," said another.

On raising up and looking through a fence, I saw they were turning a battery on General Lytle's headquarters; and at once, without heeding their shout to halt, I ran at my best speed for the foot-log over the creek. A few shots behind me had a wonderful effect in accelerating my pace, so that I never ran better than at that time. I sprang on my horse just as the Johnnies leaped out of the brush on the other side of the creek; but before they had time to fire I was off like a shot, for the hill. I at once dismounted, and leaping over the breastworks, was met by the general, who asked me what the rebels were about.

"They are," said I, "turning a battery so as to rake your position"— and I had hardly uttered the word "position," when a shell from it passed whistling between our heads. The shock caused by the current staggered the general about six feet back, and jarred me, creating a sensation such as would be produced by a stroke on the ear by a light board.

The same day, in the morning, I was passing our ammunition train, and saw on the right of it, a man sitting on a horse in an open field, scrutinizing the train closely, up and down, and around. He was in our uniform, and bareheaded, when I observed him, but I soon perceived that he held a white hat in his hand. I at once concluded that if he was a *Yankee* he had no business there; and if a *rebel* he had still less, so I "went for him," as the soldiers express it; that is, I went to kill him, if I could not take him prisoner. He saw me coming, and fled to a barn on the hill at some distance from us, and near a clump of timber.

I was about two hundred yards from the train, and could not follow directly after him, as the creek was wide, deep, and had high, steep banks; but some distance down was a ford, for which I made, and when I crossed it on the jump, I saw one of our lieutenant-colonels, a captain, and a coloured servant, watering their horses in the creek. I rode up on the hill about a hundred yards, and the barn was still about fifty yards from me, when about thirty rebels rode out from behind the building, and out of the woods, and fired a volley at me. I was not hurt, but convinced that I was too close to them, and wheeled and went back in a rather precipitate manner. The colonel heard the firing, and he and his party ran off down toward the train; but as I rode the best horse, I soon overtook them and reported the case to him. He was, fortunately, one of General McCook's staff. I told him that it was plainly the intention of the rebels to assault the train and blow it up; and this, five resolute men could have easily done, without danger to themselves.

I now went to the friendly shelter of a rail fence close by, and had a lively time with the rebs till the infantry got in sight, when they mounted their horses and left; and even then they could have destroyed the train had they known the true state of affairs; but every now and then I would fire a shot and give a yell, and I suppose they thought I had plenty of help close by.

On the second day, I was with Lytle's brigade until after the general was killed. He had sent me a long way out before the brigade skirmishers, to see for him if the enemy were coming. While on this service, I discovered an officer of the rebel army hid behind a bush that concealed him from our skirmishers; but I was about parallel with him, and of course, had a fair sight, and improved it. I fired at him three times, as fast as I could shoot a Spencer rifle; and the third bullet brought him down, his horse galloping away to a party of mounted men still further back in the timber. I hurried on in the woods, dodging from tree to tree, and from one hiding place to another, until I saw the enemy's skirmish line, which was advancing slowly, at the same time keeping well "dressed;" and instantly I was off to inform General

Lytle that they were coming.

On the line I saw a staff officer, to whom I gave my information, and who was going to the general, and he promised to report. I then took my place in the line of skirmishers, and as the rebel skirmishers came in sight, we made the fire so hot that they soon fell back to their ranks, while we, ourselves, were ordered into our breastworks.

As soon as we turned to retire to our breastworks, we were beset by a heavy fire from the enemy's columns; and one colonel made his men get down on all fours, and no doubt saved many a life by this manoeuvre.

For some reason, our first line of breastworks was abandoned after the delivery of the second volley; and as we took our position behind the second line, I placed myself behind a large chestnut tree, the top of which had been broken off by a storm, and near which I had tied my mare some time before. As I felt perfectly secure, while the rebels were coming I examined my ammunition, and laid it out on the ground by my side, and I found I had just thirty-three rounds.

When the rebels arrived within eighty yards, I began firing; and our men held them so closely there, that at one time they seemed on the point of breaking and flying from the field. As for myself, I aimed every shot at their belt-plates, and before they drove us, I had fired all my ammunition but two shots; and at that time I got a cartridge fast in my gun. A soldier was at that instant passing me, and I caught him by the leg, and without seeing who he was, I asked him for his ramrod. He jerked it out, and threw it almost directly in my face, which made me a little mad and caused me to look up, when I beheld our army flying in the utmost disorder down the hill on which they were posted. I knocked the cartridge hull out of my gun; and already the enemy were seizing prisoners, and clubbing their muskets on such as were stubborn enough to resist.

Hastily I fired my two remaining charges, almost in the faces of the advancing rebs, and I raised my gun to break it over a tree, when thoughts of prison hardships flashed across my mind, and I resolved to run for my life. The first part of the race was down hill, and I made good time. The air seemed literally full of flying bullets. I could hear them whistle close to my ear, down by my sides, and over my head; could hear them strike the ground behind me, and see them strike before me, while scores whistled, as it appeared to me, two hundred feet in the air. Far ahead I could see my comrades falling; and around me others, and yet others were biting the dust; and well I knew that the work of death was going on behind me also.

It was a terrible race, but I made it in safety, though I still feel the effects of the over-exertion in my chest. It appears, when I reflect upon it, almost miraculous that I escaped death.

As I had sent my rifle into Chattanooga, by Captain Rockwell, of the 15th Pennsylvania Cavalry, I carried a Springfield gun during the rest of the fight, but only got five shots. It was in the first part of this charge that General Lytle so gloriously fell—his body pierced with three bullets, and his sword dripping with the blood of the foe. When he saw his noble brigade break he drew his blade and rushed upon the enemy, but only to yield up his life, a precious sacrifice upon the altar of liberty, dying as he had lived, for his country.

This ended my adventures in this fearfully bloody struggle—one in which our men exhibited most heroic qualities, and which gained to us, in the end, the ground we fought for, though the cost was frightful; and it was soon after, as every reader knows, followed by stupendous results.

Long will I remember the proud look of defiance upon the face of every man when once within the fortifications at Chattanooga. As they were filing in the rebels reached the summit of Mission Ridge; and as they advanced, in full line of battle, they sent up loud shouts of victory, which were defiantly answered by our men, with cheer after cheer, as defiant and proud as ever. Soon the rebels opened, with shot and shell, upon every assailable point; but they were promptly answered, with accuracy, by our artillery, and they declined to assault us in our position, hoping to force a surrender through famine—a delusive phantom, as they soon discovered to their cost.

"When he saw his noble brigade break, he drew his blade and rushed upon the enemy, but only to yield up his life, a precious sacrifice, upon the altar of Liberty—dying, as he had lived, for his country."

CHAPTER 30

Wheeler Badly Whipped

At Chattanooga I was invited, by General Crook, to go with him up the Tennessee, as there was a prospect that Wheeler would make an attempt to get in our rear with his cavalry. Such a movement, on the part of the enemy, might well be viewed with trembling by every patriot; for, if our communications were once cut, or even if only broken three or four days, it would have compelled the surrender of the gallant army of the Cumberland, then hemmed in within the fortifications of Chattanooga, with only a single route for keeping supplies of ammunition and stores to stand a siege until reinforced.

On the 23rd and 24th of September, General Crook started, with the 2nd division of cavalry, to the vicinity of Washington, Tennessee, to counteract, or check the intended raid, if possible. When he arrived at Smith's Cross Roads, the general threw out pickets at every ford, for miles up and down the river; but at Cotton Port the enemy planted artillery and shelled our men back from the bank, and then commenced crossing. As reinforcements were not to be had, the general could not give Wheeler battle at that place; but collecting all his scattered bands, as rapidly as possible, he prepared to fall upon the rear of Wheeler's army. At the ford, the conflict was short and desperate; and, as soon as Wheeler gained the north bank of the river, he marched directly across the valley to the mountains, while General Crook pursued him rapidly. Our force, although too small to fight the whole force of the rebels, was still able to whip them on the raid, every time they came upon their rear.

Among the first who crossed the Tennessee, with Wheeler's command, was the rebel provost-marshal of Chattanooga, named William Ozier, and his object was to conscript men on the north side of the river. Major Matthews, of the 4th Ohio, had charge of the picket, and had given orders not to fire on any small parties coming over, but I had not heard the order. We had been picking them up, four or five at a time, and making them prisoners without firing a gun; and but for the fact that this party came over; and formed in line as they advanced, I suppose we should have continued to do so. I watched them closely, as they came toward us, and I thought I detected them drawing their guns for use, stealthily.

With the ring of Chickamauga fresh in my ears I may have been a little nervous; but be that as it may, without waiting for further developments, I raised my rifle and fired at the leader, killing him instantly while the next fellow caught a bullet in the temple: and then the firing became general, and the Johnnies, badly frightened, wheeled their horses and rushed them back to the shore of the river. The one who was shot in the head did not die. The ball struck the temple, and passed around under the skin, to the opposite one, where it came out—a fact which I learned from the farmer who took him out of the river. On the body of the provost-marshal was fourteen hundred dollars; but I took none of it. I laid him out decently, and handed him over to the citizens of the vicinity for identification.

Gen. Crook's force, at that time, did not exceed three thousand five hundred, while Wheeler had with him seven thousand; yet we whipped him at Cumberland mountain, on the Sequatchie River, at McMinnville, and saved Murfreesboro, and the railroad, and all our supplies; then again overtook him at Shelbyville, whipped him—then forced the fugacious rebel to a general engagement at Farmington, where he was whipped badly, taking all his cannon, a portion of his train, and five hundred prisoners; then we drove him from Pulaski, and overtook and defeated him at Sugar Creek, and sent him on the double quick over the Muscle shoals.

It was severe work; both parties displaying the most determined courage, frequently contending in hand-to-hand encounters; indeed, I saw rebels fighting with pistols when the carbines of our men would be thrust in their faces. I got a good many good shots on this raid, and had some narrow chances myself. On two occasions the rebels fired whole volleys at me, at short range, while I would be trying to ascertain their position for the general; and at Farmington, I was a target for three pieces of artillery, loaded with grape—there being not another man within cannon range. The grape struck around, over, and under me, but still did not touch either myself or horse. In the same fight a fuse shell struck immediately beneath my horse, but, although burning when it struck, it did not explode.

At a little log school-house, before we reached Farmington, the rebels made a very decided stand. I saw one fellow fighting from behind a tree, his position being secure from our men, who were unable to get at him on account of a fence which lay in front of him. I dismounted, and ran behind a little tree that was nearby, and, taking good aim, I shot him in the side, and he fell, a dead man. But such affairs happen on every battle field.

After Wheeler had been driven from Tennessee and Northern Alabama, the second division, consisting of Wilder's Mounted Infantry, went to Brownsboro, and was engaged in keeping the county clear of the enemy, and in protecting railroad works.

The amount of suffering among the citizens, resulting from this raid, was fearful. Everything eatable was seized by one or the other of the armies. The scenes witnessed called forth pity for the little children, who could not understand the nature of the calamity which had befallen them; and I also commiserated a portion of the women; but by far the larger number of the latter did not conduct themselves in a manner calculated to excite sympathy. They were vindictive, and seized every available occasion to manifest their ill nature. They were ever ready to drive their husbands and sons into the war, and they need not have expected much pity at our hands. Many, it is true, were always devotedly loyal—were ready to contribute to the success of the nation—but they did not constitute a majority.

While I was at Brownsboro, a dispatch came to Gen. Crook, by telegraph, directed to Gen. Sherman, with a request to forward it without delay. It was handed to me to carry to him, but none of us knew where he then was. Capt. Kennedy found an article in an old rebel paper which stated that he was at Corinth; but that was some time before, and we had no idea which way he was marching. Capt. Starr, of the 2nd Kentucky Cavalry, with a squadron of men, went with me to Whitesburgh, on the Tennessee, ten miles from Huntsville; and I there took a canoe and run down the river, it being about two o'clock at night when I started on my lonely ride.

About fifteen miles below Whitesburgh, I heard a noise, as if a party of men on the south bank were bailing out a ferry-boat; and, as I thought I would have time to pass it before it could be got ready to cross, I pushed on down. I could easily hear them coming as I proceeded, so that I paddled my very best; but on they came, faster and faster; I did my utmost, but still they gained on me; another stroke of their long sweeps, and they would be on my canoe. It was a critical time, but fortunately at this moment a man on the shore called out to them: "You all look as if you were going down the river; you don't look like you were coming here to me." I glanced over my shoulder, and there on the bank, at the edge of the water, sat the captain of a band of rebel cavalry; while just above him I could see forty or fifty men with their horses.

There were six men in the boat, whom I saw distinctly—two at the oars, one steering, and three standing gazing over the sides, at me. They were so close on my canoe at this time, that I raised my hand to catch the ferry-boat, in case she struck my little craft, to prevent her from dragging me under.

When the captain hailed, they headed a little more up stream, and she missed my canoe about the length of my paddle. As they passed by, I could see them watching me eagerly, but they said not a word; while I plied my paddle with all my strength, and was soon out of their sight amid the darkness. The gap I ran through between the boat and the company on shore, was not more than thirty yards wide. I could not possibly have passed it safely had I made the least possible noise with my boat; but I approached them so quietly, that the party on shore did not discover me until I was speeding past them.

A few miles above Decatur I was overtaken by daylight, and knowing very well that the river was well picketed by the rebels all the way to Tuscumbia, I did not try to travel, but pulled ashore under a steep bluff, and hid my canoe under some overhanging willows, and hid myself in a cleft in the rocks to sleep and rest till the next night. It was in the latter part of October—about the 26th or 27th, I believe—and I had rather a cold time of it, among the stones. During the day a company of rebel cavalry rode along the top of the bluff, just over my head, but they did not see me, and I rested well till dark, when I pushed out in the stream and resumed my journey. I passed Decatur while the lights in the houses were still burning, and as I rowed by the foot of the main street, a single shot was fired on the bank—the flash of the gun being toward me—though I did not know what they were shooting at, nor did I call to inquire.

In the neighbourhood of Lamb's Ferry, just at the head of Muscle Shoals, I laid down in the bottom of my boat to rest a little, as I was very tired and sleepy. How long I slept I do not know,—not more than an hour, I think—when I heard a chicken crow, and waking up, I found I was floating by a house on the bank. I picked up my oar and began to paddle leisurely on, too tired and sleepy to work hard, and in a short time I passed another house. It was dark, to be sure, but still I could see that it bore a striking resemblance to the first one. Two brothers, I thought, live on adjoining plantations; or perhaps an old man and one of his children, and have built houses alike. I still pulled on, but lo! in a short time I passed another just like the other two. This was unaccountable for a minute, but I remembered I had seen a big cottonwood tree on the bank at each of the other houses, and now I thought of it, they too were as the houses and fences—all, all exactly alike; what could it mean? Was I bewitched? I started directly across the river, to the opposite bank, resolved to leave a country where such sameness prevailed. It savoured too much of enchantment to suit me, so I would go elsewhere; but as I approached the channel, I discovered that I was in a big eddy, caused by an island on one side, and a sweeping curve in the bank on the other, and that I had been floating around in a circle—how long, I could not tell.

Shortly after I pulled ashore on an island, to pass another day, hiding my canoe under the overhanging boughs, which projected far out over the water, and lying down in my boat to sleep. After taking a long nap, I was awakened by a rattling in the chains of my boat, and raising up and peering over the gunwale, I espied a large, fat raccoon, reared up on his hind legs, playing with the loose end of the chain, as it dangled from the limb it was tied to. His look was astonishingly intelligent, and he enjoyed the sport till the swinging of the iron hit him on the nose, when he hustled off up the bank and was seen no more. Scarcely, however, was he away, before a mink came trotting down to the end of my boat, and cast an inquiring look into it; but one glance sufficed him, and he was off like a shot.

Nothing more occurred to disturb me, till I discovered a company of rebel cavalry on the north bank of the river. Nearly opposite where I lay; on that side, was a house; and as the cavalry approached it, I saw an old man bring an officer down to the water's edge, and point out to him where I was hid; after which the latter rode back to the company, when they all moved off down the river, and I began to flatter myself that I should not be disturbed. Still, I thought it best to keep a good look out for them, and I soon saw them about three-fourths of a mile down the river. They came to the bank and I was satisfied now that something was to be done. They dismounted, and six of them got into a large canoe, and pushing off, set out toward me, coming a considerable distance, when they appeared to be called back by the party on shore. A brief consultation then ensued, and they again pushed out in the river; but this time they steered below the end of the island, and again I was almost ready to believe I would not be disturbed.

In about half an hour I heard them paddling up the river on the opposite side of the island, which was here very narrow. I watched them closely, and discovered that they were not more than seventy-five yards off, and coming rapidly; so, quickly loosening my boat, I pushed out in the stream, and was away down the river. I put out all my strength until I passed the men on the shore, and as I was sailing by at a safe distance from them, they hailed me with the order, "Come ashore with that boat;" but I could not see it in that light, and redoubled my efforts at the paddle. I heard their guns, *bang, bang, bang*, in rapid succession, but it was a useless waste of ammunition, for I was now flying through one of the swiftest shoals on the Tennessee, and was out of range with almost lightning speed.

The Muscle Shoals are forty miles long, and I was now in the head of them. In some places the river is very wide—perhaps two miles—while in other places, far more narrow, and there is a long series of cascades, down which the water rushes foaming and roaring, dashing and thundering, among the rocks—sometimes for miles—lashed into foam by its own impetus, and then pouring over perpendicular falls, and breakers in the rocky bed. It was a fearful ride in the dark, as several of the cascades were five or six feet from top to bottom, and one, known as the "big jump," was ten feet in perpendicular height; or so, at least, I was informed by men who followed boating over the shoals. The most dangerous ride I had was by a point on the south side of the stream, called Green's bluff. By running on that side, I avoided the highest part of the "big jump;" and I made my way over it in safety, though not without some bruises, and a thorough drenching.

At South Florence I saw innumerable camp fires, and was at a loss to account for it. During the day, while laying up on an island, I heard the reverberations of cannon on the water, and now here was a camp in full view—perhaps the very one I was searching after. I was in a swift, but not turbulent part of the shoals, and I determined at once to reconnoitre, and therefore pulled my boat around, in full view of the camp fires—some of which were near the water's edge—and discovered the gray uniform of the sentries, and I was, of course, off again in the distance, knowing that I had passed an army of rebels.

I well knew that at least a portion of our army was near them, or why the firing I had heard? A little further down and I discovered the

"It was a fearful ride in the dark, as several of the cascades were five or six feet from top to bottom, and one, known as the "big jump", was ten feet in perpendicular height."

piers of a railroad bridge, the woodwork of which had been burned; and I felt satisfied that it was on the road leading to Tuscumbia. Still, however, I did not see any suitable place to land, till a long way below that point, when I discovered a narrow road leading out from the water's edge, and up to it I pulled my little craft, resolved to find a house and get some information about the movements of troops in that part of the country.

While hunting for a house, I heard the beating of a single drum off in the distance; and shortly after, followed a "reveille," but far away from where I was. Advancing carefully to reconnoitre, I discovered a picket just before daylight, and stealing up toward him, behind a thick growth of weeds—for he was near a fence, the corners of which had not been trimmed—I was soon near enough to touch him with my gun, when I called out to him to know his regiment, and he responded: "The 5th Ohio."

What weight and doubt was now removed from my mind! He was a friend! I had feared that I was approaching a rebel camp, but now my misgivings had vanished into air! I now told him that I had dispatches for General Sherman, and wanted to pass into camp, and he called the corporal, who sent me in without delay.

I found Tuscumbia in possession of General Blair's troops; and the general furnished me a good breakfast and an ambulance to Cherokee station; and from here, by order of General Wright I was conveyed on a special train to Iuka, where Sherman then was; and I at once delivered my dispatches, which were not yet three days old. No sooner had I delivered the documents, than my strength utterly failed me, and I sunk down exhausted, before I could reach the place assigned me to rest.

The service I had performed was most arduous and dangerous; but let General Sherman himself describe it, and its importance, which he does in the following document:

> Headquarters Military Division of the Mississippi,
> Nashville, Tenn., April 16, 1864.
>
> Corporal James Pike, Co. A 4th Ohio Cavalry, in October, 1863, carried a message from General Grant to me at Iuka. He got a canoe at Whitesburg, opposite Huntsville, and came down the Tennessee, over the Muscle Shoals, all alone, for over one hundred miles of river, every mile of which was picketed by the enemy, and reached me safely, as stated, at Iuka. It was

that message that hastened my movement to Chattanooga. The whole affair is highly creditable to the skill, courage and zeal of Corporal Pike.

    (Signed,)   W. T. Sherman,
                 Major General.

The same dispatch reached him in two other ways. Corporal Brant and private John Wakefield, of the 4th Ohio, went down the north bank of the river with it, and Lieutenant Fitzgerald, with a hundred 4th Regulars, got through with it; but I do not believe either of these parties could have been successful if I had not first made it by the river.

In about two hours after I delivered the dispatch, General Sherman put his army in motion for Chattanooga; and as soon as the first division began to cross over, the rebels who occupied the north bank, crossed over on the shoals, and joined Wheeler on the south side, thus opening the way for the other two parties to reach the general, which they could not otherwise have done.

As soon as I rested a day, I started back up the country, with Brant, and Wakefield, to report the advance of Sherman's army to General Crook. I told General Sherman that I needed a horse, and he replied that I should take the best animal there was in Tishamingo or Lauderdale counties; but after careful search and patient inquiry, I found that his own men had not left a single one in the country that was able to go; and when I reported the result of my investigation to the general, he kindly borrowed one for me, with saddle, bridle and blankets; and I need hardly state that I forgot to return them.

In an incredibly short time the army reached Chattanooga, and in two days participated in the battles of Lookout mountain and Mission Ridge; and in the glorious victories won on those stoutly contested fields, I felt myself amply repaid for the dangers I had encountered in my journey over the Muscle Shoals by night.

CHAPTER 31

Raid in North Carolina

On our return, we found Elk River exceedingly swollen; so, leaving our horses with a Union man in the neighbourhood, named Hugh McLamore, we walked up the bank of the stream in search of a boat, as an attempt to swim it would result in almost certain death. We proceeded at least ten miles, when we saw a canoe on the opposite side, which was the property of a notorious old rebel; and immediately two of us hid, while the third called the boat over. Not dreaming who we were, but evidently supposing the hail was from a rebel soldier, he sent one of his negroes over with the craft at once; but no sooner did it reach the shore, than we all three sprang in, to the astonishment and terror of the darkey.

On reaching the stable, we confiscated two fine mules and a carriage horse, the old rebel raving and swearing all the time. We laughed at his passion, and rode off, without damaging his property or injuring him, our seizure of the animals being merely for the good of the service.

At this house we learned of a Capt. Richardson, who commanded a company of guerrillas, and who was at a place called Bethel church; and immediately we set out for the point indicated, but found only one of his men and two horses, as someone had given notice of our approach. This fellow was just leaving the camp with two very fine animals; and as soon as he discovered us, he darted off down a narrow road, with us immediately after him. Before we reached the road, a man turned into it with a pair of wild young steers hitched to a cart; and as we charged down, the steers ran off, following closely the guerrilla. The chase now became exciting. Away we all went, pell-mell, the wild oxen making about equal time with the flying rebel, and we doing our best to dash by them, and the vehicle to which they were attached, to catch the Johnnie.

The driver of the steers was short, thick, and fat; and when the cart was thumping over roots and stumps, he threw himself down on the bottom of the bed, and fairly roared with fright and pain. The punishment he endured must have been severe; for sometimes he would be thrown three or four feet up in the air, and then fall back again into the cart with a thump that made him roar again. But as we lost the guerrilla by his team getting in our way, we pursued him on, chasing him another mile or so—indeed, until the cattle were completely exhausted, and could run no more. We then reached the Athens road, and there gave him a little parting advice; for we felt sure that he was the man who had warned the guerrillas of our approach; and after concluding our admonition, we struck out toward Athens.

This was once a handsome little town, the buildings possessing taste, and being of a substantial character; and it has been rendered somewhat famous as the first place where one of our commanders promulgated the doctrine of retaliation. At the time we passed through it, it was almost in ruins; the chief buildings having been burned by order of Gen. O. M. Mitchell, in retaliation for guerrilla depredations.

From Athens we proceeded to Huntsville, and thence to Brownsboro, where we found Gen. Crook, who was highly pleased with the success which had attended our efforts.

As the general expected to remain for some time in command of the second cavalry division, he at once made a detail of scouts to operate with me; his plan being to have them well drilled in their business, and then employ them in acquiring information of affairs within the enemies lines; and also as flankers and flying sentinels when the command was on the march. The men detailed were a gallant set of fellows, and they did a great amount of good service; but Gen. Crook being ordered to Virginia, was succeeded by Gen. Garrard, who did not approve of our "style," and so disbanded our organization.

Soon after being detailed on this service, we were sent out on a scout by Gen. Thomas, the object being to burn the big railroad bridge at Augusta, Georgia; and if it were possible to do so, the one across the Congaree, on the road between Branchville and Columbia. Aiken was another desirable point to reach, where we might do incalculable mischief to the enemy's communications; but Augusta was the grand objective point, as here was located the most extensive powder mill in the entire Confederacy, as well as one of the largest, best, and most important bridges. To destroy either the powder mill or the bridge,

"THE PUNISHMENT HE ENDURED MUST HAVE BEEN SEVERE; FOR SOMETIMES HE WOULD BE THROWN THREE OR FOUR FEET UP IN THE AIR, AND THEN FALL BACK INTO THE CART WITH A THUMP THAT MADE HIM ROAR AGAIN."

was to inflict irreparable injury upon the rebel cause, and hence the importance of success.

We set out in the winter, and succeeded in getting as far as the little town of Murphy, in Cherokee County, North Carolina, where we found the snow was so deep in the mountains that it was impossible to proceed farther; and we accordingly turned our attention to affairs in the immediate vicinity of where we then were. We were accompanied by a party of citizens, who aided us to the extent of their power, and gave us all the information we needed. We ascertained that one Col. W. C. Walker, who formerly commanded a brigade at Cumberland gap, but who was now at home with plenary conscripting powers, was creating much trouble in the county; he being engaged in carrying into effect his sweeping powers, with all the energy at his command, and all the cruelty of his nature.

He had already sent a large number of unwilling conscripts to his camp, on Notely River, some of whom, however, managed to desert, and reached our lines, reporting to Col. Long, then commanding the forces at Charleston, on the Hiawassee, in Tennessee. Nothing discouraged, however, Walker continued to pick up men wherever he could find them; and although he had but forty or fifty men in camp upon whom he could rely, he had a full set of officers in camp for a maximum regiment—that condition of officers being the result of the inordinate ambition of the *Southern*, or perhaps I should say *secesh* heart.

After mature deliberation, we concluded to abandon our original mission altogether, and take the "dashing" colonel prisoner, and conveying him back with us to Chattanooga. Subsequent events, however, convinced us of the truth of the old adage, that it takes at least two to make a bargain; for the Colonel refused to be taken.

As soon as it was dusk, on New Years' night, of 1864, we sallied out from a place of concealment, and went to Walker's house, and after surrounding it called upon him to surrender. He immediately demanded to know who we were, and we replied that we were Yankee soldiers; and that if he gave himself up he should be treated like a gentleman, and "as a prisoner of war;" but he replied with an oath that he would do no such thing. I then informed him that resistance would be useless, as his house was surrounded, and that we would take him, dead or alive. He responded to this threat, with:

"*I will surrender when I please.*"

Knowing that he had constantly about him a body guard, I concluded to storm the house, before they had time to rally to his assistance. Seizing the door step, which was a short, heavy log, I broke in the door, in front, while the men behind the house proceeded to demolish that in the rear. Walker retreated to an inner room, and made a stand to sell his life as dearly as possible, twice more refusing to surrender. We soon demolished the two doors to this room, as we had done the outer ones. Still anxious to save his life, I drew a bead on him with a pistol, and ordered him again to yield himself a prisoner. He was standing with a Sharp's carbine, almost ready to shoot, before I succeeded in drawing my pistol; but, fortunately, I was too quick for him. Seeing I had the advantage, I again called on him to surrender, when, after a moment's hesitation, he replied:

"Yes, boys, I'll surren———," and partly turned to lay his carbine on the bed, when his wife caught my arm, and, by a violent jerk, destroyed my aim. Quick as thought he wheeled, and raised his gun to shoot me, but the other men had got in, to assist me, and as his wife still clung frantically to my arm, his daughter, a beautiful young lady, threw herself partially between us; still, however, he appeared bent on shooting me, and I told the boys to fire on him; and Jack Cook, of the 37th Indiana, discharged his piece, and sent a bullet through his heart, and he fell dead at our feet, without a groan or a struggle.

The work had been more quickly done, than it requires me to relate it; and as we had no time to lose we prepared for defence. We heard quite a large party in another part of the house; we formed before the door of the room occupied by his body guard, and rushed at it; and I succeeded in throwing myself, and log of wood, on top of the shattered door, in the middle of the room, and directly among the rebels, who were now prepared for a serious resistance; but our onset was so impetuous, that for a moment our enemies were paralyzed, and in that brief interval we gained a decided advantage, being the first to come to an "aim" and the Johnnies at once surrendered. There were six or eight of them, including Walker's son, who was the sergeant major of the regiment; and we captured the entire party, without firing a shot.

After we had secured our prisoners, we took the colonel's horses, as well as all that we could gather up in the neighbourhood, and started on our return to Chattanooga. Our route was a tedious and laborious one, over the Frog mountains, which were then covered with ice and snow—the cold being intense.

The view from the top of Frog Mountain, is one of the grandest in

"And Jack Cook, of the 37th Indiana, discharged his piece, and sent a bullet through his heart, and he fell dead at our feet, without a groan or a struggle."

North America; but we had no time to enjoy the magnificent scenery, as there was every prospect that we should be rapidly pursued. At Murphy, seven miles from Walker's house, were about thirty home guards; at Ducktown, five miles away, were also about the same number; and at Blairsville was Young's whole battalion, while there were but ten men in my party, besides a few citizens—rather a small number to venture so far in the enemy's country. We were, however, well armed and equipped, and bountifully supplied with ammunition.

After nearly freezing, two or three times, in the mountains, and suffering severely from hunger and fatigue, we at length reached Charleston, and turned over our captives to Colonel Long, who was still in command at that place.

We travelled so fast that young Walker was seized with a violent pain in the breast, so I thought rather than be hard on him, I would parole, and leave him, which I did at the house of a noted secessionist; and he promised to nurse him till he became well enough to return to his family.

Sometime after this I was in South Carolina, and heard, incidentally, that young Walker had run off to that State, in order to save himself from being killed by his Union neighbours. He might as well have braved it out at home, for a Union man in South Carolina killed him on Tiger Tail Creek, and sent his body to Walhalla.

Before leaving North Carolina, I turned another prisoner loose, with instructions to notify every officer of Walker's command to leave the country at once, or I would return with a stronger force and send them all after their colonel; and while passing through the country some time after, I learned that they had all obeyed my injunction. We likewise, in one place, called for a certain Captain Stanhope Anderson, but he was not at home; so we took down his knapsack from a nail where it hung, inspected his papers, and then threw the whole outfit it contained on his own fire; then took his pistol and ammunition, broke into his apple holes, and helped ourselves to all we could carry with us; after which we directed the overseer to inform the captain that if he didn't quit the rebel service, and turn to be a good Union man, we would come back and take his life. On going back, I found that he, too, had heeded our admonition, and that he was then thoroughly loyal, and the original Unionists in the vicinity all spoke well of him since his change of views.

When he entered the rebel service, he swore, in a public speech, to come back with death in his hand, or victory on the point of his sword; and I think he owes me a real debt of gratitude for working his conversion without driving him to extremities.

I only relate this incident here as an illustration of a view I have always entertained, *viz*: That public opinion is an article of manufacture, as well as boots or shoes.

After reaching Colonel Long's camp at Charleston, and resting ourselves, we started for Chattanooga, taking canoes at Cottonport; and on arriving at my place of destination, I reported to General Thomas, after which I returned to Huntsville, to General Crook.

CHAPTER 32

Bridge Burning Expedition to Augusta

We scouted awhile for General Crook, then for Colonel Miller, and Gen. Logan; and upon orders from the last named, we burned up nearly all the distilleries in North Alabama; but when Gen. Garrard took command, as already stated, the scouts were disbanded, and I returned to Gen. Thomas again.

Nothing worthy of narration occurred to me now, till the advance from Chattanooga upon Rocky-face Ridge, when I participated in part of one day's fight.

The project for the destruction of the railroad bridge at Augusta had been recently revived. If that structure could be destroyed, it could not be repaired for months, and the damage to the enemy's communications would be worth an immense amount to us. Could I slip around and burn it? And then amid the confusion resulting from it, would it not be possible to give a little attention to the powder mill, and blow it to fragments?

I started for Nashville at once for an outfit, consisting of matches of a peculiar manufacture, phosphorus and steel arrow heads for throwing it; and while in the city, I was joined by a man named Charles R. Gray, who volunteered to go with me. We set out from Nashville for the front, and arrived there during the battle at Rocky-face Ridge, and we both went in. It seemed to be a free fight, and every man I saw was doing something, and of course I could not be idle. The rebels had a decided advantage in position, being at the top of the ridge; and they wounded a great many of our men, by rolling huge stones down on them. But I did not get to see all of the battle, as early on the morning of the second day, we set out on our journey—Gen. Thomas having just commenced a manoeuvre to flank the enemy on the left, as stated.

We went to Chattanooga by railroad, riding on the general's "dummy" car, and from thence proceeded to Charleston, Tennessee, on a freight train; and from that point we were compelled to fall back on first principles—to travel on foot.

From Charleston we followed the Hiawassee some distance, and then leaving the river, crossed the Frog mountains again, and then returned to the river, at Murphy, in Cherokee County. On the way we encountered some tough times and some pretty merry ones. On one occasion we stopped with an old man, whose family consisted of himself, wife, three daughters, and a daughter-in-law, all of whom were Union, except the last named, who was secesh to the back bone, and was prepared at any moment to do anything in the world for the rebel cause. We were not in the house long before we made ourselves familiar—Gray, my partner, directing his conversation to the daughters, while I entertained the daughter-in-law, and soon had her convinced that we were rebels in disguise. She was pleased that we were devoting our attention to the Hiawassee valley, and wished us every success in our enterprise, whatever it might be; and when I told her my business was ferreting out deserters, who were secreted in that region by the Lincolnites, her admiration of our patriotism was unbounded.

After thus gaining her confidence, I began questioning her as to the different bodies of troops stationed higher up the river, and through which we were compelled to pass, and I found her thoroughly posted; and the information she gave me proved, on subsequent observation, to be correct. To my inquiry about the state of the country, and as to whether there were any lawless characters infesting the mountains, she replied:

"No; there are none now, nor has there been since last winter, when Old Spikes and a lot of Yankee bushwhackers came upon Persimmon Creek and killed Colonel Walker. Ever since that time the country has been mighty quiet."

"Wasn't his name Pike, instead of Spikes?" I inquired.

"Yes, yes; that *was* it; and they say he was a mighty hard case—a perfect savage," said she.

"But what was our cavalry doing," I asked, "that they didn't pursue and capture the villains?"

"Well; a lot of Colonel Young's home guard did get after them," was the reply, "but they killed the colonel in the night, and took to the mountains right away, and our men never found them."

She was eyeing me curiously now, and presently she asked: "Stranger; what is your name?"

"Frank Barton, madam," I replied, without hesitation.

"Where are you from?" she inquired.

"Waco, Texas," said I; and I launched off into a description of Texas and its people, stock raising, agriculture, etc., and soon got her thoroughly convinced that I was really telling her the truth.

We had an excellent supper here, and pushed on up the river. Whenever we found a friendly neighbourhood we would stop at houses; but, when we wouldn't like the appearances, we would hide out in the woods. When we lay out we would steal chickens and take them into the woods with us; and if we failed on poultry, we killed a hog: and as for bread, we never thought of it. When we got into the neighbourhood at the base of the Blue Ridge, we found the people very much exercised in regard to their stock.

The rebels had sent them word to have their cattle gathered, as they would be after them in two or three days, to take them off to the army. It was Colonel Thomas—the notorious Bill Thomas, commanding a legion of Indians, who sent them the order; and the people were fully determined to resist the seizure of their stock, and sent Thomas word that if he got their cattle he must gather them himself. There were perhaps sixty able-bodied men, who were armed and willing to resist if the rebels came into their neighbourhood to enforce the order; and Gray and I joined the insurrectionary forces and helped to promote the spirit of resistance among them. We waylaid the pass in the mountains, through which the rebels must necessarily come, for a couple of days; but Thomas must have learned, by some means, that the people were armed and awaiting for his arrival, as he did not come.

We practiced target-shooting, one afternoon, with several of these mountaineers, just for the sake of making a favourable impression among them. Gray held a cap box between his thumb and finger for me to shoot at, and to show the confidence we had in each other we exchanged positions, and I held the box as a mark for Gray's bullet. The distance was fifty yards.

Early on the morning of the 20th of May we scaled the Blue Ridge—a very severe undertaking, and one which caused us great labour and fatigue. When one stands at the foot of the mountain and looks up, the summit appears wrapped in a blue haze; and when on the top, looking down, the foot appears belted in blue, a shade or two deeper than azure.

From the summit of this ridge the view is indeed grand and picturesque. Other mountains rise up in every direction, to meet the vision—"Great Smoky," in East Tennessee, being among those distinctly visible from the point where we then stood. It is no unfrequent occurrence for it to be raining down in the valleys, while on the summit of the ridge the sky is perfectly clear and the sun shining. Going along the top of the Long Ridge, or as the natives call it, the Ridge Pole, we were astonished at its height and singular formation—it being, I believe, the most elevated point of land in the Alleghany mountains, though my data on this subject is by no means positive. The summit of the ridge is extremely narrow—being not more, in many places, than six or ten feet in width—the descent on the west side being regular, but steep, while on the east it is little else than a precipice for a thousand feet down.

One particular feature of these mountains is the fact, that both sides and tops are covered with a deep, rich soil, of very dark, or black colour, the tops, however, being so high as to be destitute of timber.

Descending to the foot of the ridge, on the eastern side, we came to the head waters of the Tallulah River—so called by the Indians, on account of its extraordinary falls, which are, perhaps, the highest in the country, though no single fall is as high as others which might be mentioned. There are five cataracts in a quarter of a mile, the water descending four hundred feet altogether. The roaring of the waters can be heard an incredible distance; and no wonder that the red men named it Tallulah—thunder river.

We followed the stream to its junction with the Chattooga, where the two form the Tugalo, being conducted on the route by a man named Ramy, whom we hired to pilot us through the most dangerous sections of the country, the distance being twenty-eight miles. He was a perfect specimen of a backwoodsman, and loyal, after the most rigid definition of that word. Near the mouth of the Chattooga a brother of his lived, who had a son in the rebel army and who was a violent secessionist. He was member of Young's Georgia cavalry, which was at Clayton, then only six miles away.

On the west side of the Blue Ridge, we had frequently passed off as rebel soldiers in disguise; but generally for Union men—always suiting ourselves to the company we were in, or as our interests demanded; but on the east side, we knew that we had nothing to expect from citizens if we claimed to be Yankee soldiers, as they were nearly all against us, and, therefore, we almost uniformly represented ourselves as rebels on our way to Augusta to join our regiments. We belonged, we stated, to the 4th (confederate) Kentucky Cavalry. But we had as little to do with the people as possible; but when we could not avoid meeting them, we told this simple story with occasional variations, to satisfy the curious and the doubting.

Young Ramy was at home when we reached his father's house, and in the morning we left early, telling the people we were going to Walhalla, to get on the morning train; but as soon as we were out of sight, we turned down the Tugalo, and stole a canoe, below the first shoals, and travelled constantly till we ran our boat aground on a shoal, and were compelled to abandon it and wade ashore, trusting to our chances to obtain another craft.

When daylight overtook us, we hid out in the mountains, on Brasstown Creek—a stream noted for its high cascades. Travelling on the river by night or by day, as best suited our purposes, we finally reached the head of the canal, seven miles above Augusta; one day, at noon time, we passed through a section of the country where a large number of Col. Bill Thomas' Indians were quartered—some farming, some tending stock, while others were making baskets, and yet others were fishing. All appeared busy, in a lazy sort of Indian way; and most of them had been wounded in the rebel service. Being unfit for active duties, they had been sent to this part of South Carolina to recruit themselves, and to raise something to support the tribe who were entirely helpless. They were Cherokees, who have always lived on the Tuckasege River, and at Qualla Town, on the Qualla River, in North Carolina. They were the saddest appearing Indians I ever saw, and seemed to have lost the last vestige of that firey independence which characterizes their race: and as far as I could discover, they had not been benefited by intercourse with the white race.

The Tugalo is one of the most beautiful streams I ever beheld. Its banks are finely diversified with mountain scenery, generally in the distance; while the bottoms are in the highest state of cultivation—indeed, some of the finest plantations, and best built mansions in all the southern country, are on this river. At times, the water, which is always clear, runs smooth and deep, for some distance, when suddenly it is broken by shoals, miles and miles in length; the current roaring and dashing among the rocks, with astonishing velocity; so that to navigate the surging waves, required all the skill and presence of mind we could muster.

After the Tugalo makes its junction with the Seneca, the stream takes the name of Savannah, or as the mountaineers call it—the Sav-a-naw. Below the mouth of the Seneca, the river rapidly widens, and the water assumes a yellowish or muddy colour, and it is full of wild and dangerous shoals. The bottoms, on either side, are wide and well cultivated; but on account of the fearful freshets, caused by the rising of the mountain streams above, there are no houses built near the river—they generally being from two to three miles back, and sometimes even farther than that; so that we seldom saw any one, save the slaves, and their overseers—the former being the most abject human beings I ever saw. Occasionally, the overseers themselves were black, and as far as I could see, they were equally severe on the labourers, with the white men.

There are no towns at all, immediately on the Savannah, above Augusta. Occasionally we would meet a keel boat coming up to the plantations after corn for the rebel army, they being propelled by poles, and manned by negroes—the man in charge occasionally being a white man; usually, however, he was as black as a crow. Almost every boat contained half a dozen rebel soldiers as a guard; and these would sometimes hail us as we passed; but as they could not stop without "losing deal" with the current, we would not, for fear of losing deal with them, and therefore, our conversations were of brief duration. If we happened to meet on a shoal, they had always as much as they could do to climb up over it, and we had all we could do to keep from being dashed to pieces among the rocks, so we paid little attention to each other.

There appeared to be a continual falling of the river from the mountains to Augusta; but from there to the coast, I believe that the stream is exceedingly smooth and placid. Some of the shoals above, are miles in extent; and each is known to the keel boatmen by some significant name. Among those which we deemed from observation to be the most dangerous, are the Little River shoals, so called because they are just below the mouth of Little River; the Elizabeth Shoals—but why so called I am not aware; and the Trotter Shoals, named from the fact that on ascending them with a keel boat, the crew is compelled to trot with their poles to make headway.

This last named rapid is seven miles long, and is one continuous hill in the river, down which the current rushes with frightful velocity, the channel winding back and forth from shore to shore, while the stream itself winds around, with zigzag curves, and is thickly besprinkled with rocks; so that the water is lashed into white caps and foam—the waves rolling short, quick, and angrily, to an incredible height.

Another dangerous rapid is the Ring Jaw Shoal, not far from Augusta; the river here being almost dammed up by great rocks, among which the current forces itself with a short twist, from right to left, and back again with such power that the passing boat is nearly wrung in twain, as it proceeds. Another shoal, about the last in the river, is near the head of the canal, and is called Bull Sluice, and is somewhat after the fashion of Ring Jaw, and about as dangerous.

To add to the dangers we encountered in navigating the stream, we had to run over several mill dams, some of which were from six to eight feet in perpendicular height; and there was but a single method of passing them, and that was to go over. These dams were invariably built of loose rocks, of great size, piled on the shoals, sometimes from shore to shore, but occasionally only forming a wing, partially across. These mills were almost the only signs of habitation; the structures being generally strong frames, and they were kept constantly running; but as they had all been seized by the rebel government, it was with the greatest difficulty that the people could get either meal or flour. Still the citizens of this section of South Carolina lived far better than did those of any other section of the South which I have visited during the war. They all seemed to enjoy plenty, and it was of the best quality; but the white women, as a general thing, were not good cooks—from a lack of practice, I presume—and the negroes were usually too careless to prepare a meal properly.

CHAPTER 33

Bloodhound Chase

On the night of the 3rd of June, 1864, we arrived in Hamburg, opposite Augusta. The first thing necessary now, was to see how affairs stood in town, and we accordingly ascended a hill immediately back of it, where we could see, not only all that was going on in Hamburg, but much that was transpiring in Augusta. We secreted ourselves under a dogwood tree, which was low, and covered with vines, thus forming an excellent hiding place. If no one passed, and made it a special business to look in, we were perfectly secure; and at that place we patiently awaited the approach of daylight. We had learned on the day previous, that the powder mill was so closely guarded, that nothing could be accomplished there, so that we directed our best efforts to the destruction of the bridge.

My plan, before leaving camp, had been to float down under it in a boat, and throw burning arrows into it, provided I saw no chance to *mug* the guard, and do it boldly. At the foot of the hill we heard a good deal of talking, and could not account for it; but when it got light enough to see, judge our astonishment to find ourselves within seventy-five yards of the railroad, and right before us was a long train loaded with federal prisoners; while farther down in the town we could see several other trains of the same kind. The town was full of captured Union soldiers, and as near as we could guess, there were twelve hundred rebels guarding them. The situation was most embarrassing; to stay where we were was almost certain destruction, and an attempt to go elsewhere would be certain to be discovered. But the best we could do, was, evidently, to keep quiet in our hiding place, bad as that was. We hoped that in a little while the trains would fire up and leave; but on the contrary, they lay there all day.

We could see, too, that there was a strong and vigilant guard upon each end of the bridge; and we could discover patrols walking the streets in each town, and in every direction. The prisoners, as usual, looked half starved and sickly; some were clad in bright, new uniforms, and looked well, and it was easy to divine that *they* were only recently captured. These were in tolerably good spirits, too, which was a sure sign that they had not been long in the hands of the cruel enemy.

Others, again, were not quite so well dressed, and looked meagre and thin, but were not despondent. These had probably been prisoners for some months; but by far the greater number were clothed in rags, which were in the most filthy condition. They looked very much emaciated and weather-beaten, and their dejected and hope-forsaken countenances, spoke plainly of a long and soul-sickening captivity. Poor, wretched, starved, dejected and sick, they were being moved to that loathsome den, and wholesale place of murder—the Andersonville prison. Of course we did not know their destination for certain, but we judged it from the fact that all the engines headed west.

It was now clear that we were to be unsuccessful. Nothing could escape the vigilance of that guard, either on land or on water. It was positive that we were played out on *that* string, and what to get at next, we did not know; and even a chance of escape at all argued extremely doubtful. We remembered that on the Tugalo River we had passed under a very fine frame bridge, for ordinary travel, across the Tugalo; and we thought we must do something to damage rebeldom, and we therefore made up our minds to go back and try to burn it, but we had better have gone straight through to the coast and made our escape, as I believe we could have done, without detection.

From our place of concealment we could see the arsenal in Augusta, the powder mill up the river, and nearly every important building in the place; nevertheless, we dare not move from our retreat, for fear of being seen. The poor prisoners were kept under the strictest surveillance, lest they should attempt to escape, and a great many of them, as we could see, were prostrated and helpless from disease. We almost, ourselves, sickened at the sight of these poor, suffering men; and at the certainty that we were powerless to help them. They were crowded into the cars and on top of them, as thickly as they could be packed; and to hear the sick pleading for water, was most heart rending. Poor fellows! some of them would beg until they exhausted themselves, before it would be given them, and what added to the cruelty of this neglect, and to the torture of the men, was the fact that there was plenty of water but a few yards away.

The day wore on, and long awaited night closed in at last; and we then stole from our hiding places, and took the road back up the river. About four miles from Hamburg we "confiscated" a couple of fine horses—the property of a man named Rambo. I am inclined to think we were discovered, just as we led the horses out of the stable, for I heard someone speak at the house, though it was after midnight. On the following morning, we stopped at a blacksmith shop, to have one of the horses shod; and while there, were overtaken by a pursuing party of four men, who demanded the animals. I felt confident that quite a force was after us, and that this was but the advance guard; and as our object was to gain time, and get into the swamps, and timber, we gave up the horses, unconditionally, and without reluctance; saying at the same time that it was very hard to have to foot it clear back to Franklin.

"What are you going to Franklin for," said the leader of the party.

"Why, our command is there," I answered, in an offhand manner.

"What are you doing here, in this State," he demanded.

"We are on special service for Col. Thomas."

"What is the nature of your service," he asked.

"O, we are making preparations to move the Indians all over the mountains, into South Carolina; they are about to starve to death up there in Qualla town. We are compelled to do something to keep them from suffering."

"Well, if you are soldiers, and going back to your command, we don't want to stop you, but really we can't let you take the horses," they replied.

It was such a common occurrence for Rebel soldiers to steal horses, that nothing was ever thought of it, so after recovering the animals, this party was satisfied to start back. We could have whipped out the squad, for they were unsuspicious, and gave us every advantage; but we knew very well that if we did even kill every one of them, it would do us no good, for the whole country behind us was now alarmed, and before night it would be aroused far ahead of us.

As soon as this affair was settled, we took the big road, until out of their sight, and then turned into the woods. We then took every precaution to break our trail; wading mile after mile in swamps, and up creeks, picking our way on rocks and hard ground; but all to no purpose; for it was only a couple of hours until we heard the deep mouthed bay of the blood hound, running on our track. When we heard the dogs, we were laying down to rest, and had taken off some of our clothing to wring the water out of them. Hastily putting on our clothes, and accoutrements, we sprang off through the woods, at our highest speed, practicing every art known to woodsmen, to break our trail; but we were unsuccessful; the dogs were unerring. At one time the hounds would be within distinct hearing of us; and then we would run our very best, until we came to water, and then wading through, or up, or down it, we would break the trail so badly that we would balk the hounds for some time; but occasionally we had to stop to take breath, and then in a brief time we would hear them coming again.

Once we made a large circle through the woods and doubled on the trail; and this time we started them to running a back track, and thought we were rid of them entirely; and as it was late in the afternoon, and we hoped to escape in the darkness, we rested a few minutes, and then travelled till nearly dark; when, being tired and hungry, we concluded that it could not make the matter much worse to stop at a house and get some supper; but just as we approached one, we heard the dogs close behind us. We sprang over the fence, and across a ploughed field, and for a while succeeded in baffling our pursuers.

We then crossed two fields, and gained a dry swamp, the brush and timber being very thick and dense, so that it was with difficulty that we could make our way through it; and it was not long till the dogs struck the right trail, and quickly we heard them crashing through the bush, close behind us; and we were compelled to make a stand at once, and fight with dog, or man, or anything that approached us. On came the hounds, through the thick undergrowth, making the deep forest echo with their savage baying, until, with a sudden bound, their leader was upon us, his eyes glaring, and his mouth foaming. For an instant he paused, as he saw us through the gloom, and the next made a spring directly at Gray's face. He was large, and snow white, and this made him the better target; and as he sprang at my companion, I turned upon him, and fired, and he fell dead in an instant.

But at that moment the whole pack rushed upon us, more like demons, than even dogs; and it was with difficulty that we could see their dusky forms amid the gloom, but their glaring eyes served as guides for an almost unerring aim; and when we had discharged nine shots, we had killed one dog and wounded four more. The flash of the pistols kept the dogs at bay, wonderfully, but did not drive them off; and scarcely had we fired the last shot, when the men came up, forcing their horses through the bushes, cursing and swearing like madmen. When they got within about a hundred yards of us, we halted them, saying that if they did not stop, we would fire on them.

"Who are you?" demanded one of the men.

"Yankee soldiers," I answered.

"What are you doing in our country?" they inquired.

"We are here by order of our general," was the response.

"How many are there of you?" they next wanted to know.

"Two."

"Are you up a tree?" asked one.

"No; we are not the sort of men to take to trees," we informed them.

"Have you killed any of our dogs?"

"No," said I, and then whispering to Gray, we moved out toward them, some distance from the dead animal; then hailing the men, I said:

"There are but two of us, but we are well armed, and can do you a great deal of damage, if you drive us to it. We know that you have a strong force after us, for we have seen you two or three times to-day; we know that resistance on our part would only result in useless bloodshed; still it is our privilege to sell our lives at as dear a price as we can make you pay; but we don't want to hurt you, nor do we want you to hurt us; and, therefore, if you will agree to treat us as prisoners of war, we will surrender without a fight, because we see that one would be useless."

"You will soon be made to surrender on our terms," was the response.

"Then approach us at your peril," I answered, "for we intend to shoot as long as we can crook a finger."

During this parley, another large party had joined the first, and we could now hear them disputing among themselves, when presently they hailed us cheerfully:

"Halloo, Yank."

"Halloo yourself," we replied.

"If you will surrender, we will treat you as prisoners of war, and there shall not one hair of your head be touched," said the commander of the party.

"All right, sir," said I; "on these conditions and no others, you can have our arms."

I then invited two of their men over to take our weapons, but they asked that we should fire them in the air first; but I objected, as evincing a lack of confidence in our honour; but the truth was, the loads had all been tried on the dogs, but they failed to go, and I did not want them to know how helpless we were. They then told us to stand still, and they would all come to us; and they at once flanked out on both sides to surround us, every now and then uttering assurances that we should not be hurt.

Finally they approached us direct and demanded the arms; and while the process of surrendering was going on, Gray, who was one of the coolest men I ever met, began to crack jokes with them to give them confidence in our intentions—inquiring the "news from Virginia," and asking them what they were going to feed us on, and if they had any coffee; and on receiving a negative answer to his last question, he next asked for whisky; and to this they replied "plenty," and promised us a drink. But no sooner were our arms delivered, than they changed their manner. One of them, named Chamberlain—a Massachusetts Yankee, as I afterward learned—swore by his Maker that if we had shot one of the dogs, he would have retaliated by killing a man; and at once they commenced looking around among the pack to see if any of them were hurt; but it was so dark, and the dogs were so restless, that they were unable to ascertain what damage was done; nor was it ascertained till next morning.

The party that captured us, after a little parley, got the other squad pacified and set out on the road to return; and on the way we stopped at the house where we had intended to take our supper—the name of the owner being Serles—and it is located on what is known as the river road to Abbeville court house; and here we were met by another pursuing party, madder and drunker than either of the others. Indeed it was the most excited and drunken mob I ever saw; and I never expect to look on its like again. It required all the address we possessed, to save ourselves from the infuriated crowd—seventy-five in number, while a glance at the dogs, showed that there were thirty-six of them—a very respectable force to capture two men. Our surrender had been made to Lieut. Col. Talbot, and Capt. Burt, commanders of the party.

Mr. Serles was a gentlemanly old man, and I am persuaded, did what he could to pacify the crowd. His wife, a good old lady, also did what she could for, and seemed to sympathize with, us; but their two daughters were of a different style altogether. They ran through the excited and drunken crowd, begging and pleading with the infuriated wretches to hang us, exclaiming: "Don't let them live, men! don't let them live!" and these expressions were not without their effect upon our captors. For once in my life I saw the "*secesh*" heart thoroughly "*fired.*" The drunken mob rolled around us with pine-knot torches flickering in their hands; and the smoke and glare added to the hideousness of their excited countenances, and gave to the scene an additionally diabolical appearance.

We told them that if we had to die, it would at least be generous to give us a good supper, before sending us on our long journey to the other world; and on hearing this, the old man Serles walked around among the crowd and invited them to dismount, and take supper with him; and in this, I could readily perceive that he was anxious to gain time for us. Looking at their jaded horses, he took care, further, to remind them that they had ridden very hard, and were killing their stock; and added that he had plenty of corn, and that he would take it as a favour if they would all stop to eat. A number then began to dismount and feed their horses, while some of them, who had cooled a little from the effect of passion and whisky, began to ride off, in twos and threes, to their respective homes. Some twenty or thirty militiamen remained for supper, keeping a strict guard over us all the time.

A Col. Harrison who belonged to the party, now took the lead, and questioned us strictly, but failed to elicit any information as to the whereabouts of our troops. We were examined separately, but our stories agreed exactly, as we had conferred together, and concluded to "plead guilty" of being scouts, in order to keep down suspicion as to what we really had been commissioned to do. We had driven our arrow heads all down in the ground, at Hamburg, when it was discovered that we should have no more use for them; and when we saw escape impossible, we threw away everything but our arms and ammunition; so that nothing was found upon us to cause our real mission to be detected.

At length the party finished their supper at Serle's house, and remounted, starting for Col. Talbot's house, ten miles distant; and this we reached before daylight. Here a part of our captors left us, and we were turned over to another guard, who allowed us to lie down in the parlour, and sleep till dawn.

On waking, we saw not one of our captors—all being gone; our guards being entirely new men. The whisky bottle was in circulation, and it was not hard to discover that trouble was brewing. Fortunately, however, they had not patience to *wait* to get drunk, before they attempted to carry out their projects. It was plain to see that we had been entirely abandoned by those to whom we had surrendered, and who were in duty bound to protect us; and that we had been purposely left in the hands of a party who had made no stipulations; and we therefore prepared for the worst.

When they roused us up, which they did in a rough, insulting manner, they told us to get ready to go with them; and as soon as we raised to our feet—which it was very difficult for us to do, on account of the race we had made the day before—they commenced to tie Gray with a rope; and after getting him secured to their notion, they put him under a strong guard. Turning to me next, they took another cord, and pinioned my arms behind me as tight as they could draw the rope. It was a severe operation, and it was performed by a muscular negro, who did it under compulsion; and when completed, they led me out to a big tree, in the edge of the woods, taking the negro along, carrying an extra rope.

When at the tree, they asked me if I had any confession to make; but I replied I had none to make to *them*; and they then said, if I desired to pray, they would allow me a few minutes to prepare for eternity. I told them that I did not want to pray; that I was ready to die, and that I did not fear death.

"Have you nothing to say?" they asked, with astonishment.

"Yes; I have a few words to say that may interest you," I said quietly.

"Out with it," replied their spokesman; and I went on:

"You perhaps have never been concerned in military affairs; you are not soldiers, and have nothing to do with the Confederate army. You are citizens. You are now about to commit an act that will meet with the severest punishment that military law can inflict. We are United States soldiers, acting in discharge of our duties. You, as citizens, have no right to interrupt us. Now, I perceive that you are all old men; and have sons in the Confederate Army, perhaps. Our general will retaliate if you hurt a hair of our heads. If you hang one or both of us, he will hang man for man. How do you know but he will select some of your sons. He will be sure to do it if he learns the part you are taking here; and you will find it impossible to keep him from discovering this. Then you are all rich men, for I have heard your talk in the house, and your appearances indicate you to be men who do not labour.

"Now we are members of separate regiments; I belong to the 4th Ohio, and Gray belongs to the 5th Iowa Cavalry. If we are hung, and our regiments ever find you out, as they will be sure to do, if ever they come into this country, they will burn every dollar's worth of your

"When at the tree, they asked me if I had any confession to make; but I replied I had none to make to them; and they then said, if I desired to pray, they would allow me a few minutes to prepare for eternity."

property they can discover; and they will hang every man they can catch who was concerned in the transaction. If you are prepared to make this sacrifice, I am."

A little *nonplussed*, they now left me under guard a short time, and went off into the woods, as I supposed, to talk the matter over; and when they came back they took me to Talbot's house again, and untied us both. Talbot then brought out a decanter of whisky to treat all hands; but in his conversation he made an insulting remark, to the effect that he wanted to drink first, as he would rather drink after the blackest nigger he had than after a Yankee, whereupon we refused to drink with them.

On the night previous, as they were marching us along, one villain tried to shoot me in the back; but although the cap bursted loud and clear, the gun missed fire. He told his companion, and I overheard him, that his piece was loaded with twelve buck shot in each barrel; and when he made the attempt to fire, he was not more than the length of the horse behind me.

While Talbot's folks were preparing breakfast for us, they made an estimate of the distance we had run the preceding day, reckoning from place to place, and they reached the conclusion that we had travelled at least eighty miles. I had myself, already estimated the journey at sixty miles, after we left our horses, which was at a place eighteen miles from Hamburg. The time consumed in this trip, was from two o'clock of one morning, till the same time the next—twenty-four hours in all; and it was the roughest day's travel I ever had; it being doubly severe from the fact that we had to be wet so much, wading through the swamps to throw the dogs off the trail.

I was much pleased with Talbot's wife. She was a perfect specimen of a southern lady, in her demeanour, and appeared to sympathize deeply with us. She was large, and portly, but very fair; had very long hair, of glossy blackness, and large, brilliant black eyes, which, when they turned upon us, seemed to be struggling to speak; and they did speak, though not in words; for as I watched their deep expression, they seemed to say: "Poor fellows, I pity, but am powerless to help you!" She presided at the table and saw that we were bountifully fed.

After breakfast, Chamberlain came up, and he and Talbot agreed to take us in their buggies, to Edgefield. When Captain Burt was about to leave, the night before, he whispered to me that he could do nothing more for us; and that he was afraid the mob would not let us live; and he further informed us that men were then scouring the country for the purpose of raising a crowd to waylay the road for us next morning; so that if we even escaped death at the hands of the party in charge of us, it was almost certain we should be taken from them next day, by men who could not be appeased.

He shook hands with me kindly when he left, and said he was sorry for us, but he had done all he could do to save our lives, and keep with us; and that the excited fools were now getting angry with him. I then thanked him, and he left us. Chamberlain's manner had altogether changed since his night's sleep. When he left us he was the most vindictive man in the party; but now he was one of the most mild, and considerate.

A pair of handcuffs were put on Gray, and he was put in Talbot's buggy; after which I was securely tied with a rope, and given over to Chamberlain.

When about to start, Chamberlain asked Talbot which road they should take—the upper or the lower; when I turned around and said:

"You will do us a favour by taking us on the upper one."

He looked at Talbot as if in doubt; but he soon perceived that I knew the danger, if we went the other way, and Talbot turned and took the route we desired, and we arrived safely at Edgefield Court House. On the way, Chamberlain was full of talk; and I soon perceived that he was a very vain man, and I plied him so well with "soft soap" that, by the time we reached Edgefield, he was almost a friend.

The town was full of excited men, and fearing the mob, our keepers hurried us off to jail, and turned us over to the sheriff, until an assistant provost marshal could be found; and on entering the jail we were at once put in solitary confinement; and in a short time we were separately taken before the provost marshal's agent, who I soon discovered was a consummate villain, conniving at our seizure by a mob. He was about to refuse to receive us at all from the militia, but there happened to be a rebel lieutenant near, and who said he was on duty there, and that he would represent the confederacy; and he ordered us in jail, subject to the orders of the military authorities at Augusta. Failing to get us to "blow" on each other, or our officers, they put us in solitary confinement again.

The jail at Edgefield is the strongest one I was ever in in the South; and that is saying a good deal, as I have been kept in several, and am therefore competent to judge. We had a sorry time of it—the jailor telling us once, that the people outside were so infuriated, that he feared they would tear the jail open, and take us out and lynch us.

Detectives were employed to quiz, and even lawyers sent to examine us; but they found out nothing. They got hold of our journal in cipher, and that gave them the greatest uneasiness, as they imagined it contained some great military secrets.

About the 9th of June, our cells were thrown open again, and we were allowed to come out in the light; and then at once transferred to Captain Dearing, and a guard of twelve well armed men, whose duty it was to escort us to Augusta. After introducing himself and stating his business, the captain informed us that the citizens were swearing that we should not be taken from Edgefield alive; but he said that he would take us, nevertheless, at the risk of his life.

"You shall not be mobbed," said he, "while you are under my care."

We were heavily ironed, and chained together, and then put in a wagon, which was driven rapidly away from town before the crowd of citizens could rally.

It was forty miles to Augusta, and before we had got hardly away, our mule team broke down, and we had to walk several miles with our handcuffs and chains, a very fatiguing process; but aside from this, our guard was kind, and supplied us with provisions from their rations.

"Our mule-team broke down, and we had to walk several miles in our handcuffs and chains; a very fatiguing process."

Chapter 34

The Whipping Post

At Augusta we were put in close confinement again, under the tender auspices of a man named Bridges—a New York Yankee. He certainly can boast, hereafter, of one thing: the discovery of the smallest amount of food which is required to support human life. We were in the jail at Augusta 57 days, and at the end of that time, were so starved as to be mere shadows of what we were. I could no longer walk steadily, and felt as weak as when just beginning to walk after a severe attack of typhoid fever.

At the end of that time, Captain Bradford, the rebel provost marshal, came to see me, and we had a very pleasant conversation. He said that he used to be a scout in their service, and had been promoted for meritorious service. He informed us that our case had been submitted to their Secretary of War, and that the order was "close confinement during the war." Capt. Dearing also used to call and see us, once in a while; and the Catholic priest there, Rev. Father Dugan, once called to see me; aside from these, we never saw any one but the turnkeys, unless it was a prisoner, or someone who wanted to see a prisoner, while we were there. In the cell opposite mine was a man confined for whipping a negro to death, while in that on my right, was a negro charged with murder; in a neighbouring cell was a Yankee confined for bigamy; nearly over my head, in the second story, was a negro woman, held for attempting to poison her mistress; and somewhere near her was an Italian soldier, in the Federal service, whom the rebels claimed as a deserter from their army. The "big room" was filled with rebel deserters, thieves, pickpockets and all sorts of petty villains.

In the next cell above mine, was an "institution" which has been a curse to our country, and a disgrace to our own character as freemen; and an "institution" which has been the witness of more agonizing torture in the South, than any of us can imagine—*the whipping post*—that ready means of inflicting terrible and summary punishment, without any trial or other law, than the caprice of the master, or mistress. I did not see this machine, because I never got up there; but managed to draw an accurate description of it from Luck, a negro, who was undergoing sentence upon it, and had been whipped upon it repeatedly. He described it as being made of heavy square timbers, in the form of a cross; and at the ends of the arms were iron fetters, made to clasp around the wrist, and hold them outstretched; and at the bottom were similar irons to secure the feet. The victim is first stripped naked, then stretched upon the cross, and made fast, when a turnkey plies a whip, with a short handle, and a broad heavy strap, punched full of holes for a lash, and which is, altogether, about two feet and a half long. The strap strikes flatwise, and wherever there is a hole through it, a blister raises in the skin; and if it be a heavy blow the edge of the leather around the openings cuts the skin open, around the blister, and the wounds bleed profusely.

There was scarcely a day that there was not one whipped, while I was in that jail; and sometimes there were as many as six flogged in one day; and generally from three to five. I have counted the blows at times, and once they numbered one hundred and eighty-seven, when the punishment was stopped, by the victim becoming insensible. He must have been a very robust man, for most generally when they were whipped so hard, they would faint under from twenty to forty lashes—according to the force with which they were laid on. It was the custom, the turnkey said, for the careful master to stand by, to regulate that matter to suit himself. I could generally give a close estimate of the age of the slave they were punishing, by the sound of the voice. Sometimes the pleading would be heavy and strong, as though it came from a large man; at other times I could hear the wailing cries of a feeble, and sometimes of a healthy young woman; and occasionally I heard children screaming under the terrible torture; and once in a while I would recognize the trembling voice of an old man.

Their struggles would, at times, be almost superhuman, as they writhed in their iron manacles; and I have often stopped my ears to shut out their heart-rending supplications for mercy. This whipping was generally done by a young man named Evans, a turnkey, and the head jailor Bridges, who, as previously stated, was originally from New York. The young man, who was in jail for helping to whip the negro to death, said that they only struck him eighteen blows; but that after he was let down, they allowed him to drink too much water, and that killed him.

"Oh," he said, "they kin stand several hundred, ef you don't let 'em git too much water, while they are hot."

Filled, as this jail was, with all sorts of villains, guilty of every degree of crime, it was certainly a hard place for any man to find himself.

When we had been there fifty-seven days, we were taken by a Captain Gunn, under a strong guard, to Charleston, and there turned over to Maj.-Gen. Jones, who, I am sorry to have to say it, robbed us of two hundred and eighty dollars in Confederate money. Well, it wasn't much in quantity, and was worth perhaps less in value, but it really looked mean for a *Major general* to steal from us what even the militia allowed us to keep. At Gen. Jones' quarters, Captain Gunn and guard left us. They had treated us like gentlemen, and when we were hungry they divided their own rations with us, for the authorities gave us NONE to travel on. I wonder how they would have liked their men travelled on empty stomachs? On the train I saw Dr. Toddd, President Lincoln's brother-in-law, and he seemed like a very clever man and a gentleman. He gave each of us a nice, light roll and some ham; nevertheless, he was a strong "secesh." When a command of rebel soldiers began to talk roughly to us, he would say:

"Come, boys, let us be generous to prisoners."

He had charge, as I learned, of a very large hospital, at or near Charleston.

Gen. Jones (oh! the villain,) sent us down to Charleston jail, with orders to have us kept in close confinement, and he allowed us no liberties whatever. At the jail, the guard turned us over to the keeper—one John Simes—who, though not a very clever man—that is, I do not believe he would steal anything he could not carry off—had some good traits about him (for what thief has not)? He put us in the "tower," which is the strongest part of the building, and the reader can, perhaps, imagine our feelings, at thus being kept FIVE MONTHS, confined under the fire of our own guns, on Morris Island; the shells bursting around us constantly, all the time we were there, and when one of the shells from the huge three hundred pounders would explode in the vicinity of the jail, it would rock the tower to its foundation.

In a few days after we were incarcerated in this place, twelve hundred of our officers were brought to the city, to be put under fire of our own guns, in retaliation for the shelling of the city; and among them, was Lieut. Henry, of my own regiment, who had been captured at the battle of Chickamauga, and with him was Major Beatty, of the 2nd Ohio infantry, and from them I obtained a knife and a small file, to make some keys with, for the purpose, if possible, of making my escape. I had intimated my desire to them, and they tossed the instruments into my cell, through the grating, as they were going up into the drum of the tower to sleep.

I saw them once, after, for a few minutes, "on the sly," and learned that they had been brutally treated, as had been all their comrades, since the Battle of Chickamauga.

In my prison were about thirty coloured soldiers, belonging to the 54th Massachusetts Infantry, who had been captured in the attempt to storm Fort Wagner. Poor fellows! they had a sorry time of it, as the rebels had a particular spite at them; and some of their number, I learned, had been sent off to the country, to men who claimed them as slaves.

One—a fine looking fellow, named George Grant—had so far gained the confidence of the rebels, that he was made a sort of turnkey over the prison; and he succeeded in getting a Union woman to bring him a piece of thick brass for us to work into keys. It was a piece of stair carpet bar, and was just the thing we wanted. Through a man named Leatherman, I got a note to Lieut. Stokes, of the navy, and requested him to write to my father, and let him know how and where I was.

Stokes had been brought to the place for exchange; and I will take occasion here to say that I have it in my power to vindicate our officers from the charges so often brought against them by our enemies, of not caring for the welfare of the soldiers, and that they were selfish, and ambitious, and were indifferent as to what became of us, if they only could get place and power, and were able to make money out of the war. Here was an officer of another arm of the service than that to which I belonged, who had never seen me before, who knew nothing in the world of me, but who interested himself deeply in my case; for as soon as he was exchanged, he wrote the following letter to my father at Hillsboro, Ohio:

New York, October 26th, 1864.

Sir:—I have just returned from the South, a paroled prisoner. While I was confined in Charleston, S. C., I saw your son, James Pike, who was in solitary confinement in the jail, together with his comrade Charles Gray, and was able to correspond with them. They told me they were captured near Augusta, Ga., in uniform, and under arms, and on "special duty" for General Thomas; and also wished me to write to you when I was released, and tell you that he was quite well and in good spirits; but they were looking rather pale, poor fellows, from their long imprisonment and short rations of food. I was kept in the jail yard, while they were in the building. I communicated by means of a negro boy who carried water to them.

I promised them when I got out, I would do all I could for them. I have just written to Col. Mulford, Assistant Agent of Exchange, and to Gen. Thomas in their behalf. I cannot promise they will be able to effect your son's release, but they will do all they can, I think.

I had an interview with Col. Mulford on the flag-of-truce boat coming down the James River, and he told me to make the statement in writing, and it would receive attention.

"I saw your son last on or about the 6th of this month. I trust, sir, he may soon be restored to you. I am, respectfully,

Your obedient servant,

Thomas B. Stokes,
Acting Ensign, U. S. N.

This letter was received on the 4th of November; but my father had previously written to the War Department, and received the following answer:

War Department, Washington City,
October 5th, 1864.

Sir:—Your communication of the 28th *ultimo* has been received, and I am instructed to inform you, in reply thereto, that the Department will use all the means in its power to effect the release of your son, Corporal James Pike, of the 4th Regiment Ohio Cavalry, now held in confinement, as you state, at Charleston, South Carolina.—Very respectfully,

Your obedient servant,

Louis H. Pelouze,
Ass't. Adjutant-General.

Mr. Samuel Pike, Washington C. H., Ohio.

From Gen. Grant he also received the following note:

Headquarters Armies of the United States,
City Point, Va., October 24th, 1864.

Mr. Samuel Pike, Washington, Ohio:

Sir:—I am directed by Lieut-General Grant to acknowledge the receipt of your letter of September 28, and to say that he perfectly recollects the services rendered by your son. In regard to an exchange, Gen. Grant hopes during the coming winter, or perhaps earlier, to be able to effect the liberation of all our soldiers now in the hands of the enemy.—I am, sir, very respectfully,

Your obedient servant,

Adam Badeau,
Lieut-Col. and Mil. Sec.

The man who, above all others, has always been most systematically abused, is General Butler. He has ever been represented by his enemies as a cold-hearted tyrant in his dealings with our soldiers, and has been constantly blamed by the rebels with retarding all their pious(?) efforts to effect speedy exchanges; but the following letter completely vindicates him from such slanders, if nothing else would:

Headquarters Dep't of Virginia and North Carolina,
Office Commissioner for Exchange,
Fort. Monroe, Va., Dec. 18th, 1864.

Sir:—In reply to your communication of November 14th, the commanding general directs me to inform you that he has ordered a rebel prisoner, now in Fort Delaware, to be held a hostage for your brave and gallant son.

The prisoner is of the same rank as your son, and is to be subjected to the same treatment as your son receives at the hands of the rebels.

He sympathizes deeply in his sufferings, and hopes by these means he may soon be released.—Very respectfully,

Your obedient servant,

Henry H. Bennett,
Private Secretary.

Samuel Pike, Esq., Washington C. H., Ohio.

My father also received a very kind letter from Gen. Thomas, promising to render me all the assistance in his power; and the correspondence ought to satisfy any one, that our officers, so far from neglecting my interests, were really bestowing more attention to my case than I deserved; nor do I believe they ever neglected the interests of any soldier whose situation was properly brought to their notice. But to return to my narrative, after this digression.

We remained in Charleston jail for five months, and during that time I communicated with a Georgian, named Jim Robinson, who agreed, that if we could make the keys, he would show us a sewer under the tower, leading out beyond the prison walls and the guards; and with this understanding we laboured for weeks, making in all about thirty different keys, out of tin, bone, etc., besides eighteen out of brass. These latter were filed so as to fit the locks, and with them we were enabled to open every door leading to the sewer. We then opened the cell doors, and let the Georgian out during two successive nights; but each time, when he got out, he was seized with fear, and, trembling, would excuse himself, promising go if we would wait another night; but in the meantime he communicated the whole affair to the jailor, who searched for the keys, and found them in Grant's cell.

In prospecting about to get the keys, they seized Grant by the throat to frighten him; but he struck the traitor Robinson with a large pocket knife, and cut him through the instep of one of his feet. After this failure we were too closely watched to get any chance to escape, and so had to "sweat it out" as long as the rebels could keep us in that jail.

Our rations were a pint of meal, and half a pound of meat per day, and when we failed to get the former, we had rice or cow peas dealt out in their stead. Much of the time, however, we failed to get meat, and often our meal would be so musty that we could scarcely swallow it, although always ravenously hungry. The rations were always cooked for us, and brought once a day; and we had our choice either to eat them up at once, or set part of them aside. We could not, however keep it long, as the foul air in the cells would spoil the best of food in a few hours; and we, therefore, speedily acquired the habit of eating but once a day. The quantity of food given us, to tell the truth, was not more than sufficient for one light meal.

The Sisters of Mercy came to see us, after they found out our condition, as often as the jailor would allow them to do so, or as they could find time. They always brought some little delicacy, and to them we were indebted for about all the medicine we got. We were badly afflicted with scurvy, and they sent us potatoes and vinegar, which nearly cured us; while a priest—Father John Moore—supplied us with books, thereby giving us an opportunity to spend our time profitably and agreeably. We were enabled to get light enough to read, provided the sky was clear, by sitting at the grating door, which we were allowed to do four or five hours each day; but if the sky was shrouded in clouds, the gloom of the tower was like that of a dungeon.

In cell No. 8 was a Union man named Webb, in No. 10, an old fisherman, and in No. 11, an Irishman, all of whom had been incarcerated aiding our officers to escape; and it was through Mrs. Webb that the Sisters of Mercy heard of us.

During the first sixty days of our imprisonment we could get no water with which to wash our clothing; and during the entire Winter we slept on the floor without covering, but a short time before we left Webb was released, and he gave us his blanket, and a Mrs. Trainor got an opportunity to smuggle in another one. The jail, too, was literally swarming with vermin, and to add to our discomfort, the inmates of the jail were keeping up a continual noise, so that rest was nearly impossible. In addition, when the air was full of fog or clouds, the inner work of the jail was always streaming with water, which collected on them, and which caused the floors to be continually damp.

The cell in which we were confined so long had a front of eleven feet, with a rear six feet four inches broad, in the tower, and its width was also six feet four inches; and often, for weeks together, we were not allowed to step beyond the doors of this narrow cage.

But why add more relative to the horrors of this filthy pen? He who has never experienced the torture of a Southern prison-house can form no idea of the wretchedness inclosed; while the tens of thousands who have been incarcerated therein, but who have been fortunate enough to escape death, need no words that they may appreciate the cruelties inflicted.

CHAPTER 35

"Adieu" to Charleston

"*It is a long lane that has no turn,*" says an old adage; and our captivity, like all things earthly, came to an end. When Gen. Sherman moved upon Branchville, the evacuation of Charleston became a military necessity; and when the rebels left the city, Gray and myself were sent to the jail at Columbia, the capital of South Carolina. The presence of Sherman's army appears to have almost worked a miracle, for from the time we were lodged at Columbia, we received the best possible treatment. Our keeper was Capt. Semmes, whose whole conduct toward us was that of a gentleman, though a bitter rebel; and I got along finely, except in a single instance.

We were put in a room in which there were about twenty-five persons, twenty-one of them being deserters from our army, and the remainder prisoners of war. Of course, we could never agree with the deserters; and they put at me to convert me to their "faith," or rather lack of faith, which occasioned me to insult them, and for this I was soundly whipped for it in less than three minutes. I was not strong enough to fight them, for they were just from the north, and had been well fed and were in good health; while I had been shut up so long on short allowance and unwholesome food, that I had little strength left; nevertheless I went in whenever opportunity offered, and always came out second best.

Fearing if ever I got north again I would report them, they concluded to take time by the forelock, and reported me to the rebels as a spy; and either Capt. Semmes or his lieutenant, gave an order that my hair should be cut off as a punishment: and accordingly four of them seized me and held me down, while a fellow named Jim Brown, a deserter from the 31st Illinois, hacked off my hair. This miscreant is a man about six feet high, with dark hair and eyes, and swarthy complexion—a very talkative man—and, I believe, a fiddler. He was raised in the Sequatchie Valley, in Tennessee, but for several years has been living in Franklin County, Illinois; and he, together with the whole vile crowd, took the oath of allegiance to the Southern Confederacy, and were sent back north as a reward for their rascality. They should forever be excluded from society for their crimes.

When Gen. Sherman's army invested Columbia, the rebels took us out of jail, and put us under fire of our own guns; but what for, we did not know. There were about sixty of us altogether, and among the number was the Colonel of the 1st Georgia Federal regiment; also a Capt. Harris, of the 3rd Tennessee Cavalry, who had been in close confinement for two years and a half—heavily ironed all the time; and during the whole period had been kept in one room, outside of which he had never been.

While we were under fire, a piece of one of our Rodman shells, weighing about five pounds, struck me on the left shoulder; but as it was a glancing blow, it did no other damage than to stiffen my arm a little.

That night (I believe it was the 17th or 18th of February), the rebels started us off for Winnsboro, to put us on a train and run us to Salisbury, North Carolina. This was the first time they had tried to do anything with us on foot; and about three miles from Columbia, as we were going down a hill, where on the left hand side of the road there was a bluff several feet high, almost perpendicular, Gray sprang down the bank and escaped to the woods. The rebels fired about twenty shots at him; but I afterward saw him, and he told me that although several balls cut close, none of them touched him; and he told me that he got to the Congaree River, and swam over it next morning to our army.

I went on with the rebels till the next night, and then I left them; and the way I escaped was this: we had been marching hard all day, and at night all hands were very tired. We only had one skillet for the whole party to bake bread in, and I rose about two o'clock in the morning and began to cook. After awhile I wanted wood, and going up to the dead line with an axe on my shoulder, I got permission from the guard to step over to a tree top that lay just at their feet to supply myself. They thought, I suppose, that I would not attempt to get off, and they allowed me this small privilege; I had struck but few blows with the axe before they turned their heads to watch the other prisoners; and as that was my only chance, I was off at once, and made the best time I ever did.

After running about three hundred yards, I halted and looked around; but I had not yet been missed, and I then felt perfectly safe. I took the best course I could through a swamp and wood, and then struck out for Columbia. I did not, however, proceed far before I came in sight of camp fires; and immediately I commenced a reconnoisance. Stealing close to their pickets, I discovered rebel cavalry, and away I went once more through the woods, like a race horse—keeping all the time, however, in sight of the camp fires; for I knew that if I followed their direction, I would soon pass the rear-guard of the rebel army and stand a chance to fall in with our own troops.

It was not long before daylight overtook me, and I was obliged to conceal myself in a little cane-brake, in a narrow swamp. When I entered it I felt sure that nothing but an accident would save me from discovery; but there was no other chance, and into it I went, waist deep in water. After travelling about a considerable time, I discovered a place which afforded as much security as, and a little more comfort than, any other; and after arranging the brush I laid down on a little knoll of dry earth to rest.

From my hiding place I could distinctly see a brigade of rebel cavalry, encamped on a hill but three-quarters of a mile from me; and from the arrangement of the camp I knew it was on some road. All day long, not daring to move, I laid and shivered in my hiding-place; and at one time a number of soldiers approached near me, while driving out cattle from the brake—eight of them coming within a few feet of where I laid; but I was not discovered.

That night I struck the railroad, and travelled—sometimes near and sometimes on it—as my judgement dictated most prudent, until I was at length interrupted by a body of water, which I took for a river. The railroad bridge over it was very high, but was in flames and rapidly falling down; so I crept up to it to consider the chances of crossing the stream. I saw a picket post about a hundred yards from the stream, but there appeared to be no guard at the bridge itself; so I hastened up to it, mounted the lower timbers, which did not appear to be on fire, and on them I made my way nearly across, when I discovered that a portion of them had already been burned out, so that I was compelled to go back again, and I was fortunate enough to escape detection, and was soon once more in the woods.

Near the bridge, at a mill, were three hundred rebel cavalry; and just above were camp-fires enough for a division of infantry.

Before I struck the railroad, I slipped up to a house to inquire something about the country; for I did not know for certain that I was travelling in the right direction to strike our troops; but I was under the impression that Sherman had taken Columbia, and was therefore aiming for that point. Creeping quietly up to this house, I was just about to rouse the inmates, when a man on the opposite side shouted:

"Halloo, the house;" and in a minute he was answered by a woman.

"We want," said he, "to get some feed for our horses; we have been riding all day, and our stock is very tired and hungry, and if you have any corn or fodder we want to get it."

The woman asked what they belonged to, and they answered: "Wheeler's cavalry."

"Gentlemen," she said, "we have no corn or fodder, only what we buy and pay the money for. We did not raise any this year; our crop failing entirely. If we let you take what we have on hand we will have to pay out more money to replace it, and that would be rather hard, you know."

"O, yes, madam;" was the reply, "we know that; but you might as well let us have it as the Yankees. They will be along here to-morrow and take everything from you they can find."

This was news to me—just what I wanted to learn.

"Are the Yankees that near?" asked the woman.

"Yes, madam; they are not more than two miles in the rear of our army now, and will be along here sure, tomorrow."

"Why, I thought they were away the other side of Columbia," responded the woman.

"O, no; they captured Columbia day before yesterday," said one of the party.

"Well, if that is the case," she answered, "you can take all the corn and fodder we have got. You will find it down at the barn."

Now the barn was almost behind me; and when the woman told them where the forage was they started instantly for it. Just on my right hand was a low shed, that had been built to shelter sweet potatoes, which had been buried under it; and the hills were covered with pine boughs, which made it very dark under the roof; and as it looked like a good hiding-place, I dodged down there, but fell headlong on an old sow with a litter of young pigs, and some half a dozen full-grown shoats. Here was a rather unpleasant situation! The hogs, alarmed and indignant at the unceremonious intrusion, made a great noise, of course; and, as they rushed out, they threw down a part of the shanty on my head.

I now laid myself down flat on my face, in one of the ditches, alongside of a sweet potato "hole," and hoped to escape detection; but that hope was a fallacious one. Scarcely had I straightened myself in the ditch before two enormous dogs leaped over the fence and made directly for me. There was no time to lose, I thought, and I sprang from under the shed and was off, like a race-horse, over the white sand; nor did I stop to look behind until I had cleared three fences.

On turning around, finally, I discovered the rebels at the barn, some dismounted, but others on their horses looking for me, as if exceedingly anxious to discover my whereabouts; but none of them attempted a pursuit. Nor would it then have been any use, as I had reached the edge of the brush, through which they could not have ridden. I suppose they believed me one of their own men, as their camps were so near.

After my attempt to cross the burning bridge, I picked my way around a great swamp, and came to a large plantation; and hoping that I might get a boat to cross the supposed river, before daylight, I went to the house, which was not more than a quarter of a mile from the largest camp I had seen; but when I reached it, I looked up and thought daylight was approaching and I must secrete myself till the following day, when I felt sure our army would pass by and I could join it.

I looked all around, and the best hiding-place I could discover was under the house; so I laid down on the ground and rolled over and over till I got to the chimney, where I thought I was pretty well secured from observation, and then fell asleep. Presently, however, someone in the house began to stir the fire, and that waked me up; and, on looking about, I saw immediately above me a wide opening in the floor, so that the inmates of the house could certainly see me if I remained where I was; and of course I had to "evacuate" the position.

When I got out daylight still appeared no nearer, and I consequently, concluded I must have been mistaken, and I therefore at once determined to rouse the people, and standoff in the dark and talk to them, and learn what I wanted about the country and the armies. First, however, it was necessary to reconnoiter the position, and I went to the end of the house, where I found a little hole in the window, which was curtained. Through this hole I thrust a finger, and was enabled to gradually remove the curtain so as to see the fire-place; and there was an old darkey down on his knees, with his back to the fire and his breast resting on a low stool. He was very old and very fleshy; and he evidently had not been to bed that night. I wondered at this, and went around to the door and opened it very gently and put my head into the room, which contained two beds, in each of which were two white men. On the posts were gray coats, and at the head of each bed were two guns, and on one was a sabre; so regarding this as a rather dangerous place, I did not pursue the "reconnoissance" further, and I closed the door and left.

On the other side of the yard a light was streaming through the window of a negro house, and I went over and peeped in and found a black man sitting by the fire, half asleep; but with a low "whistle" I brought him to his feet as quickly as if he had been bitten by a rattle-snake, and I at once called him, in a whisper, to the window. I told him I was a Yankee soldier in great distress; that I wanted to come in and warm myself, for I was nearly frozen, and adding that I was very hungry.

"You can't come in heah, sah," said he; "my boss is in de nex' room wid four or five soldiers, an' if dey ketch you, fore God, dey kill you."

"Can you not, then, give me something to eat?" I asked.

"Ain't got a bite cooked, sah; soldiers dun tuk all we had, sah," he replied.

"Then, you can tell me a good place to go and hide, can't you?"

"Right down dar, sah; across dat ole fiel'; dar's an ole house you can go an' git inter."

I only asked him the question to make him believe I was going in one direction, when I would strike out in the contrary one as soon as I was out of his sight.

From this plantation I continued to follow the course of the water I wanted to cross, and in a short time I came to another plantation. In each corner of the yard at this place, there was a large log cabin standing; and selecting the one I judged to be occupied by the blacks, I approached it, and knocked at the door, and almost instantly a huge house-dog came bouncing at me from the other building; and as I thought there might be rebel soldiers sleeping there, I declined an engagement with the animal, and ran off down to the stables, and climbed up in a loft, after which the dog returned to the house, apparently well satisfied with his exploits.

As soon as he became quiet, I got down and stole up to the house again, and softly opening the door, went in. The first thing I now did was to feel around over the beds to see if anyone was sleeping in the house; but they were all empty. I then examined the table and cupboard, trying to discover something to eat, but found nothing. Then I stirred the ashes to see if I could raise fire enough to warm and dry myself, and while doing this, I heard someone in the other house opening the door. Knowing that it is always best to meet danger half way, I went out into the yard, and as soon as I showed myself, was challenged by a female voice from the porch.

"What are you doing in my house at the dead hours of the night?" she fairly screamed.

"Don't be uneasy, madam," I said calmly, for I was afraid she would alarm the camp which was within easy hearing distance.

"Who are you?" she screamed again.

"I am a soldier, madam, and I want to come in your house, and warm myself."

By the time I said this I was close enough to see her, and discovered that she had on no article of dress but one of those short-sleeved, low-necked garments, made of muslin, which I have often seen on clothes-lines, while in her right hand she had a vicious-looking rifle, and she looked angry enough to use it. I now determined, if possible, to get near enough to snatch the gun from her, if she made any attempt to shoot. As I drew close enough for her to see the colour of my clothing, she hallooed out:

"You're a *Yankee*, that's what you are!"

"No, madam," I answered, "you are very much mistaken; I am no Yankee, I am a Texan."

"Well, what were you doing in my house this time of night; why didn't you come to the house we live in; what did you go there for? you might have known there was nobody in there."

"Madam, I am a stranger; how should I know which house you were in?"

"Well, what do you want here, this time of night?"

"Why, I want to come in and warm, and get something to eat, for I am hungry, and very cold and wet."

"Why don't you go over there to the camp, and get something to eat?' she asked; "haven't they got plenty over there?"

"Madam," I said solemnly, "there are men over there who have not had a bite to eat for three days."

"Is that so?" she asked in a relenting tone, and I saw at once that I had gained the point I wanted—her sympathy.

"Yes, madam, that is true, and for my part, I have been wandering about all night to find something to eat; but the boys all said they had nothing, or else that they couldn't spare it, so I came off over here."

"Poor fellows!" she said, "why, I didn't know our soldiers were so hard up as that."

"Madam, I must come in and warm," I said; "for I am really freezing," and suiting the action to the word, I started in.

"Well, wait," she said, half scared, "till I make a fire, and you may come in."

In a few moments she had a bright fire of fat pine blazing, and she called me in. She had also put her clothes on, and wrapped a shawl around her. I sat by the fire some time and warmed, when she called to a younger woman, and told her to go out in the kitchen and find me something to eat. In a little while she returned, bringing a large, "flat cake" of corn bread and a piece of raw bacon, which she gave me, and I proceeded to appease my appetite. When I got through eating, I resumed the conversation with,

"Madam, these are troublesome times, and these are days when we all need friends; you, perhaps, need friends, and so do I. You befriend me tonight, tomorrow I may have it in my power to help you."

"Why," said she, "what do you want?"

"Madam," I replied, "I don't believe you could find it in your heart to injure me, and so I shall make a confidant of you, for I need your assistance. I am a United States soldier."

"There now," she said, in an excited tone, "I said you were a Yankee, and you told me, no. Oh! just think! what if some of our soldiers should step in; and a body never knows when to look for them. What *did* bring you so close to the camp? Why if they should catch you here they would kill you, and may be me, too; at least, they would take everything I had in the world. Oh! if I had known you were a Yankee, I wouldn't have let you come in."

"Madam, I am no Yankee;" I answered, "I am a western man; I told you no lie."

"Oh, but you are the same thing; you know we call all your men Yankees; that is the only way we always speak of your men in our country."

"Well, madam, you help me tonight, and tomorrow I may be able to do you a favour."

"What do you want me to do?" she asked.

"Why, all that I want now, is for you to tell me how to get over this river down here," pointing in the direction of the water.

"Why, bless your soul, that is no river; it's nothing but a mill pond. Where do you want to go?" she asked.

"I want to go to Columbia, or to the nearest camp of Sherman's army."

"Well, I can put you in a path that will take you out on the Columbia road," said she; and without more ado about it, she went out some distance from her house, and showed me a path, by following which through the fields, woods, around a swamp, and over a ridge, I would eventually come to a big road that led to Columbia.

I thanked her, and she asked me my name, and told me she was a lone widow, and her name was Mary Jones; and she certainly was young and beautiful as one could wish. I followed her directions to the letter, and found the big road she described; but lo! there was a big cavalry camp on it. I picked my way around this, well satisfied that the woman did not know they were there; so I struck out across woods, and plantations, in the direction I wanted to go, and was soon so far from the camp that I believed myself safe, and travelled in daylight, though I still kept off the road.

I was making very good time across a piece of low swampy timber land, to a ridge, a short distance before me, when all of a sudden, I heard sharp skirmishing on the top of the very hill I wanted to reach, and knowing our men were there, I was sure that all I had to do was to conceal myself till the rebel rear guard was drawn back, and I soon found a hiding place in a tree top nearby. Covering up my blue clothes in the green boughs a while, I found the skirmish had ended, but still the rebels did not pass me, as I expected, and I therefore came out and started on my journey, and soon found our infantry tearing up the railroad at a rapid rate. I was now free once more, after a long and tedious captivity! Those who have never been captives, can little appreciate the feelings of one in my situation at that time. The sight of friends, and of the old flag, and the prospect of soon again being able to revisit home and friends, called up feelings too deep for utterance, too intense for description.

CHAPTER 36

The North Carolina Campaign

On reaching our camp, I reported to Col. Fairchild, who treated me with great kindness, and sent me, as soon as I was well rested and refreshed, to Columbia, which place I reached at night, and on the following morning I reported to Gen. Sherman. He was just marching out of town when I found him, and he appeared highly gratified at my escape, and expressed a hope that Gray would reach him all right. He then sent me to Gen. Kilpatrick's command, to get a horse and outfit, which was soon obtained, among which was a Spencer rifle—the latter given me by Col. Starr, of the 2nd Kentucky Cavalry.

It was not long before I had an opportunity to "see service" once more. Capt. Northrop, of Kilpatrick's scouts, went with his men to Wadesboro, North Carolina, and although there were but about thirty of us, we charged the place without hesitation, and drove out about two hundred rebels. It was a gallant little fight, but our lieutenant was killed—the only man hurt in the engagement, on our side. We captured a great many prisoners, horses, and negroes, which we carried back to the camp.

A day or two after this affair, Wade Hampton mustered up pluck enough to give Gen. Kilpatrick battle. Early in the morning the Johnnies charged on our pickets, on every road leading to camp; but when they met the main body of our cavalry, they got handsomely repulsed.

When Gen. Sherman reached Cheraw, I went there, in obedience to orders, to carry dispatches to certain points, within the enemy's country. I travelled with the army, to Laurel Hill, in North Carolina, when the general started me from that place on the 8th of March, in the night, to go to Wilmington, with dispatches for Gen. Terry, who was in command at that place. It was raining hard, and intensely dark, when I left camp; and, as might have been expected, I got lost in the first swamp I came to, and wandered around till morning, without getting anywhere; but finally brought up at Gen. G. A. Smith's tent, in another part of the swamp.

Being exceedingly tired, and sleepy, I arranged some rails by his camp fire, and laid down to rest. When I did so the ground was dry; but when the General woke me up, I found the water four inches deep, all around the rails. He then gave me a good breakfast, and a pass, as the "bummers" were not familiar with Gen. Sherman's chirography, and had arrested me on the previous night. Some of them even seemed to doubt the general's ability to write, urging as a reason for their opinion, that they had never seen anything he had written. I talked to them, but they were inexorable, and I was compelled to go back to a picket partly to prove my identity.

Gen. Smith gave me a horse to ride to the river, and I then made good time. Twelve miles above the mouth of Rock Fish Creek, I stole two negroes, and a boat, and abandoned my horse; and at dark I was at the mouth of the creek, on Cape Fear River, down which I proceeded rapidly. This is not a wide stream, until it passes Wilmington; but it was very high at that time, and the current was swift; and below the mouth of Rock Fish, as far as the town of Elizabeth, it is the straightest natural water course I ever saw; indeed it was almost as straight as a canal.

My contrabands worked very hard at the paddles, for they knew that I was going to make them free, as soon as they reached Wilmington; and we got along remarkably well, considering the fact that it was extremely dark. We came near being stove to pieces several times, by snags, and once were caught in an eddy, in the middle of which was a whirlpool—an ugly place, in which we came near being drawn under. We laboured assiduously, however, with all our strength, and finally succeeded in escaping, but our boat was nearly full of water, and our strength almost exhausted. Although the largest whirlpool I ever saw, I do not think it is always there, but is the result of an extraordinarily high water, sweeping by the curve in the bank.

When daylight overtook us, we pulled ashore, and hid ourselves and went to sleep, thinking we had passed the town of Elizabeth, which was the only point on the river at which we anticipated danger; but when it got entirely light, we discovered that the place was yet a little below us, and on the opposite bank. If we remained where we were, in close proximity to the town, we knew that detection was certain; and I therefore got my black crew on board again, and dropped down a little, to the mouth of a creek, and then pulled into it; and we soon found it widened into a timber swamp, and in this we hid our boat, and then took ourselves to what we deemed a secure place. We were, however, soon astonished to find ourselves within a stone's throw of a rebel camp; but there was now no help for us, and we were compelled to do the best we could. The town, also, which was in full view, was full of rebel soldiers, and refugees; and these, to add to our unpleasant feelings, were constantly engaged in running off stuff and hiding it in the very swamp in which our boat was concealed. There was, also, on our own side of the river, a body of cavalry and infantry, some eight or nine hundred altogether—and two pieces of artillery; but the latter were taken away during the day.

Notwithstanding all these difficulties, we escaped detection, but were obliged to abandon our boat, and take to the woods, which we did as soon as it was dark. Our course was up the creek, and through the woods, until we concluded we were far enough away to have no more to fear from the rebel camp, when we struck out, and soon came upon a big road, where we crossed the creek or rather swamp, on a big log; but only to find ourselves on an island, and in the midst of a company of rebel infantry. Men were passing, and repassing; and near us, were at least a dozen brilliant camp fires. We at once threw ourselves flat on the ground, to study what we should do; and while laying there, a company of cavalry passed so near us, that we might have touched their horses "with a ten foot pole."

"Now is our chance," I whispered to my negroes, as I heard the horses splashing through the water, while some of the men were swearing. We immediately bounded up, ran to the log, and crossed, immediately behind the cavalry, and when we cleared the water, we sprang for the brush, and were soon out of sight. I was sure that if we were seen by the infantry, they would conclude that we belonged to the cavalry, and had dismounted for some purpose; and if the cavalry observed us, they would take us for infantry men, and pay no attention to us. However, I do not think they saw us at all.

We now made a wider circuit around the town, and by dint of exertion and much wading, accompanied by enormous fatigue, we reached the river bank again, two miles below the place.

At the next plantation, we got a negro guide to pilot us across another swamp that was very deep, and could only be crossed with difficulty in a boat, as it was fully a mile wide and densely timbered all the way. He landed us at an old road which was now out of use, and took us a mile or so further to a ferry, where we stole another boat, and went on our way rejoicing. We now travelled as fast as we could paddle our *bateau*, until within about twenty-five miles of Wilmington, where we met with the gun-boat *Eolus*, which we hailed and were taken on board.

About three hundred yards above where I got on board, she stopped and captured four rebels who were in a *bateau* trying their best to escape her, and who appeared to have been following us; but of that I am not certain. I reported to the captain, whose name was Young, that I was carrying dispatches for Gen. Sherman. He was delighted to hear from the interior, and was ready to afford me any assistance in his power. The men crowded around me, and for a few minutes I was besieged with questions about the welfare of the army, and the nature and extent of its achievements; and then hurrying me down into the hold, they quickly had me rigged out in clean clothes—shirts, drawers and socks—and they were hunting for pants, blouse and hat, when the "dinkey" was lowered to the water, and the captain gave me a letter and told me my craft—which was his own light boat—was ready. I was surprised when I found that the *Eolus* had carried me fourteen miles up the river again in the little while I had been aboard of her; but our boat ran very light, and we soon regained the distance. As we had been fasting nearly two days, her hospitality was well timed.

That afternoon we got to Wilmington, and leaving the "dinkey" with one of the gun-boats, according to Capt. Young's order, and my negro crew at the provost marshal's office, I went immediately to Gen. Terry's headquarters, and delivered my dispatches. He received me very kindly, and satisfied all my wants, and gave me a fresh supply of ammunition. The same dispatch had already arrived a few hours before me by two of Gen. Howard's scouts—a sergeant Amich, and a man whose name I do not recollect. Their route was much shorter than mine, and they beat me through half a day. They had made the trip in the disguise of rebel officers, and met with no opposition, though they often met pickets, and squads of men on the way.

My journey by the river, however, was an important one, as by that means the practicability of ascending it with gun-boats was established. I was fully able to report every obstruction on the stream, and informed the commanders of the fleet that at Elizabeth was an immense raft, which the rebels deemed sufficient to check the progress of the boats; but that hope turned out a delusion. At some points, they had the river nearly blocked up by trees, which they had chopped into it; but the inevitable Yankee couldn't be stopped.

My work, however, was not done when I reached Wilmington, as I had yet other dispatches to deliver to Gen. Schofield, at Newbern, or Kingston; and as my orders were to proceed to the former place by sea, Gen. Dodge gave me transportation on the *Weybossett*, a very large vessel loaded with soldiers.

While off the coast, we experienced a severe storm, and though the waves did not roll "*mountains high*," or anything like it, they did rise about twenty feet, which was sufficient to make everything about the ship crack, and to put me out of all fancy for sea travelling. Everybody on board, of course, was sea-sick, except a few chaps who, I observed, were plunging about in heavy boots, pea-jackets, and uncouth looking hats; and who were chiefly employed in pulling, first at this rope, and then at that, as though they might have imbibed too freely of old Bourbon. The gunwales of the boat were lined all the time with men holding their heads over the water, and acting very much as if they had all taken rather freely of an emetic. For my part, I discovered that the most comfortable position I could assume, was with my stomach across a water cask.

The ship didn't appear to care a cent about the muss it was raising, but kept on, like a wild mustang, when under the saddle for the first time; every few minutes contriving to duck down so low that the wind would dash the water over us, which did not greatly enhance our comfort. I will not say that it made us more miserable, for that would be impossible; a sea-sick man can defy all creation to add to his misery.

In due course of time we arrived at Morehead city, and from there I took the cars to Newbern, and thence proceeded to Kingston, walking the last ten miles of the way. I gave my message to General Scofield, and then, after eating a meal, laid down for a nap; but I had not been asleep more than three hours, when an orderly woke me up, saying the general wanted me. I went immediately to him, and he said he desired to have me carry a dispatch back to General Sherman across the country; and I took the document and started.

At these headquarters, I met an old scout and friend, named McIntyre, who went five or six miles with me—a man from the escort accompanying us to take back the horse I rode. We parted, and they returned to the camp, while I directed my steps through the woods toward Kenansville, and the reader may be sure I had a long, hard tramp. My orders were to go to Faison's Depot, on the railroad, be-

"The ship didn't appear to care a cent about the muss it was raising, but kept on, like a wild mustang when under the saddle for the first time."

tween Wilmington and Goldsboro, where General Scofield expected that General Sherman would be the next Sunday; and it was a difficult job to get through, as the rebels had the bridges and creek crossings all picketed. I had, sometimes, to go four or five miles out of my way to get across streams. At one point, about sixteen miles from Faison's, I wanted something to eat, and went to a negro cabin some distance from the road to get it; and while I was there, one of our soldiers went down the road on about the fastest horse, ever I saw a soldier ride; and he was making it do its best, while close behind him were about twenty Johnnies, in full pursuit, I soon saw, however, that the Yankee was bound to be winner, for his horse could out run everything the Johnnies had.

It was a pretty race, as long as I could see it; and when the party was out of sight, I took to the woods. Fortunately I did not travel far, till I discovered two horses tied to a tree, and I at once made a fair "divide" with the owner—I took one and left him the other; of course exercising my privilege of first choice. At the first house I passed I borrowed a saddle, and from there made good time, going at a run till I overtook the general. He had left the depot, and was already several miles away; and judging from the roar of artillery, was up to his eyes in a fight. Following the direction of the heaviest sound, I kept on, and found the general, as I expected, trying to force the Johnnies into a decent submission to the laws of the country. He was on the march with the 15th corps, when I overtook him, and delivered my dispatches.

As the enemy did not stand long, our army went into camp soon after my arrival, and I had the privilege of a free night's rest—and let not the reader suppose that I needed rocking in order to sleep.

On the following morning, the army was on the march early, and in a little while began fighting with the enemy's cavalry. I was with the advance, and we had a lively time, in which I got several good shots; but of course the rebels had to fly. We kept on after the retreating foe all day, skirmishing almost continually. Our route lay in the direction of Smithfield, and in the evening, we came upon the enemy in considerable force, and had a warm encounter, which resulted in the capture from them of a strong line of breastworks, on Hannah's Creek—they being carried by a charge made by the 46th Ohio Infantry. The boys went in with a spirit which was irresistible, and the Johnnies either fell before their unerring Spencer rifles, or retreated in shameful disorder, amid the cheers of our gallant men.

The army immediately went into camp, after this encounter, and

"The boys went in with a spirit which was irresistible, and the Johnnies either fell before their unerring Spencer rifles, or retreated in shameful disorder amid the cheers of our gallant men."

began to strengthen their position. Next morning, I went out and skirmished a little, but on learning that a train was to start from Kingston, that day, I returned to headquarters, and got permission from the general to go home. As I had served about seven months over my time, my request was readily granted; and he further furnished me with an order to the adjutant general, at Washington, who immediately through his assistant, Colonel Beck, gave me another order, directing me to go to Columbus for muster out; and my connection with the service, and my adventures, terminated on the 1st day of April, 1865.

Chapter 37

Personal—Conclusion

My arduous duties, accompanied as was the peculiar branch of the service to which I was attached, by far more than ever the ordinary exposure of soldier life, together with the hardships of two long terms of imprisonment in rebel slaughter pens, naturally impaired my health greatly; though, fortunately, my maladies were only of a trifling nature, and a few months at home leaves me once more able and willing to respond to a second call to serve my country, should the necessity again arise to marshal an army for its defence—which, I trust, may never be the case. As for the war of the rebellion—that practically ended with the surrender of Lee; and with it is settled the whole question of secession. Henceforth, no man will be so idle as to dream of place and power through disunion; and no man will dare to raise his hand against this government, which is emphatically the great champion of freedom.

The Union of the States—that is to be perpetual; the last rays of the setting sun, on the day that time ceases to be, must fall upon our nation united, and able to cope with all mankind, and only succumbing to the decrees of Heaven. Let malcontents reconcile themselves to this fact. Patriotic heads have decreed that treason shall never again rear its head; and patriots are ready to enforce this decree, as they have already enforced it, at fearful cost.

I have ever endeavoured to do my duty faithfully, and will never shrink from meeting any man who is a foe to my country. I chose the occupation of a scout, because it was suited to my nature, and because, while preferring those duties, I was independent, and could suit my actions to my will. While in the army directly, there was more restraint than suited me; but my duties as a scout, though accompanied by cold, hunger, and danger, were ever a pleasure. The more the risk accompanying an expedition, the greater was my ambition to undertake it.

My reward has been rich. I gained the confidence of officers, and the respect of comrades; and this was all I ever desired, and all I received, except on two occasions. One of these was when Gen. Grant paid me a hundred dollars for running the Muscle Shoals; and the other was on leaving the army, on the 21st of March, when Gen. Sherman gave me a like sum for navigating the Cape Fear River to Wilmington.

Many of the occurrences I have related may be hard to believe; some may even regard them as wholly fictitious; but those who have seen service in this way, whether officer or soldier, will scarcely question them; as there is scarcely a man who has been in the army but has experienced more or less of adventure, equally startling and romantic.

I am not disposed to be vain, nor to parade the good opinions which others have entertained regarding me, before the world; but for the benefit of those who know nothing of my character for veracity, I beg leave to append the following documentary evidence, relating to my career:

Headquarters 4th O.V. Cavalry,
Paint Rock, Ala., Dec. 3, 1863.

To his Excellency David Todd, Governor of Ohio:

I have the honour to respectfully recommend to your notice for promotion Corporal James Pike, of the 4th O.V. Cavalry, who has been a member of the regiment since September, 1861. He has, by strict attention to his duties, and by meritorious conduct in various engagements, richly earned a commission. He has also been engaged at different times in secret service, thereby gaining a great deal of valuable information, which has been highly beneficial to the government.

Respectfully yours,

O. P. Robie,
Lieut. Col. Commanding, 4th O.V. Cavalry.

Headquarters 2nd Cavalry Division,
Huntsville, Ala., Dec. 4, 1863.

Corporal Pike is well known to almost every commander in this department for the invaluable services he has rendered as a scout and on secret service. He has been with me for some two months, sometimes performing the most dangerous services. I have always found him intelligent, energetic, zealous, and possessed of a high sense of honour; and in every way calculated to make an excellent officer. I hope, if consistent with the Governor's views, this promotion will be made as a slight acknowledgement of Corporal Pike's past services.

George Crook,
Brig. Gen. Commanding Division.

Headquarters, Dep. Cumberland,
Chattanooga, Feb. 15, 1864.

Respectfully forwarded and recommended. I have known Corporal Pike for a long time as an energetic, capable, and conscientious man, and believe he would make a good officer.

George H. Thomas,
Maj. Gen., U. S. V., Commanding.

Headquarters of the army in the Field,
Nashville, Tenn., March 14, 1864.

The recommendation of Gen. Thomas is cordially concurred in by me. Corporal Pike has proved himself brave and energetic, and I believe would make an efficient commissioned officer.

U. S. Grant,
Lieut. General.

General Sherman, who is a man of few words, and who is not readily imposed upon while acting in a military capacity, gave me the following, which is in his usual terse and comprehensive style:

Trust the bearer.
W. T. Sherman,
Major General.
March 8, 1865.

I did not enter the fearful contest, which raged so unremittingly for four years, from any sectional prejudices. I fought no man because he was a *Southerner*, but because he was a *rebel*. I hated secession, but have ever loved and been ready to protect the loyal men of the South. The war was not of my seeking, but was the inevitable result of the fact that those who entertained a certain class of principles were unwilling to submit to the arbitrament of reason. The secessionists forced the contest upon the country, and I had but to choose the cause I would espouse. In every conflict there is a right and a wrong side; and when the war began I chose the right. When I enlisted, I fully resolved never to abandon the struggle, if my life was spared, till the great wrong, beneath which the country was suffering, should be righted; and if the work of rendering every foot of my native country free, has not yet been accomplished, I am ready to fight again.

When once it is determined to engage in a war, it is the part of mercy and humanity to wage it with all the energy a belligerent possesses. The more sanguinary the conflict, the shorter will be its duration, and the sooner peace will be restored to bless the land. The more lives lost in battle, the fewer the victims of camp life; and a sharp and decisive campaign is far less wasting to an army than one of idleness and inactivity.

Hoping that our country has endured its last great trial; that perpetual peace and prosperity may bless its people, and that henceforth reason, and not passion, may be the arbiter of all differences, I bid the generous reader a kind

Goodbye.

ALSO FROM LEONAUR
AVAILABLE IN SOFTCOVER OR HARDCOVER WITH DUST JACKET

LIFE IN THE ARMY OF NORTHERN VIRGINIA *by Carlton McCarthy*—The Observations of a Confederate Artilleryman of Cutshaw's Battalion During the American Civil War 1861-1865.

HISTORY OF THE CAVALRY OF THE ARMY OF THE POTOMAC *by Charles D. Rhodes*—Including Pope's Army of Virginia and the Cavalry Operations in West Virginia During the American Civil War.

CAMP-FIRE AND COTTON-FIELD *by Thomas W. Knox*—A New York Herald Correspondent's View of the American Civil War.

SERGEANT STILLWELL *by Leander Stillwell*—The Experiences of a Union Army Soldier of the 61st Illinois Infantry During the American Civil War.

STONEWALL'S CANNONEER *by Edward A. Moore*—Experiences with the Rockbridge Artillery, Confederate Army of Northern Virginia, During the American Civil War.

THE SIXTH CORPS *by George Stevens*—The Army of the Potomac, Union Army, During the American Civil War.

THE RAILROAD RAIDERS *by William Pittenger*—An Ohio Volunteers Recollections of the Andrews Raid to Disrupt the Confederate Railroad in Georgia During the American Civil War.

CITIZEN SOLDIER *by John Beatty*—An Account of the American Civil War by a Union Infantry Officer of Ohio Volunteers Who Became a Brigadier General.

COX: PERSONAL RECOLLECTIONS OF THE CIVIL WAR--VOLUME 1 *by Jacob Dolson Cox*—West Virginia, Kanawha Valley, Gauley Bridge, Cotton Mountain, South Mountain, Antietam, the Morgan Raid & the East Tennessee Campaign.

COX: PERSONAL RECOLLECTIONS OF THE CIVIL WAR--VOLUME 2 *by Jacob Dolson Cox*—Siege of Knoxville, East Tennessee, Atlanta Campaign, the Nashville Campaign & the North Carolina Campaign.

KERSHAW'S BRIGADE VOLUME 1 *by D. Augustus Dickert*—Manassas, Seven Pines, Sharpsburg (Antietam), Fredricksburg, Chancellorsville, Gettysburg, Chickamauga, Chattanooga, Fort Sanders & Bean Station.

KERSHAW'S BRIGADE VOLUME 2 *by D. Augustus Dickert*—At the wilderness, Cold Harbour, Petersburg, The Shenandoah Valley and Cedar Creek..

AVAILABLE ONLINE AT **www.leonaur.com**
AND FROM ALL GOOD BOOK STORES

ALSO FROM LEONAUR
AVAILABLE IN SOFTCOVER OR HARDCOVER WITH DUST JACKET

THE RELUCTANT REBEL by *William G. Stevenson*—A young Kentuckian's experiences in the Confederate Infantry & Cavalry during the American Civil War..

BOOTS AND SADDLES by *Elizabeth B. Custer*—The experiences of General Custer's Wife on the Western Plains.

FANNIE BEERS' CIVIL WAR by *Fannie A. Beers*—A Confederate Lady's Experiences of Nursing During the Campaigns & Battles of the American Civil War.

LADY SALE'S AFGHANISTAN by *Florentia Sale*—An Indomitable Victorian Lady's Account of the Retreat from Kabul During the First Afghan War.

THE TWO WARS OF MRS DUBERLY by *Frances Isabella Duberly*—An Intrepid Victorian Lady's Experience of the Crimea and Indian Mutiny.

THE REBELLIOUS DUCHESS by *Paul F. S. Dermoncourt*—The Adventures of the Duchess of Berri and Her Attempt to Overthrow French Monarchy.

LADIES OF WATERLOO by *Charlotte A. Eaton, Magdalene de Lancey & Juana Smith*—The Experiences of Three Women During the Campaign of 1815: Waterloo Days by Charlotte A. Eaton, A Week at Waterloo by Magdalene de Lancey & Juana's Story by Juana Smith.

TWO YEARS BEFORE THE MAST by *Richard Henry Dana. Jr.*—The account of one young man's experiences serving on board a sailing brig—the Penelope—bound for California, between the years 1834-36.

A SAILOR OF KING GEORGE by *Frederick Hoffman*—From Midshipman to Captain—Recollections of War at Sea in the Napoleonic Age 1793-1815.

LORDS OF THE SEA by *A. T. Mahan*—Great Captains of the Royal Navy During the Age of Sail.

COGGESHALL'S VOYAGES: VOLUME 1 by *George Coggeshall*—The Recollections of an American Schooner Captain.

COGGESHALL'S VOYAGES: VOLUME 2 by *George Coggeshall*—The Recollections of an American Schooner Captain.

TWILIGHT OF EMPIRE by *Sir Thomas Ussher & Sir George Cockburn*—Two accounts of Napoleon's Journeys in Exile to Elba and St. Helena: Narrative of Events by Sir Thomas Ussher & Napoleon's Last Voyage: Extract of a diary by Sir George Cockburn.

www.ingramcontent.com/pod-product-compliance
Lightning Source LLC
Chambersburg PA
CBHW031615160426
43196CB00006B/146